Parents and Tea

ukra

Parents and Teachers Together

Proceedings of the Twenty-Third Annual Course and
Conference of the United Kingdom Reading
Association,
Part of the Eleventh World Congress on Reading of the
International Reading Association
Institute of Education, University of London,
July 1986

Editor: Peter Smith
(Editor for Part III: Joyce M. Morris)

M
MACMILLAN
EDUCATION

© United Kingdom Reading Association 1987

All rights reserved. No reproduction, copy or transmission of this publication may be made without written permission.

No paragraph of this publication may be reproduced, copied or transmitted save with written permission or in accordance with the provisions of the Copyright Act 1956 (as amended), or under the terms of any licence permitting limited copying issued by the Copyright Licensing Agency, 7 Ridgmount Street, London WC1E 7AE.

Any person who does any unauthorised act in relation to this publication may be liable to criminal prosecution and civil claims for damages.

First published 1987

Published by
MACMILLAN EDUCATION LTD
Houndmills, Basingstoke, Hampshire RG21 2XS
and London
Companies and representatives
throughout the world

Typeset in Great Britain by
Wessex Typesetters
(Division of The Eastern Press Ltd)
Frome, Somerset

ISBN 0-333-44416-7

Printed and bound in Great Britain by
Anchor Brendon Ltd, Tiptree, Essex

Contents

Acknowledgements viii

Introduction ix

PART I AN OVERVIEW OF THEORY AND PRACTICE IN PARENTAL INVOLVEMENT IN READING AND LANGUAGE DEVELOPMENT

1 Parents and Teachers in Reading Education: Let's Get Our Act Together! 3
John E. Merritt

2 A Review of Research into Parental Involvement in Reading 21
John Bald

3 Partnership with Parents in Children's Reading: How Close is the Partnership? 31
Wendy Bloom

4 A Critical Look at the Advice Given to Parents Helping Their Children to Read 42
Eleanor Anderson

5 Working Together: Teachers and Parents 53
Flo Robinson

6 Parents of the Future 61
Rosemary Bacon and Alan Porter

7 Children Choosing and Reading 68
Dina Thorpe

8 Cross-Age Tutoring in the Primary School 80
Margaret Litchfield

9 Using Volunteer Helpers as Scribes 94
Brigid Smith

PART II EXAMPLES OF GOOD PRACTICE

10 The Problem of Underachievement in School 105
Moira G. McKenzie

11 Play with Literacy: A Home–School Liaison Project to Support School Beginners 122
Helen C. Tite

12 The Literate Home Corner 134
Nigel Hall, Elizabeth May, Janet Moores, Janette Shearer and Susan Williams

13 Intonation in Early Reading 145
Elizabeth Goodacre

14 Letterland: Changing the Language of Reading Instruction 154
Lyn Wendon

15 Parents and the Writing Process 165
Roger Beard

16 Teaching the Catching of Spelling 175
Margaret L. Peters

17 Adult Attitudes to Children's Handwriting 183
Peter Smith

18 Individualised Spelling: The Spellbank Project 187
Frank Potter

19 Computer Essentials for Home and School 195
David Wray

20 The Personal Computer as a Vehicle for Home–School Liaison 204
Jonathan Anderson

PART III   ACHIEVING LITERACY IN A MULTILINGUAL SOCIETY

21 Challenge and Opportunity for Literacy in the English-Medium, Multilingual School   215
   Joyce M. Morris

22 Responding to Language Diversity   219
   John Singh

23 Focus on the Multilingual Primary School   225
   David Houlton

24 Focus on the Multilingual Secondary School   231
   Mohammed Nazeer-Ud-Din

25 Bilingual Children and In-Service Education   236
   Silvaine Wiles

26 Training Bilingual Teachers to Support and Develop Pupils' Bilingualism   243
   Arturo Tosi

27 Teacher-Training for Bilingualism in Wales   247
   Beryl Thomas

28 Ideas Behind the Congress Display of Work by Teachers and Pupils in Multilingual Classrooms   252
   John Broadbent

List of Contributors   261

Acknowledgements

The United Kingdom Reading Association wishes to thank the following individuals and institutions for their sponsorship of the World Congress on Reading, London July 1986, at which the papers which form this book were delivered.

British Airways
British Gas
Commission for Racial Equality
Department of Education and Science
Dr. Michael Morris
Hilden Charitable Trust
Hounslow Education Authority
Inner London Education Authority
London Montessori Centre
Macmillan Education Ltd.
Midland Bank PLC
Pan Books Ltd.
Richmond College, London
Scholastic Publications Ltd.
Thomas Nelson & Sons Ltd.
Viscount Alexander Macmillan
W. H. Smith & Sons Ltd.
William Collins Ltd.

The Association would also like to express its appreciation to the following individuals who served on the **Local Arrangements Committee:** *Chairperson* Joyce M. Morris, *UKRA President* Peter Smith, *Treasurers* Ron Johnson and Jack Morrish, and *Members* Joe Hammond, E. W. Freeth, Patricia Dodds, Jill Haye, Jean Evans and Jeanne Nickson.

The editor thanks Joyce M. Morris and Jean Evans for their generous help with the work of editing the proceedings.

Peter Smith

Introduction

The UKRA Annual Study Conference for 1986 was arranged as part of the International Reading Association's (IRA) Eleventh World Congress on Reading at the University of London Institute of Education. This was the first time the UKRA had hosted the World Congress and we were pleased to welcome over 1600 delegates from all over the world.

The UKRA's contribution to the Congress was less than a quarter of the total programme with over forty United Kingdom educators presenting. It was, of course, possible for all delegates to attend any session they chose and this added to the richness of the occasion. The theme of the whole Congress selected by the IRA President, Roselmina Indrisano, was 'Gladly Lerne, Gladly Teche'. I chose the theme 'Parents and Teachers Together' for the UKRA strand of the Congress and this was, in effect, our annual study conference.

The IRA does not make a practice of publishing the proceedings of its conferences but it was decided to publish the UKRA strand in the normal way, hence this volume – *Parents and Teachers Together*. The majority of the UKRA presenters submitted papers relating to their sessions so it has been a challenging task for me to decide which of the many excellent and relevant papers to include.

The theme 'Parents and Teachers Together' was selected in order to draw attention to some of the many successful cooperative ventures currently pursued in the United Kingdom and to encourage their further spread. This togetherness is seen as operating in two main ways. On the one hand a need is perceived to explain school policies and programmes to parents as a whole and to inform individual parents about their children's progress, while, on the other hand, there is a wish to capitalise on the benefits that can be gained through parental support and co-operation, both at home and at school. It has been found that, where parents are made sincerely welcome and given adequate information, a large proportion of them are ready, willing and able to help by sharing reading experiences with their children at home and/or by coming into the classrooms to assist the teachers. Several of the papers in this volume describe ways in which parents are also able to contribute to children's development as writers through similar schemes of co-operation.

There would appear to be no one universally successful strategy for involving parents and teachers in these ways so knowledge of a variety of proven methods is useful. There is, however, clear evidence of the need for careful planning before embarking on such a project and for regular monitoring procedures. There are, too, obvious resource implications, including funding for the additional books needed for use in shared reading programmes. Perhaps even more vital is the resource of time, non-contact time for teachers so that they can undertake essential discussion with parents and children without neglecting other aspects of their work.

Peter Smith

Part I

An Overview of Theory and Practice in Parental Involvement in Reading and Language Development

Chapter 1

Parents and Teachers in Reading Education: Let's Get Our Act Together!

John E. Merritt

Do parents really have an important part to play in reading education? If they do, is there anything more we could be doing to take advantage of what they have to offer? If there is, what exactly is it – and how can we best go about it? These are the questions that are addressed in this paper. The last question provides the main focus. Specific strategies are suggested for raising standards of achievement by drawing more effectively on the existing knowledge and experience of both parents and teachers within a context of genuine partnership.

The importance of parental influence

The powerful influence of parents on the educational achievements of their own children has been widely demonstrated over the years in investigations of many different kinds. More recently, research has shown that parents from a wide variety of social and ethnic backgrounds can actually learn to contribute to their own children's progress in reading – if we give them adequate help and encouragement. It may be argued, therefore, that parent education should be given much more attention than it has been given to date (see Greaney, 1986).

Within the school, the contribution of parents can also be seen as a resource of great potential value. In many schools it is an easy matter these days to find excellent examples of how parents can help both to complement and to supplement the work of the classroom teacher (see Ree, 1985). They contribute to the routine administration. They help to provide the kind of individual attention that children of all ages need from time to time during each day and which a teacher with a class of normal size cannot possibly provide. They provide a means of amplifying the work of the teacher by supervising group activities. They also provide a source of special knowledge and expertise not otherwise readily available or affordable.

It is abundantly clear, then, that the contribution of parents, both in the home and in the school, is potentially very large in scale. It far outweighs anything that might be expected from any foreseeable improvements in educational funding. Even more important, we have to recognise that the increased involvement of all parents in all aspects of education is a matter of principle – an area of serious long-term neglect – rather than a mere expedient to be adopted in straitened economic circumstances.

But how many schools do not provide the kind of help and support that would enable parents to do more for their own children? How many schools do not make full use of parents as allies? And in how many schools are the staff not involved, periodically, in a serious examination of all the relevant issues and a review of their own priorities? Clearly, these are matters for each school to resolve. Getting all schools to work on these issues, however, is no easy matter.

The need to get our act together

There is already a great deal of knowledge, experience and expertise quite widely available. What we are concerned with is a process of 'getting our act together'. That is to say, we have to develop a partnership that includes:

- **student teachers** – because if parents are to be involved in education on an increasing scale then students must learn how to handle this as an integral part of their initial training
- **teachers** – because they need to learn how to work with parents and see them as much needed allies and supporters

rather than as a threat either to their jobs or to their professional self-esteem

- **advisers** – because direct experience of the partnership is essential if they are to provide the kinds of support that are most needed in particular schools at particular times
- **tutors in teacher-training institutions** – because they need extensive direct experience of the process if they are to guide their own students effectively
- **other professionals in the educational and social services** – because a process of the kind envisaged will inevitably impinge on many areas
- **parents** – because the education of their children is their business and education is not something that can be left to a school that merely functions as a wayside service station.

If we are going to develop a process that leads to increasing co-operation between all these different parties we must accept that everyone concerned will feel vulnerable until procedures for working together are well developed. This kind of co-operation calls for a far greater understanding on the part of parents of the work of the schools than exists at present. It also calls for an increased awareness on the part of teachers of what can be done in the home. It calls for increased mutual tolerance on the part of parents and teachers – a willingness in parents to recognise and accept the professional skills of the teacher and to accept the guidance of the school; a readiness by teachers to accept the contribution that parents can make in their own classrooms.

Here, as in any other area of education, there can be no prescriptions or sure-fire recipes for success. What succeeds in one context may not succeed so well in another. The process of 'getting our act together', therefore, can only succeed if it is developed by those directly concerned.

This paper, then, is concerned first with getting the actors themselves together at appropriate times and places – and with enough support to enable them to undertake their own development in areas of need which they themselves identify.

It is also concerned with how we can most easily move from what has hitherto been an essentially *ad hoc* approach to one which seeks to establish more systematic procedures for initiating and supporting self-generating development. As a first step, however, let us take a closer look at some of the underlying issues.

Humpty-Dumpty and the Emperor's clothes – or – who is the expert?

At this point, I should like to reveal the answer to a problem that has taxed some of the world's greatest minds. Ever since Humpty Dumpty fell off the wall we have not been able to find out why he could not be put together again. The answer – like most good answers – is quite simple. Experts on different aspects of Humptology, or Dumptology as it is sometimes known, took the individual organs on which they specialised and grew them as entirely independent cultures. That is why you can't get them back into the original shell. And because they were nourished and developed in isolation from each other it is almost impossible nowadays to establish any organic links between the separate parts of the original Humpty – or Dumpty.

Naturally, I would not want to draw too close an analogy with reading. Reading, however, like every other aspect of curriculum, has been carefully broken down into its various knowledge components, skills and sub-skills. Each of these aspects of reading has also been carefully nurtured with its own separate instructional materials. This process of fragmentation is increasing year by year and by the turn of this century, according to current estimates, it will take the average child some 73.5 years to complete the instructional programme that will then be necessary to become an effective reader – provided, of course, that he or she does nothing else but work on skill development in reading.

In the face of this monumental contribution to reading on our part, is it not truly appalling to find so many children with so little regard for our work on their behalf that they learn to read before they come to school? What is even worse – they are often encouraged, or even taught, by parents who have not had the benefit of any specialist training whatsoever in the teaching of reading (Durkin, 1966). Some children are even taught by older siblings who have barely begun their own education. This sort of thing does make even the most devoted teacher sometimes wonder why we bother.

So what about the people who ultimately pay for all the reading research, teacher training and instructional material that provides us with a living? If they had a chance to examine this state of affairs they might just think of asking if we have all been barking up the wrong tree. Furthermore, if parental influence is so great in its effects, they might ask, why are we not spending more of our resources on parent education so that all parents can provide what is at present only provided by the few?

We do know our business, however, and we can, of course, offer a reasonable explanation for this apparent paradox. We can point out, for example, as we noted earlier, that a child in a good home gets a great deal of individual attention. The parent is constantly available to provide comfort and support as well as specific help when help is needed. The parent can also provide a wide range of activities in which reading forms as natural a part as spoken language. There are letters to be read and messages to be 'written', birthday cards to make and shopping lists to check, menus to follow, calendars and TV programmes to consult, brochures on visits to this place or that, signposts and adverts, stories to listen to, 'stories' to write, and so on, and so on, and so on.

Now it is obviously impossible for any teacher, in a class of normal size, to provide that kind of opportunity for each child. The only way out is for the teacher to find out all there is to know about the process of learning to read. S/he can then decide what, realistically, can be done. S/he needs this knowledge, and s/he needs the relevant instructional materials, so that s/he can make up for the absence of all the realistic opportunities for reading that are found in a good home. It is quite obvious, therefore, that we must support a substantial teacher training programme in the teaching of reading. It is equally obvious that we need a substantial research establishment to provide an appropriate scientific basis for all the instructional methods and materials which the teacher must have at his or her command.

Perhaps, however, you have spotted a slight flaw in this defence. We seem to be suggesting that we can achieve success in school by means of methods and techniques that are very different indeed from those that lead to high achievement on the part of the child from the good home. What we are saying, to borrow a phrase, is, 'We have our own ways of making them read'.

Unfortunately, there is little evidence to support the view that all this panoply of expensive expertise is justified. For example, Corder (1971) reviewed a very wide range of studies and found no research support for the view that any particular method or approach to the teaching of reading in the early stages is significantly better than any other. Vaughan (1982), in a review of studies of instructional strategies at the secondary stage, drew a similar conclusion. Samuels (1981) reviewed the characteristics of exemplary reading programmes. His summary of the more important features contains little that refers specifically to reading. His recommendations could, in fact, be applied with little change to teaching in any area or aspect of the curriculum. In study after study in different aspects of education it is the teacher, and the climate within the school, that emerge as being of overwhelming importance, rather than any specific programme.

More generally, there is little evidence to suggest that the vast expenditure on maintaining the reading establishment itself is justified. Here we may draw on the work of Thorndike (1973) in an international study which looked at the differences between reading standards in different countries. From the results obtained we can compare the United States, where there is a hugely expensive reading establishment and reading industry, with countries which had not at that time provided substantial resources for reading *per se*. The results showed that reading achievement was no higher in the United States than in other developed countries which had not put resources into reading on anything remotely approaching the same scale.

In the light of all these insights, the time has surely come when we must ask, in all seriousness, if the reading establishment is perhaps wearing the Emperor's clothes. If parents, and even older children, can help youngsters to learn to read without the benefit of help from the reading specialist, what right have we to think that teachers cannot do the same – provided we get off their backs?

Teachers obviously need help of some kind – after all, they do have the problem of the large class. That is precisely why we need parents in the classroom – so that they can help teachers to replicate the conditions in the good home.

Teachers also need to develop in themselves the confidence of the good parent – the confidence to draw on their own resources as human beings. For this reason, we need to make it very clear indeed that the academic or researcher is not a superior being who invents strategies that are in any way superior to what teachers themselves have to offer.

The researcher's strategies come all too often from a situation which rules out the very factors that are most important – a genuine purpose, texts selected by the reader expressly to satisfy that purpose, an outcome format relevant to the reader's purpose rather than that of the researcher, and so on. It is the practical requirements of realistic reading situations that must determine our strategies – not some *a priori* theoretical perspective. This is why the overall curriculum context and the wisdom of the teacher are the critical factors in reading development.

What we seem to be providing at present is clearly not what is most needed. By various means, however unconsciously, we have kept teachers locked into our patronising academic and administrative life-support systems. Fortunately, the pattern is gradually changing with the growth of school-based and schools-focused approaches to in-service education for teachers. The obvious problem we must now tackle is just how we can most effectively help teachers to grow in stature and self-confidence in the full knowledge of the primacy of what they themselves do, and can do, by their own efforts.

Are we doing this already?

First, let us consider parent education. Many schools are already involving parents in a lot of activities that contribute, directly or indirectly, to parent education. We have to recognise, however, that the actual numbers of parents we reach is very small indeed. In many cases, also, we are not reaching the parents who most need it.

Apart from this, the mere fact of parental involvement in schools does not, of itself, provide any guarantee of effective progress. It is all too easy to get parents in and then to sit back – complacently assuming that all is well. The question is, what are the parents actually doing? What are they learning? How are they benefiting? What are the children learning as a direct result of parental involvement? How are *they* benefiting – at home and at school? And how many parents and children are actually involved for how much of their time?

Then there is the further question – can we even afford to wait until parents have children of school age before we take action? Here too, there is a lot of excellent work being done – but again, the number of parents we reach is relatively small.

Even more important, perhaps – does it make sense to wait until someone is in the throes of looking after a child before we do anything? It takes years to develop the sensitivity, self-reliance and insight that is needed in bringing up another human being. If the social experiences of the parents have been less than satisfactory what is the point in waiting until the years of child-rearing have been reached? Why do we not provide experience in parenting throughout the school years?

Yes, of course, we are already doing something about this. There are certainly courses on aspects of parent education in almost every school at the secondary stage. But most of this is essentially cosmetic. You do not change the habits of a lifetime by providing a few lessons on this or that aspect of parenting, or by the odd discussion period, or even by the occasional bit of practical work. Parent education is a lifelong task. Our present provision, I would suggest, is not only too little and too late – it is not even well designed as a collection of learning experiences from which any appreciable transfer of learning could reasonably be expected. A great deal of what is currently being done would be rejected out of hand by anyone who knows the first thing about the conditions necessary for transfer of learning. The trouble is that we preach in our traditional courses about what makes for effective learning but fail to apply what we know with any degree of rigour when it really matters.

But we are not even talking simply about parent education – not, that is, as a purely individual concern. The lack of adequate parent education affects the community as a whole. Our contemporary society, with its isolated one-parent families and unstable family groupings, provides a basis not only for a discontented and divided family but also for a discontented and divided community. We are developing, indeed we have already developed, into a community in which there is a great deal of mutual contempt between the 'haves' and the 'have nots'. There is also a widespread mutual contempt between groups which, for historical reasons, just happen to be different in life-styles and beliefs. We are developing – we already have developed – into a community in which too many groups of people now combine both for mutual protection and for mutual aggravation, rather than for mutual support in positive and constructive action in the interests of the whole community.

Certainly, we have come quite a long way already in recognising many of these problems. Certainly, there is a lot of experience around. But we are still faced with the Heineken problem – the task of reaching all those parts that other beers cannot reach. We also have to be sure that we are satisfying the Sale of Goods Act – that what we are providing does in fact achieve the degree of effectiveness expected of us by those who entrust us with their children's education.

What I would propose is that learning to live with other people of all ages in a caring community must be a fundamental aspect of each child's education. I do not mean that we should pay lip-service to this idea. I do not mean that we should dutifully include it as a concept to be covered in one or two of the lectures in courses of initial training. I do not mean that we should make it an element in the latest booklet on curriculum development. I do not mean that we should introduce a handful of time-tabled periods for 'looking at' the problem. And I do not mean that we should simply have the occasional project to develop an understanding of other people's quaint customs. *I mean that the curriculum itself should embody in everything each child does each day, activities which provide continuous opportunities for developing those insights and attitudes which are necessary for participating as an effective, caring parent and as an effective, caring member of the community. This is not something we can inject once our other planning has been done. It is something that must constantly inform all of our thinking.*

Those who focus on reading development within a narrower context are simply conditioning children in low level skills that damage their ability to cope with the very problems which reading should help them to solve. The effects of educating children in low-level thinking skills in narrow educational settings are brought sharply home by Marton and Saljo (1976). Glaser (1984), in reviewing a wide range of research on education and thinking, shows just how essential it is to link thinking skills directly to relevant areas of application.

But where do we start if we want to engage children with the realities of life and living instead of cossetting them like battery hens? And are we up to it? Our own education has not necessarily been altogether satisfactory in this respect. We ourselves are not necessarily the products of homes that have been idyllic in every respect. We cannot look to experts in any particular field for solutions because no one has really cracked this problem. What we do have, however, is our own experience of life, the experiences of our colleagues and the experiences of parents and others in the community. These experiences must always provide our starting point.

As every child, every parent, every teacher and every community is unique in so many ways then a 'do-it-yourself' approach seems unavoidable. This 'do-it-yourself' philosophy must also include the child – not as a patient in an educational surgery and not as a rather advanced ventriloquist's dummy – but as a human being with a right to gain experience in defining his or her own priorities. Clearly, then, there is no alternative, in practice, but to adopt a 'do-it-yourself' philosophy and, happily, that is also what is actually required in principle.

In this kind of approach there must obviously be a great deal of sharing of experience. Effective sharing does not just happen, however. There are skills to be acquired. It is a case, then, of 'learning-to-share' as well as 'sharing-to-learn'. Here is another area that calls for development. First, from the point of view of teachers, there is a need to legitimise the concept of sharing on a very large scale. We must then make sure that there is adequate support for teachers who set out to initiate and maintain this kind of development until the whole process develops a life of its own. Some strategies for providing such support will be described later in this chapter.

Research projects on parents and reading

What can we learn from projects which have involved parents in reading? Here, we have to be rather careful. There has been a good deal of useful research from which we can derive some benefit. It is easy, however, to focus on the specific research activity and take a too narrow view of what is really needed.

Let us, for example, consider the Haringey experiment as reported by Tizard et al. (1982). Here, following an analysis of earlier research they decided that the single most important feature in learning to read in the good home was for the parent to hear the child read. They set up an experiment, therefore, in which parents were simply encouraged to hear their own children reading to them each day after school.

As you know, this experiment was very successful, whatever its limitations may have been. Almost every parent participated and useful results were achieved even in cases where the parents themselves could not read in English. Similar results have also been reported by Widlake and McLeod (1984) in a very extensive experiment of a broadly similar kind in Coventry. There have been numerous other experiments in this general area in this country and elsewhere.

Now all this is fine as far as it goes. But are we really developing reading in this kind of exercise? Or are we merely pushing up scores on word-recognition tests and pseudo-comprehension tests at the expense of what really makes for effective reading? And is the implication that we should concentrate on getting more parents to listen to their children reading? Surely not. This simply distracts attention from all the other kinds of reading that could be going on in a partnership between children and their parents. What we are concerned with is purposeful reading in all the different varieties that can be found in a good home – the kind of reading referred to earlier.

Most researchers – but, alas, not all – would be appalled at the thought that their findings were to be interpreted so narrowly. Certainly, those cited above were as much concerned with the many and varied educational 'spin-off' features as with reading scores. In many cases, however, the researcher identifies reading with what can be most easily measured by standardised tests. If teachers allow themselves to be dominated by this kind of 'expert' they will never provide children with an adequate education in effective reading.

Building from the ground up

So where do we start? At this point I would like to make a few suggestions based on work that I am currently doing with the support of Cumbria Local Education Authority and Charlotte Mason College, Ambleside. This project is concerned with reading, language and personal development. The main thrust in this project is to get older children to work with younger children. The purpose here is to develop sound, caring relationships between children of different ages.

The context is one in which the older children need to study the needs and interests of the younger children and to decide for themselves how to provide for these, taking account of what they regard as being in their, that is, the younger children's, best interests. In other words, we are creating opportunities for these children to relate to each other in ways that form the very basis of family life. They are, in effect, acquiring the skills of the good parent. More immediately, however, they are building up increasingly sound relationships within the school community. The younger ones look on the older ones as their friends, and as responsible elders deserving of respect, instead of potential bullies or intimidators. The older children look on the younger children as friends for whom they have responsibility, rather than as inferiors to be pushed around or as pests to be kept out of their hair.

The actual reading and language activities in this project are of a kind that would hardly cause any thoughtful teacher to raise an eyebrow. Progress to date has been modest because we are largely concerned with supporting what is already going on – with organic development rather than organ transplants. So far, we have had children preparing *tape-recorded stories* for younger children, *reading to* younger children, and *writing stories for* younger children. Among the other starting points we hope to cover in each school are the following:

Story Telling   Making up stories to tell to younger children.

General Interest Project Work   Helping younger children to decide what information to collect, helping them to decide on a suitable format for organising information (a simple list, a comparison table, tree diagram, or whatever), reading to them from source books that the younger ones can understand but could not read for themselves, and so on.

Functional Project Work   Identifying individual, group, class or community needs that can be achieved by co-operation within classes and/or between classes; following these through to satisfactory achievement of the objectives set; recording and reporting; communicating to interested parties by whatever means are most appropriate.

Information management   Helping younger children to decide what they want to keep and in what form, then helping them to record this information in personal dictionaries, in encyclopaedias, on individual reference cards, or in other appropriate formats.

Puppet work and creative drama   Some of this had been going on before the project started – as had most of the other activities – in one form or another. We are simply beginning to develop the cross-age sharing element on a more regular basis.

As part of this process we are working out how best to increase the involvement of parents – again on a more systematic basis. The best way, as so many teachers already know, is to let the children take some of their problems home with them so that the parents can help. They can help to select stories from the library, help in rehearsing and tape-recording stories, write stories themselves, contribute to projects, and so on. We hope gradually to develop this so that parents start getting together in groups to work on some of these activities for the benefit of other children in the school and not simply for their own children alone.

In all this we start where the teacher is and where the school is, where each child is and where each parent is. And we are trying, all the time, to move at whatever pace is comfortable for all concerned. It is a highly integrated approach to reading, to language development, to personal development, to curriculum development and to parental involvement. We are not trying to break down barriers. Some barriers are no doubt important. Rather, we are finding ways through and across barriers whenever there is a worthwhile educational objective to be gained by doing so.

Back to sharing

One kind of barrier is the one that leads teachers to say to themselves 'I can't do that – it's so and so's idea'. But there really can be no ownership in educational ideas – ideas are there to be shared. They belong to children. And we are certainly not entitled to sacrifice the educational needs of children on the altar of professional possessiveness!

Unfortunately, sharing takes time – and more expertise than we yet possess if we are to do it effectively. Here, then, are some of the ways in which, I suggest, we can help to bring it about.

Sharing within schools

This sharing of experience through regular discussion is usually most effective when there is adequate preparation. Every teacher must be willing, therefore, to produce some kind of material from time to time to provide a focus for discussion. This will usually need to be circulated in advance to save precious time at the actual meeting. After all, we can read faster than we can talk or listen and these 'advance organisers' are likely to make any discussion that much more effective.

The material itself might simply consist of a sample of classroom work, a brief, illustrative case study – or even a cartoon. It might be designed simply as a 'one-off' contribution. Alternatively, it might be produced so that it can be referred to later. In this case it will go into the school's resource unit where it will be indexed in whatever ways are appropriate so that colleagues can find it easily at a later date. Resource materials of this kind might then be used for:

- **occasional browsing** – for inspiration, perhaps
- **curriculum development** – as a means of developing the repertoire of all the teachers in the school
- **curriculum evaluation** – as a record of the variety of work that is going on
- **more systematic study** – as part of some kind of course work, perhaps
- **the induction of recently qualified teachers**
- **familiarisation studies for new members of staff**
- **raw material for inclusion in a booklet for parents** to provide insights into what the school is trying to achieve
- **sharing with other schools.**

One rather nice element in all this is that teachers themselves gain experience in 'writing for an audience' – a pre-requisite, you might think, for helping others.

The role of teacher training institutions

The current level of involvement of the majority of teachers in in-service training falls well below what would be necessary to bring about any substantial improvement in the quality of teaching across the board. One way of bringing in increasing numbers, however, is the possibility of recognising school-based in-service activities within some system of awards or credits that lead to a postgraduate qualification of some kind. Teachers would not have to go in for credits if they chose not to do so – but at least they should have the opportunity of getting some kind of credit if they so wished.

If we do go down this road we have to recognise that there are many teachers who involve themselves in activities of the kind I have been talking about without any thought of reward – either personal or professional. Their primary motivation is simply the well-being of their pupils. And then again, there are many teachers for whom the pressures of the classroom are such that they have little energy or enthusiasm left over at the end of the day for the creative and constructive processes of professional development. This kind of activity can even be seen as self-indulgent. Attitudes need to be changed, therefore, and one way of changing attitudes is to link professional development to professional qualification. This also has the advantage of providing a powerful incentive for teachers to raise their own professional standards as a healthy counterbalance to the more negative aspects of accountability.

The changing role of the school

When we consider the various activities that I have been briefly sketching in it becomes clear that schools will need to develop in a number of significant ways. As a result, the head must obviously carry increased responsibilities. It would be the head's responsibility

(a) to encourage the involvement of all members of staff as members of the professional team;

(b) to see to the continuity and co-ordination of the various activities; and
(c) to ensure the professional and academic quality of whatever takes place as a result of teacher participation of this kind.

This continuing attention within each school to the development of professional competencies, underpinned by relevant academic insights means, in effect, that every school, or group of schools, becomes a professional college with its own principal. It also means that an in-service curriculum, both for teachers and for their various partners in education, must be given an appropriate degree of priority in the allocation of time and responsibilities in every school or college. This process has already begun. If we are to take advantage of all that children, teachers, parents, and other members of the community have to offer then we have to make sure that it continues to develop. I hope that the comments I have made will serve as a stimulus for further thinking about what will be needed to bring this about – and as an incentive to action on the part of those who command the resources to make it happen.

References

CORDER, R. (1971) *The Information Base for Reading*, National Center for Research and Development, Project No 0–9031 (Berkeley: California Educational Testing Service).
DURKIN, D. (1966) *Children Who Read Early* (New York: Teachers College Press).
GREANEY, V. (1986) Parental Influences on Reading, *The Reading Teacher*, vol. 39, no. 8, pp. 813–18.
GLASER, R. (1984) 'Education and Thinking: the Role of Knowledge', *American Psychologist*, vol. 39, no. 2, pp. 93–104.
MARTON, R. and SALJO, R. (1976) 'On Qualitative Differences in Learning: I – Outcome and Process', *The British Journal of Educational Psychology*, vol. 46, no. 1, pp. 4–11.
REE, H. (1985) 'Breckfield Infants and a Liverpool Experience', in Rennie, John (ed.), *British Community Primary Schools: Four case studies* (Lewes: The Falmer Press) pp. 23–43.
SAMUELS, S. J. (1981) 'Characteristics of Exemplary Reading Programs', in

Guthrie, John T., *Comprehension and Teaching: Research Reviews* (Newark, Delaware: International Reading Association).

THORNDIKE, R. L. (1973) *Reading Comprehension in Fifteen Countries: An Empirical Study* (New York: John Wiley).

TIZARD, J., SCHOFIELD, W. N. and HEWISON, J. (1982) 'Collaboration between teachers and parents in assisting children's reading', *British Journal of Educational Psychology*, vol. 52, no. 1, pp. 1–15.

VAUGHAN, J. L., JR. (1982) 'Instructional Strategies', in Berger, Allen and Robinson, H. Alan (eds), *Secondary School Reading* (Urbana, Illinois: ERIC and NCRE).

WIDLAKE, P. and MCLEOD, F. (1984) *Raising Standards: Parental Programmes and the Language Performance of Children* (Coventry: Community Education Centre).

Chapter 2

A Review of Research into Parental Involvement in Reading

John Bald

Following the Thomas Coram Research Unit's Haringey Project, there has been a great deal of small-scale action research designed to investigate the benefits of involving parents in their children's reading. This work has, however, met with problems encountered by action research in other fields, including difficulties with sampling and assessment. This paper is an attempt to relate action research to earlier work and current long-term projects, and to suggest ways of improving its reliability.

Early research into the influence of parents

In 1966, Dr Joyce Morris's *Standards and Progress in Reading* found 'evidence of a connection between parental encouragement and the reading ability of juniors' (Morris, 1966, p. 213). Her results are contained in Table 2.1.

TABLE 2.1 *Help and encouragement and reading performance – third year juniors*

		Mother	Father	Both parents
Lots of encouragement	Poor readers Good readers	9% 76%	3% 61%	2% 52%
No encouragement	Poor readers Good readers	54% 6%	74% 12%	46% 4%

SOURCE: Morris (1966) p. 212.

In addition, among parents of 'good' readers, 61 per cent of fathers and 49 per cent of mothers were members of public libraries, while the corresponding figures for poor readers were 15 per cent and 13 per cent respectively (Morris, 1966, p. 205). There was, however, no investigation of the nature of the 'connection' between encouragement and performance, and the study did not attempt to identify those patterns of encouragement which might prove to be most beneficial.

In the same year, Dolores Durkin's *Children Who Read Early* found that the relationship between support and achievement was not simple, especially when instruction was attempted without reference to the child's interests. Dr Durkin considered, moreover, that there was no clear connection between early reading and social class. Instead:

> What is much more important, the research data indicated, is the presence of parents who spend time with their children; who read to them; who answer their questions and requests for help; and who demonstrate in their own lives that reading is a rich source of relaxation, information and contentment.
>
> (Durkin, 1966, p. 136)

This opinion is echoed in *Young Fluent Readers* (Clark, 1976), which ends with a plea for reading to be considered in the context of a child's experience at home as well as in school.

Research up to this point is descriptive and analytic, and does not involve the researchers in assessing the effects of changes which they themselves have introduced. Bridie Raban's doctoral thesis, *Observing Children learning to read and write* (Raban, 1984), based on research carried out in the context of the Bristol Language Development Study, is within this descriptive tradition, combining case studies with statistical analysis to identify patterns of interaction between parents, children and teachers which contribute to the long-term process of literacy and language development. The methods and evidence yielded by such studies must be borne in mind when considering the results of the large number of studies which have sought to investigate the benefits of extending parental support to pupils who may not previously have been receiving it, as most of this work has been conducted on a more limited time-scale. There is an additional *caveat* in J. E. Collins's (1960) *The Effects of Remedial Education*, which describes a controlled experiment in which the immediate benefits of an intervention with nine-year-old children had disappeared when the sample and control group were retested at the age of thirteen. The fact that these results related to an improvement produced by remedial teaching by students rather than to one produced by parental involvement does not alter the need for evidence of the long-term effects of any intervention which is designed to improve children's reading.

Experimental studies

Experimental studies may be considered in two groups, one stemming from the Thomas Coram Research Unit's project in Haringey and the other based on the 'paired reading' technique, which is derived from behavioural psychology. The Haringey project (Tizard *et al.*, 1982) was designed to investigate the conclusion of an earlier project in Dagenham, that 'child reads to parent' was the factor in parental support which was most often associated with reading success. It consisted of a two-year intervention, beginning in the final year of the infants school, with a follow-up study a year after the project's conclusion. The sample was drawn from six schools, of which two acted purely as controls. Of the remaining four schools, two were designated as parental involvement schools, with one class in each participating in the intervention and another class as a control, while the last two schools were used in a parallel project designed to compare the effect of parental involvement with that of additional help from a teacher in school. This part of the project was intended as a further control, and was based on the work of just one teacher, whose approach to the work is not described in detail. The project report states that this part of the work is 'in no way comparable in scope to the home collaboration', that 'different methods or forms of provision might have produced different results', and that 'direct comparisons of the parental involvement and extra help groups would be unjustified' (Tizard *et al.*, 1981, pp. 12–

13). Such comparisons, however, have been made, often on the basis of incomplete accounts of the research, although they may be less frequent following a recent statement by Dr Jenny Hewison that this part of the project was 'rather ill thought-out' (Topping and Wolfendale, 1985, p. 49). The problem might have been avoided at the design stage had it been decided either to investigate comprehensively the effects of additional provision in schools, or to omit the factor entirely. It does not, however, detract from the main finding of the study, which was that both home collaboration groups showed statistically significant gains over control groups in the same schools after two years. In addition, one group maintained statistically significant improvement in the follow-up study, and it is suggested that the other may well have done so but for the statistical consequences of a number of good readers leaving the collaboration group and a number of weaker readers leaving the control group.

These results immediately established parental involvement in reading as a national focal point for professional activity and for research, and studies are now appearing so frequently and in such a variety of journals that it is almost impossible to keep pace with them. Among the most important initiatives are the Belfield project in Rochdale, the Pitfield project in Hackney and the work of the Community Education Development Centre in Coventry, which began in the early 1970s but only became the object of investigative research in 1982 (Widlake and McLeod, 1984). There have also been a great number of initiatives from individual schools and teachers, of which *Read with Me* (Waterland, 1985) is an outstanding example. It is difficult to assess on a national basis the extent to which schools have changed their practice, but a survey in the London Borough of Havering (Whitelaw, 1985) found that out of 74 primary schools, 16 had an active parental involvement programme and 20 more were either seriously discussing the issue or were to launch a scheme in Autumn 1985. This is evidence both of considerable expansion and of the work that remains to be done.

Much recent work has been concerned with the social dimensions of parental involvement as well as with its effects on reading performance. A paper from the Belfield project, based on analysis of reading record cards which passed between home and school each day, shows an increase in the proportion of parents who report that they are hearing children read 'almost daily' from 38 per cent before the project again, to 90 per cent (Hannon *et al.*, 1985). Another, based on tape-recording a sample of 52 children aged between five and seven years as they read to a parent and to their teacher, showed that parents were remarkably close to teachers in their approach (Hannon *et al.*, 1986a). Further papers have analysed the ways in which teachers and parents respectively have felt about their experience of the project – of a sample of 78 parents, only 2 made negative comments and one of those changed her mind after a year (Hannon, 1986) and the effects on the patterns of communication between the school and its parents of having the record cards in daily use (Hannon *et al.*, 1986b). Unfortunately, these papers have all been published in different places, so that teachers do not have ready access to them. On the other hand, the booklet *The Belfield Reading Project* (Jackson and Hannon, 1981) which describes the process of setting up a home-reading scheme, and includes personal responses from teachers and parents, had sold over 5000 copies by the summer of 1985.

Testing and assessment

It is, however, beyond question that the growth of the parental involvement movement has been greatly helped by positive results on standardised tests, which provide evidence which is particularly convincing to those who are not directly involved in the work. Nevertheless, the variety of tests in current use and the ways in which results are obtained are both causes for concern, particularly in the case of paired reading. The essential criteria for the selection of a test in this field are that it should be appropriate to the range of reading ability of the sample and that it should reflect as closely as possible the normal reading experience of children. It is also important that the reasons for choosing a test should be set out in the study, that limitations should be acknowledged and that statistical procedures used with raw scores should be justified, particularly when these involve any form of norm-referencing or regression analysis. Where the word 'significant' in fact means 'statistically significant', rather than 'educationally significant', this should also be made clear, as the two are not always synonymous. The Hunter-Grundin Literacy Profiles (Hunter-Grundin and Hunter-Grundin, undated) which are based on silent reading of a continuous story at each level, and which generate information on a range of language development in addition to reading, are the most comprehensive instrument currently available, and are standardised to allow a school's catchment area to be taken into account when assessing results. These tests have a ceiling which is high enough to allow their use in secondary as well as primary schools, although an additional level designed specifically for school-leavers would be invaluable, and incorporate a system for monitoring children's responses to the tests. The profiles have been used on a large scale in the Community Education Development Centre's work in Coventry.

Paired reading

Problems of testing and assessment have been particularly acute in the case of paired reading, a technique which has been developed in isolation from other forms of parental involvement. The basis of paired reading is that the parent, or other fluent reader, and the learner read a text aloud, simultaneously and at a speed which is suitable for the learner. When the learner thinks he can continue on his own, he taps the book or nudges the parent, who stops reading and joins in again once the learner makes a mistake which he does not correct himself. As the child is not allowed to skip any words or to persist with an error, paired reading can be a demanding activity, although its inventor, Dr Roger Morgan, believes that the consistent availability of support results in a reduction in stress for the learner. He also acknowledges the influence of behavioural psychology in his work, as a central idea is that the fluent reader provides a model for the learner. There is now a national paired reading network, based on a project at Kirklees.

The first studies of paired reading involved small numbers of children who were having difficulty with reading, and they included results based on pre- and post-testing with the Neale Analysis of Reading Ability over relatively short periods of time. In the first study (Morgan, 1976), two children made gains of 16 months in comprehension and 5.5 months in accuracy over 19 weeks, while in the second (Morgan and Lyon, 1979), the mean scores of four children rose by 11.75 months in accuracy and 11.5 months in comprehension over 6.25 months. These are encouraging results, but they are far removed from the time-scale established by Collins's study, and have unfortunately been used as a model for a spate of studies in which children are commonly retested after a period of as little as six weeks, with results computed to provide multiples of assumed normal progress and little attention to the long-term effects of the technique. In one study of paired reading in three Sheffield secondary schools which did use a follow-up one year after a 6-week intervention, there was no gain whatever against control groups in two schools out of three. Dr Morgan, speaking at the Conference on paired reading in Kirklees, 1985, has conceded that the Neale Analysis is not being properly used in such studies and has suggested an alternative be sought. It is fair to add that a recent study proposing 'relaxed reading' as an effective alternative to paired reading used the same assessment technique (Lindsay et al., 1985).

The greatest assessment problems of all, however, are raised in the report of a study commissioned by the Department of Education and Science (Young and Tyre, 1983). This study, in which paired reading was supplemented by a range of additional techniques and by holiday schools, lasted for one year and showed parental involvement to be of great benefit to a group of fifteen pupils who had been assessed as 'dyslexic', as well as to a similar group of pupils with reading difficulties who had not been so assessed. The authors noted improvements in many areas of education, including homework and spelling, but the only evidence they present takes the form of a graph containing the scores of both groups of pupils, with a control group, on a test which is not identified, and rounded up or down – they do not say which – to the nearest 6 months. This test was in fact the *Salford Sentence Reading Test* (Bookbinder, 1976), which has a ceiling of 10.6+ and is therefore inappropriate for use with their sample of pupils, whose ages ranged from eight to thirteen at the beginning of the experiment. The claimed improvements in spelling and in other areas are supported by no evidence whatever, so that it is difficult to use the study, despite the success of the project, as an argument for further investment in this form of parental involvement.

Suggestions for future research

Parental involvement in reading probably owes more to research than to any other educational movement, but if the influence of research is to be maintained it must be conducted on a substantial scale and over a time-scale which takes account of the learning patterns which begin before school and which extends to the end of compulsory education. This is the key to the success of such work as the Bristol Language Development Study and the Rutter Report (Rutter, 1979), although it raises obvious practical difficulties as it does not fit the normal patterns of research funding or of the Ph.D. Research on a smaller scale can nevertheless benefit from the retention of sampling details in order to allow follow-up studies when children are thirteen or sixteen. They should also be constructed so as to prevent the problems of design noted above in the case of the Haringey project, and should if possible be assessed in terms of their impact on written and spoken language as well as on reading, so that the work may be seen in the context of a comprehensive programme of literacy and language development.

References

BALD, J. (1985) 'The Individual Benefits of Paired Reading', *The Times Educational Supplement*, 22 November 1985.

BOOKBINDER, G. (1976) *The Salford Sentence Reading Test* (Sevenoaks: Hodder & Stoughton).
CARRICK-SMITH, L. (1985) 'A Research Project in Paired Reading', in Topping, K. and Wolfendale, S. (eds), *Parental Involvement in Children's Reading*.
CLARK, M. (1976) *Young Fluent Readers* (London: Heinemann Educational Books).
COLLINS, J. E. (1960) *The Effects of Remedial Education* (University of Birmingham).
DURKIN, D. (1966) *Children Who Read Early* (Teachers' College Press).
HANNON, P., JACKSON, A., and PAGE, B. (1985) 'Implementation and Take-up of a Project to Involve Parents in the Teaching of Reading', in Topping, K. and Wolfendale, S. (eds), *Parental Involvement in Children's Reading*.
HANNON, P., JACKSON, A. and WEINBERGER, J. (1986a) 'Parents' and teachers' strategies in hearing young children read', *Research Papers in Education*, no. 1.
HANNON, P. (1986) 'Teachers' and parents' experiences of parental involvement in the teaching of reading', *Cambridge Journal of Education*, vol. 16, no. 1.
HANNON, P., WEINBERGER, J., PAGE, B. and JACKSON, A. (1986b) 'Home–School Communication by means of Reading Cards', paper published in *British Educational Research Journal*, revised version, May.
HUNTER-GRUNDIN, E. and HUNTER-GRUNDIN, H. U., (undated) *The Hunter-Grundin Literacy Profiles* (The Test Agency, Cournswood House, High Wycombe, Bucks).
JACKSON, A. and HANNON, P. (1981) *The Belfield Reading Project* (Rochdale: Belfield Community Council).
KIRKLEES PSYCHOLOGICAL SERVICE (1985) *The Paired Reading Bulletin*, no. 1.
LINDSAY, G., EVANS, A. and JONES, B. (1985) '"Paired Reading" versus "Relaxed Reading": a comparison', *British Journal of Educational Psychology*, vol. 55, no. 3.
MORGAN, R. T. T. (1976) '"Paired Reading" Tuition: A Preliminary Report on a Technique for Cases of Reading Deficit', *Child Care, Health and Development*, vol. 2.
MORGAN, R. T. T. and LYON, E. (1979) '"Paired Reading": A Preliminary Report on a Technique for Parental Tuition of Reading-Retarded Children', *Journal of Child Psychology and Psychiatry*, vol. 20.
MORRIS, J. (1966) *Standards and Progress in Reading* (NFER).
RABAN, B. (1984) *Observing Children Learning to Read* (Ph.D thesis, School of Education, University of Reading).
RUTTER, M. (1979) *Fifteen Thousand Hours: Secondary Schools and Their Effects on Children* (Wells, Somerset: Open Books).
TIZARD, J., SCHOFIELD, W. N. and HEWISON, J. (1982) 'Collaboration between teachers and parents in assisting children's reading', *British Journal of Educational Psychology*, vol. 52, no. 1.
TOPPING, K. and WOLFENDALE, S. (eds) (1985) *Parental Involvement in Children's Reading* (Beckenham: Croom Helm).

WIDLAKE, P. and MCLEOD, F. (1984) *Raising Standards* (Coventry: Community Education Development Centre).
WATERLAND, L. (1985) *Read With Me* (Stroud: The Thimble Press).
WHITELAW, B. (1985) *Parental Involvement in Reading in Havering Primary Schools* (London Borough of Havering).
YOUNG, P. and TYRE, C. (1983) *Dyslexia or Illiteracy?* (Milton Keynes: Open University Press).

Chapter 3

Partnership with Parents in Children's Reading: How Close is the Partnership?

Wendy Bloom

The practice of involving parents in children's reading has now been widely accepted and well established. It is based on sound theory (the process model of reading) and replicated experimentation (Haringey, Belfield, Hackney, etc., etc.). There is no doubt now as to the benefits derived for children and their reading when parents and teachers collaborate. The benefits, in fact, are not just confined to children and their reading, but enrich the relationship between teachers and parents and affect the child's whole learning experience.

It has now been well established that all *parents are able to help children with their reading and that it is done most powerfully in close co-operation with teachers. There are many schemes and projects being developed and maintained in schools up and down the country; some have received recognition and wide publicity, the vast majority have not. It follows that there must be many variations in practice. Variation and flexibility are necessary as each school or teacher tries to establish a desired degree of shared understanding. It is this shared understanding about reading that is the main focus of the question posed in the title 'How close is the partnership?'*

It would seem reasonable to suppose, and indeed it has been found to be the case, that when the teachers' and parents' understanding of and practice in reading approximate to each other the consequent benefit for children and their reading is considerably enhanced. This chapter aims to look at the closeness of the partnership between parents and teachers, concentrating mainly on the preconception and understanding of parents. From this the focus will move on to consider ways in which teacher and parent might establish a closer partnership.

The discussion is based on interviews with a sample of parents who had been involved in a home reading scheme for 6 months. These parents repesented different socio-economic and ethnic groups in an infant school in outer London. The findings are not offered for generalisation, but may give useful pointers for consideration by teachers who are working in this way with parents. Interviews were carried out in small groups of 4–7 parents where, once they got under way, discussion developed which was very informative and led to further questioning.

Before proceeding any further let us go back and look at the title of this chapter and at the term 'partnership'. It is interesting to think about the definitions. Various other terms are employed in the literature about home-reading schemes and I have used them in this chapter . . . 'involvement', 'co-operation', 'collaboration' and 'partnership'. One definition of 'collaboration' given in the Concise Oxford Dictionary is to . . . 'co-operate treacherously with the enemy' – this term might find recognition amongst some teachers who do not subscribe to the idea of parents as educators! More seriously, though, the term 'partnership' was deliberately chosen as its definition seems to reflect equality and commitment. The definitions of a 'partner' in the Concise Oxford Dictionary are as follows:

(a) . . . sharer with or in or of
(b) business partner . . . sharer of risks and profits
(c) sleeping partner . . . one partner predominates over the other.

It is on the word 'sharer' that I want to concentrate and from this to look at the amount of shared understanding there is between teachers and parents over children's reading.

The investigation, based as it was on parents' understanding of and preconceptions about reading, was biased in that it did not look into teachers' understanding of reading. It was established, however, that the school was moving towards an apprenticeship approach to reading and seeing reading more as a whole process rather than a series of hierarchical skills. This was the basis of their information and guidance to parents and the task was to try to ascertain how readily the parents had taken up this model of reading and applied the approach to their reading at home with their child.

The interviews

Question: How did parents feel initially about being asked to participate in such a scheme?

It seemed that all the parents interviewed were willing helpers in their children's reading: they referred to class sizes and the daunting task of the teacher. They seemed to think that some part of a child's education was a parental obligation and regarded reading as being the key area of learning for the young child. Who else but they had such a concern for their child's future? Some parents had memories of difficulty over reading and were all the more determined that their child should not be handicapped in the same way. They were pleased that the school took learning to read so seriously, that they wanted to structure and recognise parents' contribution.

Questions: What do you know about your child's reading at school? How often do you think your child reads to the teacher?

The majority of the parents had little idea of the various reading activities that their child would engage in during the course of the day. Almost all of them mentioned the class story time and a few mentioned the large class books which the teacher shared with the class.

Most parents did not know how often or under what circumstances their child read aloud to the teacher. When pressed to estimate this they thought that certainly once a week and perhaps twice weekly. The parents of the five-year-olds were more inclined to think that individual reading took place twice a week.

This seeming lack of awareness is interesting and surprising when seen against the alleged obsession of middle-class parents with teachers listening to children read daily and the pressure that some teachers feel. It seemed that this group of parents were quietly confident in their role in reading and there was no hint of disapproval that teachers may not be listening to their child read on a daily basis. Again, they mentioned the bustle of activity in the classroom and the consequent difficulty of teacher and child to be able to concentrate on the reading task.

The reading process

The way in which parents learnt to read is likely to have a significant effect on how they will approach reading with their child. The responses to questions about the parents' experiences of reading is considered in conjunction with responses to earlier questions in the interview. These questions concerned their reaction to the initial meeting with teachers at the start of the scheme and to the small booklet that they were all given. This booklet put across the message of a process model of reading – reading for enjoyment, and an apprenticeship approach with the emphasis on sharing books. If there was a conflict between the parents' experience of learning to read and the approach advocated by the school, parents were asked how they would resolve this in their own minds and how they would subsequently approach reading their their child.

Question: What do you remember about learning to read?

For most parents there was not a clear recall at first about the early stages of learning to read, and this was not surprising. One parent remembered very vividly a phonic approach: she stated that she was not 'able to read' until she was ten and recalled feelings of frustration and disappointment. In discussion it was evident that at school all the group had experienced a skills-based approach to reading based on phonics and/or look-and-say. Many recalled their boredom or puzzlement in these early stages. One or two parents, however, expressed the belief that this approach was necessary in order to gain later enjoyment and efficiency as it was 'structured' and 'logical'. Many parents mentioned the competitiveness in the early stages and the urge to progress from one reader to the next. Any reading for enjoyment seemed to take place at home and it was interesting to hear some mention of *their* parents reading with them in much the same way as was now being advocated by the school.

A small number of parents who learnt to read in Africa as children at school there, remembered learning to read very differently. They remembered firstly learning to read and write the alphabet. They then learnt to write and read individual words, at last coming to read whole sentences. This was done initially through the whole class reading aloud in unison from the blackboard. They well remembered their first experiences of continuous text in their first individual books which they then considered exciting and colourful. They reflected that compared to the beautiful books that their children brought home, their own first books would now seem very dull.

Question: How did you reconcile your own early experiences of reading with the approach being advocated in the new home-reading scheme?

On the whole, parents welcomed what they saw as the 'new' approach. The term 'new' is only used in the school context as those parents who had been reading with their children had mostly been using intuitively what we might call an apprenticeship approach. The fact that they welcomed the approach advocated by the school may well have been because this confirmed their practice. Furthermore, parents made comments like 'it seemed like common sense', 'it's something we could do easily'. This remark prompted two further questions –

'Did it all seem too easy when it was explained to you? Were you expecting something more complicated?'

The answer to these were in the negative. The build up to the scheme had led parents to believe that their contribution would be straightforward. They were not, however, convinced in the early stages that what they were being asked to do was enough to make any difference to their children's reading.

There was a sharp division here amongst the group of parents. Three fathers who were themselves educated in Africa, with English as a second language, obviously had different views from the rest of the group and from the teachers in the school. Having learnt to read by an approach that placed meaning and enjoyment last and discrete skills first, they employed a mixture of approaches with their children with a skill approach predominating. They not only had their own experiences guiding them, but also the fact that they read very little in English and were not able to share and discuss in the same way. They also held a much more functional and instrumental view of reading generally. It might be interesting to take this further and look at views of reading held by mothers and fathers in general.

As mentioned before, the school had employed various means to set up their home-reading scheme and promote the partnership with parents. These and other ways are returned to later in this chapter. The following questions refer to the means by which the school had sought to involve, instruct and interest their pupils' parents.

Question: Was it clear to you from the first meeting, what you were expected to do?

The meetings launching the scheme were conducted in year groups with the teachers from two parallel classes getting together and holding their meetings on different afternoons in the course of a week. The main thrust of all the meetings was that of sharing and enjoying books together. As part of the presentation, the teachers showed and read to parents some good early books for children. They went through the points covered in the booklet about timing and getting stuck on words.

Of the group of parents interviewed, most had attended a meeting. They had largely understood what the teachers had been saying, but agreed that the actual carrying out of the ideas had made things clearer than 'just listening'. They came away from the meeting willing to 'give it a go', but quite sceptical as to how much difference their efforts would make.

The three fathers who were educated in Africa and recently settled in this country did not attend the meetings. The language support teacher had been present at the meetings and had visited groups of parents at home.

Questions: Did you read the booklet? How helpful was it?

The school produced an attractive booklet with line drawings done by children. Most of the group replied that they had read this soon after the meeting, but none of the group had referred to it since! The reason for this was that they found their present task so unproblematical that they did not need the guidance of the booklet. The three fathers already mentioned could not read the booklet fully, and they were carrying out a modified version of the practice advocated in that they were not reading to their child at all, but rather listening to him or her and asking questions about the text.

Questions: Do you write in the comment sheet? Are the teacher's comments helpful?

The responses to these questions proved to be the most varied. Some parents seemed to write quite naturally – usually about the child's response to the book and noting any particular difficulties. Some parents rarely commented, they felt unsure of what was appropriate and how frank they might be. Many parents commented that now the scheme was established they were running out of things to say! The main problem of the standard type of comment sheet seems to be for those parents who do not write in English: the sheet did not represent to them a means by which a dialogue could be carried on. All the parents confined any comments to the child's reading, but interestingly, all the parents would have liked fuller comments from the teachers. (This will be returned to later.) They would have appreciated information about the child's reading in school and about the book.

Question: Is there anything else you want to know about reading?

The group were mostly quite confident at this stage in their practice. They had all seen definite improvement in their child's reading and interest in books and other text, but they did feel that they would need more guidance if they were to continue to be involved when their child was a fluent reader. Interestingly, they were all very concerned about their writing and it would have seemed from this sample of parents, that having helped to give their child a good start in reading they would appreciate the chance to help with writing also.

It would seem from these interviews, that with many parents there is a good deal of shared understanding about reading, at least at the initial learning stages. The exceptions were those parents recently arrived who were not only experiencing difficulties with English language in all its aspects, but also had vastly different cultural expectations. While most of the parents accepted the importance of enjoyment and engagement at the early stages, these people saw the child's future reading mainly in functional terms.

Some ways of establishing a closer partnership with parents in reading

The various ways in which teachers can try to establish a closer partnership with parents in reading are well established and many of these ways were being used by the school in question. Ways in which this school are planning to make the partnership more effective are also mentioned briefly:

1. Through meetings, talks and individual contacts.
2. Through written material.
3. Through home visits.
4. Through the comment sheet.

1. Through meetings, talks and individual contacts

The teacher will be aiming for four main goals:
(a) to reinforce and confirm parents as educators
(b) to show how books work
(c) to explain the process and practice of reading as it is perceived by the school
(d) to offer advice and guidance.

Schools tackle these tasks in various ways, sometimes using video or role play as an aid. This school plans to hold a whole school meeting early in the next school year to reinforce its good beginnings and to take parents on a little further in these four aspects now that they have had some common experience.

2. Through written material

Many schools compile their own short booklets. There are also an increasing number of published sources; these include ILEA's *Read, Read, Read* (McKenzie *et al.*, 1984) and various booklets and sheets from the Centre for Reading. There are also full-length books which might be loaned to interested parents: Margaret Meek's *Learning to Read* (1982) is a very good example of one such book. This school plans to compile a further booklet, discussing reading in more depth and showing parents how they can continue to help once their child is a fluent reader.

3. Through home visits

In some schools home visits are made to all parents as an extension of the teacher's role in organising a home-reading scheme. Reference to this important aspect is made in *Partnership with Parents in Children's Reading* (Bloom, 1986) as well as in many other sources. In this particular school, home visits were not the general practice, though the Language Support teacher did talk with groups of parents about the scheme, a practice which it is now intended to develop further.

4. Through the comment sheet

The success of this method of communication has been illustrated by the varied responses of the parents interviewed: The comment sheet is almost universal in its use, but there are some problems.

To help parents who do not write in English the PACT Hackney Teachers' Centre have produced comment cards in English and other languages. They use various symbols for parents to use, to give an indication of how the reading was done and the child's response.

The following extract from a comment sheet used in a scheme described in Bloom (1986) is obviously limited from the parents' point of view:

	TEACHER	PARENT
1/9	Read 2 pages aloud to your mum.	He refused to read his book to me, just grizzled and played up. G. Green, Mr
1/10	Read 2 pages aloud.	No messing about at all with me. Got down to it. He told us the story so far. Mrs J. Green

The next extract from a different scheme in the same book gives an important comment from the teacher.

Trug 1	I've offered him a free choice!	Read this through 3 times in about five minutes! He said it was a bit easy for him and he'd find something harder next time!
Trug 3 & 4	I tried to persuade him to change series but *no way*. So I've sent 2 at a time!	

In conclusion: how close is the partnership?

From the sample of parents interviewed it would seem that for many of them the partnership is fairly close at the stage of sharing and reading books together. This considerable degree of partnership seems able to be accomplished by careful and thoughtful planning, a supply of good books and goodwill on both sides. Communication is the essence of a good partnership and it seems that in this area, parents' particular needs should be looked at, if not individually then in small groups. Somehow there needs to be a monitoring and evaluation of such schemes based on feedback from parents and children. Then practice and communication can be refined and, if necessary, goals redrawn.

References

BLOOM, W. (1986) *Partnership with Parents in Children's Reading* (London: Hodder & Stoughton).
MEEK, M. (1982) *Learning to Read*, (London: Bodley Head).
MCKENZIE, M., PIGEON, S. and WARE, I. (1984) *Read, Read, Read* (Centre for Language in Primary Education, ILEA).
PITFIELD PROJECT (1984) *PACT Reading Record Cards* (Hackney Teachers' Centre, ILEA).

Chapter 4

A Critical look at the Advice Given to Parents Helping Their Children to Read

Eleanor Anderson

There has been an increase recently in the number of schemes involving parents in developing their children's reading at home. This has been as a result of the successful Haringey (Hewison and Tizard, 1980) and Belfield (Jackson and Hannon, 1981) projects. The purpose of this study was to consider the extent to which a sample of publications for parents reflected insights gained from recent research in literacy development. The findings suggested that there may be a narrowing of focus in the advice being offered and a tendency to present reading as a performance rather than as a purposeful activity.

Introduction

Nearly ten years ago Moseley and Moseley (1977), in their thorough review of research on language and reading among underachievers, drew attention to the fact that there are significant gains in reading and language performance where home and school contacts are fostered.

Since then there has been a proliferation of schemes concerned not just with fostering closer links between home and school, but also with involving parents in developing their children's reading at home.

This was mainly because of the success of the Haringey Reading Project and its precursors (Hewison and Tizard, 1980; Tizard *et al.*, 1982), the work of the Coventry Community Education group (Widlake and McLeod, 1984) and the Belfield Project (Jackson and Hannon, 1981).

These early studies all involved parents in listening to their children reading. However, in a recent review of parental involvement in children's reading, Topping and Wolfendale (1985) discuss four different categories of involvement, namely parental listening, paired reading, behavioural methods and variations of those.

Listening approaches may involve *only* listening or they may involve hearing children read very much along the lines recommended to teachers by Goodacre (undated), Campbell (1981) or Arnold (1983).

Paired reading has two strands, *simulataneous reading* when adult and child read in synchrony, and *reinforced individual reading* when the child reads independently. The child signals by tapping (Morgan and Lyon, 1979) when he or she wishes to read independently and taps again when wishing to return to simultaneous reading. A variation of this approach is Pause, Prompt and Praise which involves only partial support for the reader in order to encourage self-correction strategies (Glynn, 1980).

Behavioural methods have been used on the whole, but not exclusively, with children with learning difficulties. The approaches may involve the use of reinforcement in the form of, perhaps, a token economy, precision teaching or direct instruction. Topping (1985) includes Pause, Prompt and Praise in this category, but it appears to me to be simply a version of paired reading. It is certainly no more behaviourist in approach than is paired reading.

Robson *et al.*, (1984) and Topping (1985) claim superiority for the paired reading approach but Swinson (1986) sounds a well-argued note of caution about interpreting the source of improvement in any one approach, when, as was pointed out in this introduction, parental involvement alone is effective. He does not accept the claims that 'paired reading' is superior to the traditional 'listening' approaches, though he admits that it may be for non-readers and other special groups. In fact, there would seem to be a strong case for drawing together the practices of the home and the school.

The concern of this paper then is to examine the extent to which the advice being given to parents is similar to or different from that being given to teachers. If what is being encouraged is a genuine partnership one would expect a certain commonness of content across the advice, allowing for the fact that the roles and settings differ.

Working with teachers on initial and in-service literacy courses, over the past ten years the following are the major insights from reading and study that the teachers have found most useful in practice.

The first is confirmation from Lawrence's work (1971, 1972 and 1973) of the importance of confidence, self-concept and the relationship between reader and listener in the development of competence in reading.

The second, deriving from the work of Clay (1969, 1972) and of Goodman (1969, 1982), is the value of listening to children's miscues to gain insight into the child's construction of meaning and the increase in confidence on the part of the listener in allowing time for the child to self-correct, perhaps to miss out a word and to read on to the end of a sentence, paragraph or story before attempting it again. The literature is full of examples of this happening and there is yet another

Text	Jenna's reading of the text
Every day at nine o'clock Mr Pine went to his sign shop on Vine Street to paint signs. "What signs do we need today?" he would ask his wife.	Every day at nine o'clock Mr Pin went to his ——— shop on Vin Street to paint ———. "What sins do we need today? he would ——— his wife. ask his wife.
One day Mrs Pine looked at the list and said, "Well we need six STOP signs. Three KEEP OFF THE GRASS signs. Four SCHOOL signs. One DON'T FEED THE ANIMALS sign and two CAKES FOR SALE signs. Mr Pine said, "Signs, signs, signs, that's too many signs to paint in one day, I need a day off."	One day Mrs Pin looked at the last and said, "Well we need six STOP ———. Three KIT OFF THE ——— ———. Four SCHOOL ———. One DON'T FEED THE ANIMALS ——— and ——— ——— ——— ———. Mr Pin said, "Signs, signs, signs, that's too many signs to paint in one day, I need a day off."

FIGURE 4.1 *Jenna's miscues*

in Figure 4.1. You will notice that it is at the ninth occurrence that Jenna, who is just six years old, read 'sign' correctly.

The third insight, drawing on the work of Reid (1966, 1983) and Cazden (1983), is the need to have a language to talk about written language, to talk about the reading process as well as the content.

The fourth insight, from the work of Clark (1976, 1984) and of Payton (1984), is the importance of answering children's questions about written language.

Closely related to this is the fifth insight, from the work of Reid (1966), Ferreiro (1980, 1984), Ferreiro and Teberosky (1982), Goodman (1984) and Wells (1982), that is the role of print in the environment in children's awareness of written language.

The sixth insight, from Mackay *et al.* (1970), Holdaway (1972), Clark (1976) and Teale (1984), is the importance of reading stories to children so that they become accustomed to hearing written language, the language of books.

The seventh insight, from the work of Bradley and Bryant (1985) and Bryant and Bradley (1985), is the importance for children of playing with rhymes and letter shapes.

The study

In order to examine the extent to which these insights are reflected in the advice given to parents, a sample of 24 research reports, articles and pamphlets for parents was chosen from the Hertfordshire collection of papers on parental involvement in children's reading. The earliest was dated 1979 and the most recent 1986. These were then considered under the seven headings already introduced.

The publications were taken out of context, in as much as no account could be taken of what was said to parents, only what was written down. The sample is small and may well be unrepresentative. It is not the purpose of this paper, therefore, to provide answers about the state of the art, but to raise questions about present and future practice.

Results

1. The importance of a positive relationship

Twenty-two out of the twenty-four publications stressed the necessity for a warm and encouraging atmosphere.

2. Provision of opportunities for self-correction

Fourteen of the publications encouraged some form of self-correction, but this varied from reading to the end of the sentence then trying again, to re-reading after an adult had read correctly. Few would have permitted Jenna (see Figure 4.1) to have had nine attempts at 'sign'.

3. The importance of talking about the reading process

This was mentioned in only three of the publications.

4. The need to answer questions about print

This was mentioned in only two of the publications.

5. The use of print in the environment

This was mentioned in six of the publications.

6. The importance of reading to children

Twelve of the publications mentioned reading aloud to children and some also mentioned the use of stories on tape.

7. Playing with rhymes and letter shapes

Only four of the publications mentioned this as a worthwhile activity.

Discussion

It may well be that the poorly represented categories (*talking about the reading process, answering questions about print, the use of print in the environment, playing with rhymes and letter shapes*) are all activities that are normally associated with the very early stages of reading development and are considered irrelevant for older children or children who have made a start on reading. It would be unfortunate if this is the case, as each activity can contribute powerfully to the continued development of reading, as Donaldson and Reid (1982) and Reid (1983) argued so cogently. Indeed, the development of a language or metalanguage to talk about texts is what is made explicit in and contributes to the effectiveness of group reading, discussion and thinking activities (Lunzer and Gardner, 1979, 1984) or 'DARTS', as Lunzer and Gardner (1984) call them.

The same argument of relevance only to the early stages may also have been applied to reading aloud to, and sharing stories with, children. Though it is quite clear that listening to texts read aloud is an educationally valuable activity for all ages, not only for the development of reading and awareness of a range of styles and registers (Chapman, 1984, Chapman and Louw, 1986), but also for the development of writing (Smith, 1982).

Just over half of the papers encouraged opportunities for self-correeection. Admittedly, such provision is complex and may be difficult to handle, but at the very minimum children should be encouraged to read on to the end of the sentence, thus enabling the use of syntactic and semantic cues to support what is available from grapho-phonic cues. They will then have the chance to self-correct or to have their attention drawn to any breakdown in the sense of the passage. Since listening to a child read or reading with a child (Waterland, 1985) is such a delicate balance of providing confidence but also opportunities for independence; a balance between silent reading and oral reading; between drawing attention to errors that distort meaning and ignoring those that do not; perhaps it is too complex to communicate to parents. And yet, dilemmas of such a kind are the very essence of the childrearing and caring that occurs before schooling.

Indeed, some of the publications expressed these very points clearly and succinctly. In fact, some of the briefest accounts (two sides of an A4 sheet) were among the most wide-ranging. It was among these that two additional insights were covered. One was the relationship between talking and writing and the use of a language experience approach to the development of literacy. The other was the importance of reading right across the curriculum, not just for reading stories. These are two areas which would be included in a replication or extension of this study.

Implications for practice

In order to accommodate the subtlety of moving from supported to independent reading it may be necessary, as some projects already do, to have a series of leaflets, workshops or meetings for parents where advice changes gradually in character as confidence and success are achieved and as parent and child become more aware of the joy of mastery of print, and gain a greater understanding of its power and complexity.

There was evidence from reading through the reports that some of the more recent applications of earlier approaches were sometimes accompanied by a narrowing down of focus on a few 'Dos and Don'ts', that did not reflect adequately the theoretical base of the original work. This applied equally to 'listening' approaches and to 'paired reading' approaches. It would be disastrous for all concerned if listening was only to occur with one page of a school reading book or if paired reading was to become simply parroting an adult. It would be reprehensible if in the emphasis on performance one was to lose sight of the purpose of reading; if in straining after accuracy one ceased to question the authenticity and purpose of the text; to emphasise the role of reader and accept uncritically the product of the writer.

It is hoped that some of the issues raised in this paper may provide a wider framework or starting point for those who may be considering developing a scheme of parental involvement in children's reading. However, it would seem worthwhile at this point to reiterate Swinson's (1986) caution that it is the *involvement* of parents that appears to be effective. The detail of approach required may vary from child to child and from parent to parent. No firm evidence would seem to be available about the superiority of one method over another.

Conclusion

In a recent report, Hannon (1986) suggests, as a result of his comparison of teachers and parents hearing children read, that: 'there may be considerable similarities between parents and teachers in hearing children read' (p. 22). If this is the case, then there would appear to be hopes for partnership with parents and a genuine sharing of knowledge and of expertise. As Hannon (1986) goes on to point out: 'When it comes to providing support or advice, there could be some aspects of their strategies which we might invite them [parents] to reflect upon, and perhaps modify. However, that applies to anyone hearing children read, including teachers' (pp. 22–3).

References

ARNOLD, H. (1983) *Listening to Children Reading* (London: Hodder & Stoughton).
BRADLEY, L. and BRYANT, P. (1985) *Rhyme and Reason in Reading and Spelling* (Ann Arbor: University of Michigan Press).
BRYANT, P. and BRADLEY, L. (1985) *Children's Reading Problems* (Oxford: Basil Blackwell).
CAMPBELL, R. (1981) 'An approach to analysing teacher moves in hearing children read', *Journal of Research in Reading*, vol. 4, pp. 43–56.
CAZDEN, C. B. (1983) 'Play with language and metalinguistic awareness: one dimension of language experience', in Donaldson, M., Grieve, R. and Pratt, C. (eds) *Early Childhood Development and Education* (Oxford: Basil Blackwell), pp. 302–7, first published 1974 in *Urban Review*, vol. 7, no. 1.
CHAPMAN, L. J. (1984) 'Nurturing every child's literarcy development: a

four-pronged teaching strategy', in Dennis, D. (ed.) *Reading: Meeting Children's Special Needs* (London: Heinemann), pp. 54–65.

CHAPMAN, L. J. and LOUW, W. (1986) 'Register Development and Secondary School Texts', in Gillham, B. (ed.) *The Language of School Subjects* (London: Heinemann).

CLARK, M. M. (1976) *Young Fluent Readers* (London: Heinemann).

CLARK, M. M. (1984) 'Literacy at Home and at School: Insights from a Study of Young Fluent Readers', in Goelman, H., Oberg, A. and Smith, F. (eds) *Awakening to Literacy* (London: Heinemann).

CLAY, M. M. (1969) 'Reading errors and self-correction behaviour', *British Journal of Educational Psychology*, vol. 39, pp. 47–56.

CLAY, M. M. (1972) *Reading: The Patterning of Complex Behaviour* (London: Heinemann).

DONALDSON, M. and REID, J. F. (1982) 'Language skills and reading: a developmental perspective', in Hendry, A. (ed.) *Teaching Reading: the Key Issues* (London: Heinemann), pp. 1–14.

FERREIRO, E. and TEBEROSKY, A. (1982) *Literacy Before School* (Exeter, New Hampshire: Heinemann) (UK publication 1983).

FERREIRO, E. (1984) 'The Underlying Logic of Literacy Development', in Goelman, H., Oberg, A. and Smith, F. (eds) *Awakening to Literacy* (London: Heinemann), pp. 154–73.

FERREIRO, E. (1980) 'The relationship between oral and written language: The children's viewpoints', in Clark, M. M. (ed.) *New Directions in the Study of Reading* (Lewes: Falmer Press) (1985), pp. 83–94, first published in 1979–80 in Goodman, Y. M., Haussler, M. M. and Strickland, D. S. (eds) *Oral and Written Language Development Research: Impact on the Schools* (Urbana, Illinois: National Council of Teachers of English).

GOODACRE, E. J. (undated) *Hearing Children Read* (University of Reading: Centre for the Study of Reading).

GOODMAN, K. (1969) 'Analysis of oral reading miscues: applied psycholinguistics', *Reading Research Quarterly*, vol. 5, pp. 9–30.

GOODMAN, K. (1982) *Language and Literacy. The Selected Writings of K. S. Goodman vol. 1: Process, Theory, Research*, Gollasch, F. V. (ed.) (Boston: Routledge & Kegan Paul).

GOODMAN, Y. (1984) 'The Development of Initial Literacy', in Goelman, H., Oberg, A. and Smith, F. (eds) *Awakening to Literacy* (London: Heinemann), pp. 102–9.

GLYNN, T. (1980) 'Parent–child interaction in remedial reading at home', in Clark, M. M. and Glynn, T. (eds) *Reading and Writing for the Child with Difficulties* (Educational Review, Occasional Paper no. 8, University of Birmingham).

HANNON, P. (1986) 'Research into How Parents Hear Their Children Read', *Education*, 3–13, vol. 14, no. 1, pp. 20–3.

HEWISON, J. and TIZARD, J. (1980) 'Parental involvement in reading attainment', *British Journal of Educational Psychology*, vol. 50, pp. 209–15.

HOLDAWAY, D. (1972) *Independence in Reading* (Auckland, New Zealand: Ashton Scholastic).

JACKSON, A. and HANNON, P. (1981) *The Belfield Reading Project* (Rochdale: Belfield Community Centre).
LAWRENCE, D. (1971) 'The effects of counselling on retarded readers', *Educational Research*, vol. 13, pp. 119–24.
LAWRENCE, D. (1972) 'Counselling of Retarded Readers by Non-professionals', *Educational Research*, vol. 15, pp. 48–51.
LAWRENCE, D. (1973) *Improved Reading Through Counselling* (London: Ward Lock).
LUNZER, E. and GARDNER, K. (1979) *The Effective Use of Reading* (London: Heinemann).
LUNZER, E. and GARDNER, K. (1984) *Learning from the Written Word* (Edinburgh: Oliver & Boyd).
MACKAY, D., THOMPSON, B. and SHAUB, E. (1970) *Breakthrough to Literacy: Teacher's Manual* (London: Longman).
MORGAN, R. and LYON, E. (1979) 'Paired Reading – A Preliminary Report on a Technique for Parental Tuition of Reading Retarded Children', *Journal of Child Psychology and Psychiatry*, vol. 20 (2), pp. 151–60.
MOSELEY, C. and MOSELEY, D. (1977) *Language and Reading among Underachievers*, (Windsor: NFER).
PAYTON, S. (1984) *Developing Awareness of Print* (Educational Review, Offset Publication no. 2, University of Birmingham).
REID, J. F. (1966) 'Learning to think about reading', *Educational Research*, vol. 9, pp. 55–62.
REID, J. F. (1983) 'Into print: reading and language growth', in Donaldson, M., Grieve, R. and Pratt, C. (eds) *Early Childhood Development and Evolution* 67–8 (Oxford: Basil Blackwell).
REID, J. F. and LOW, J. (1972) *Link up Teacher's Manual* (Edinburgh: Holmes McDougall).
ROBSON, D., MILLER, A. and BUSHELL, R. (1984) 'The development of paired reading in High Peak and West Derbyshire', *Remedial Education*, vol. 19 (4), pp. 177–83.
SMITH, F. (1982) *Writing and the Writer* (London: Heinemann).
SWINSON, J. M. (1986) 'Paired reading: a critique', *Support for Learning*, vol. 1, no. 2, pp. 29–32.
TEALE, W. H. (1984) 'Reading to Young Children: Its Significance for Literacy Development', in Goelman, H., Oberg, A. and Smith, F. (eds) *Awakening to Literacy* (London: Heinemann).
TIZARD, J., SCHOFIELD, W. N. and HEWISON, J. (1982) 'Collaboration between teachers and parents in assisting children's reading', *British Journal of Educational Psychology*, vol. 52, no. 1, pp. 1–15.
TOPPING, K. and WOLFENDALE, S. (eds) (1985) *Parental Involvement in Children's Reading* (London: Croom Helm).
TOPPING, K. (1985) 'An Introduction to Behavioural Methods' in Topping, K. and Wolfendale, S. (eds) *Parental Involvement in Children's Reading* (London: Croom Helm), pp. 163–72.
WATERLAND, L. (1984) *Read With Me: An Apprenticeship Approach to Reading* (Stroud: The Thimble Press).

WELLS, C. G. (1982) *Language, Learning and Education* (Centre for the Study of Language and Communication, University of Bristol).

WIDLAKE, P. and MCLEOD, F. (1984) *Raising Standards: Parent Involvement Programmes and the Language Performance of Children* (Community Education Development Centre, Coventry LEA).

Acknowledgements

Access to relevant papers was provided by Mrs Pam Rivaz, Advisory Teacher of Reading for Hertfordshire. Teachers following the Advanced Diploma in Reading provided critical comment and the miscue example. Their support is acknowledged with gratitude.

Chapter 5

Working Together: Teachers and Parents

Flo Robinson

This paper outlines the research and rationale of teachers and parents working together, and then describes some of the initiatives that have been taken successfully by teachers to promote this and effect change dealing with:

1. THE IMPORTANCE OF PRE-SCHOOL INITIATIVES because it is at this stage that the climate for partnership should be established.

2. THE PARTNERSHIP IN SCHOOL where there needs to be an open sharing of information, skills and goals.

3. THE DEVELOPMENT OF THIS PARTNERSHIP AT A LATER STAGE, where the partnership may change but does not stop, and a summary of the benefits.

Research and rationale

Research evidence shows that where teachers and parents work together to help children to learn to read, on the whole children do very much better.

One piece of research carried out in Haringey (Tizard, *et al.*, 1982) has shown that if parents are encouraged simply to 'hear their children read' the effects on reading in school are very pronounced indeed. They found that children whose parents heard them read on a regular basis did significantly better in school reading tests than those children who had received extra help at school, and this finding was consistent across all ability levels.

For many years now, schools in Coventry have given top priority to involving parents throughout the school, particularly in the areas of reading and language development. A recent survey covering eight schools and nearly 1000 pupils revealed good levels of achievement in oral and written language and in reading comprehension. A very high proportion of the pupils tested had positive attitudes towards reading. Children in these schools, mainly from so-called disadvantage backgrounds, were doing as well as, and often better than their 'middle-class' peers. In all schools, a clear-cut linear relationship was found between the amount of parent support provided and children's reading performance. The results of this survey are published in *Raising Standards* available from the Community Education Development Centre (CEDC).

Teachers involved in the Parent and Child and Teacher (PACT) scheme in Hackney not only found improvements in children's reading ability and attitudes to reading but also that this contact between home and school led to improved relationships between the two.

These examples and other well-documented work in this area, including the Belfield experiment in Rochdale, all reinforce the belief that there is much to be gained by parents and teachers working together. As far as reading is concerned, children who are at an advantage usually have the following sort of background: parents who themselves read at home; books in the home; books bought for birthdays and Christmas, or with the shopping; a regular bedtime story; parents who take them to the local library, talk and play with them, encourage them to discuss and argue, take them on outings and provide a stimulating environment; parents who have the confidence to find out how they can support the school and do so; and above all somebody at home, parent, grandparent or older sibling, willing to give time and encouragement to hear the child read.

Many children do not have these advantages, and sadly, many schools have seen the disadvantages as a result of their attitude. The reality is that many parents have been let down by the system, have little or no confidence in schools nor in themselves as people, as parents or as educators of their own children. There is little spare money for books (and it is important to own books), libraries are often far away, it costs money to get there and bookshops are even further away. Even regular bedtime stories may be a counsel of perfection in a household where parents are continually exhausted by social problems and have little inclination because of the pressures of their own lives.

Over the past few years many teachers have effected changes in their own attitudes and those of parents in two main areas – in attitudes towards each other and in working together in ways we would not have thought possible twenty years ago. I will now outline some of the changes that have taken place.

Pre-school initiatives

Since the early years are so important, we have begun to recognise the need to establish a climate for partnership before children come into school, and although we are specifically considering a partnership in reading we would see it as only one aspect, albeit a major one, of parental involvement. It is best carried out in a climate of good home–school relationships where parents are encouraged to become partners with teachers in the education of their children.

We have also seen the need to acknowledge, appreciate and value in a non-judgemental way the job that parents do right from the start. You have only to observe parents with their children in public places to appreciate that the vast majority of parents of young children are teaching a lot of the time, but we are mostly unaware that that is what they are doing. They count as they climb the stairs, read the writing on grocery packets, bottles and signs, count out money, point out colours, and make their children aware of time. It is from parents that a child first learns about the world. We need to stress it and value it. It is vital that we help all parents to see how important their role is in the education of their children, and how it will develop and change as children grow. Our job is, I believe, to *enhance* that role.

Over the past few years, dedicated teachers and heads of schools have taken positive steps to welcome parents into schools, shown friendliness and courtesy, and a willingness to listen. Every opportunity has been taken to break down the barriers and develop a relationship so that a genuine partnership can be undertaken.

Regular family assemblies where young children accompany their parents, join in, and stay to have refreshments in a very informal way with opportunities to get to know the staff and school, coffee mornings, social occasions such as discos, craft sessions for summer fairs and bazaars where skills are shared, are some of the opportunities that have helped to change attitudes. It does mean a more 'open door' policy giving opportunities for parents and teachers to get to know each other.

Many teachers and parents would testify, however, that for them the biggest breakthrough came when home visiting was undertaken, especially before the children came into school. Indeed, this outreach work has been one of the greatest changes, for it has changed attitudes – which is the most difficult change of all – attitudes of parents to teachers and teachers to parents. It has been the means whereby many parents who were nervous of coming into school for various reasons and did not respond to the messages sent home, however welcoming, came to feel much more at ease.

As far as reading is concerned, it has, for many, meant making it easier for families to borrow and buy books, through parent and toddler groups, 'getting ready for school' groups, family libraries, regular book shops and book clubs, and having tapes of stories available as well as room and opportunity for informal adult education. Above all we have seen the need to stress that children 'get the message' about books from their parents – the example, the enjoyment and the habit, and we need to offer every encouragement to make it easier for them to do so long before the children come into school.

Working together in school

Once children are in school, teachers need to share information about how they help children to learn to read. Many parents have felt themselves excluded from helping because of the mystique that surrounds learning to read, as well as lack of information and their lack of confidence. The truth is that we don't really know how children learn to read, but we *do* know some of the things that help them. Since many of those things involve parents it is important that we work with them.

To be effective in communicating what we are doing means an open sharing of information, goals and skills, and great changes have taken place here. Instead of the mass lectures on 'How we teach reading' or the scanty bits of information gleaned at 'open evenings' we have invited parents a few at a time to observe reading activities in the classroom and to join in when they feel confident, with the guidance of the teacher. Reading evenings with exhibitions, materials and videos showing the children in the classroom, and where teachers are available for discussion, have proved to be very effective, but perhaps one of the best ways is through a series of workshop sessions where parents can:

(a) Find out something of the school's approach to reading.
(b) Learn in an active learning situation some of the stages and problems a child may experience.
(c) Make games and materials to take home for parents and child to do together.
(d) Have an opportunity to hear their child or another child read, with teacher at hand to support and help.
(e) Discuss topics like the importance of talking with children, the importance of story telling, use of libraries, etc.

Details of the organising and running of reading workshops need careful staff discussion and planning.

Home reading schemes

Traditionally, many teachers have always sent books home

for the parents to hear the child read, and know that where this has been done conscientiously the child has benefited. This strategy has been taken much more serously by many schools: following initial meetings organised by the schools, parents have been asked to hear their children read at home, and to comment about how they got on, on a card or booklet prepared by the school. Inviting the parents to comment either verbally or in writing has proved to be effective both in obtaining a serious commitment to the task and in communicating effectively.

Later stages

As confidence in each other and as skill grows, other intiatives that have been taken up include parents accompanying groups of children with a teacher to and from the local library, and parents publishing a regular school magazine with contributions from children, families, staff and the local community. Some parents have discovered an ability to write stories for children, others have written about their own experiences of jobs, illustrated with photographs. Such books provide a new dimension to the reading stock in the school, are seen as immediately relevant by the children, and enhance the confidence of the parents who produce them.

There is a wealth of knowledge about the local community which needs to be recorded, and parents and older children have successfully interviewed people within the community, used tape recorders to collect information and experiences, and the school has then produced books illustrated either by the children or with photographs. These books mean that the community is reflected in the curriculum of the school and local language and experience is validated.

Some parents have taken part in 'reading extension skills' workshops and have been involved in devising materials for these, whilst others have undertaken training to help devise and make simple early learning materials and games which they then take into homes where discussions are held on the importance of the early years.

The school library needs to be readily accessible to children and parents. This means regular opening times and a fixed location. Schools should have a selection of books which reflect the lifestyle of the neighbourhood. This is particularly important in disadvantaged or multi-cultural areas. Many parents are involved in operating the library and parents and children are encouraged to select books together. In some areas a large stock of popular adult books can be borrowed from the local library and changed every month. Other books can be added through donations from friends and from jumble sales. Swop shops are very popular.

Every encouragement is given to buying books or book tokens for birthdays and Christmas or prizes and a special effort made in Children's Books Week and a few weeks before Christmas when a display is mounted. Lists are available for parents and children to guide choosing, and staff are at hand and willing to help. Once books are chosen a weekly instalment scheme is put into operation and the books collected just before Christmas.

Where parents are welcomed, their skills valued and they are taken into partnership, *everyone benefits*. The children on the whole do better and are happier knowing that home and school are working together; many parents have become more confident in themselves as people, as parents and as educators of their own children, and many have been helped to enjoy their children more.

Teachers too have benefited because they have begun to realise that they need the help and support of parents; that having to explain what you are doing increases professional skill and confidence and above all, that by *working together: teachers and parents* teachers' work is made more effective and ultimately more enjoyable.

It does not devalue a teacher's role – in fact, it enhances it – but it does mean a *change* in role. It is necessary to advise parents and children, organise materials, stimulate and encourage, diagnose and help with weaknesses, and become involved in informal adult education. For some teachers this change in role is difficult and we believe that the change can only come about with training. It is not acknowledged in initial training.

The Community Education Development Centre offers such

an in-service training programme to local authorites. For further information contact:

Mr Phil Street
Assistant Director
Community Education Development Centre
Briton Road
COVENTRY CV2 4LF

Tel. No. (0203) 440814

References

CEDC's publications on readings

Raising Standards
Reading: How to involve parents (for teachers)
For Parents
Beginning reading (Pack of 10 books)
Improving reading (Pack of 10 books)

Other publications

GRIFFITHS, A. and HAMILTON, D. (1984) *Parent, Teacher, Child – Working together in children's learning* (London: Methuen).
JACKSON, A. and HANNON, P. (1981) *The Belfield Reading Project* (Rochdale: Belfield Community Council).
TIZARD, J., SCHOFIELD, W. and HEWISON, J. (1982) 'Collaboration between teachers and parents in assisting children's reading'. *British Journal of Educational Psychology*, vol. 52, no. 1, pp. 1–15.
WATERLAND, L. (1985) *Read With Me* (Stroud: The Thimble Press).

Chapter 6

Parents of the Future

Rosemary Bacon and Alan Porter

An account of the 'cross-age tutoring' project being carried out in Lancashire by the Reading and Language Service. The project was introduced with the expectation that it would be of benefit to the educational progress of the junior school children who were involved. It was not originally envisaged that important developments would also take place within the teenage tutors – the parents of the not-too-distant future.

Cross-age tutoring, as developed in Lancaster, is a system which uses 'failing' fourth-year secondary school pupils as individual tutors to first-year junior school children who are experiencing great difficulty with their reading and language skills.

It has now been in operation since 1984 and is proving to be extremely successful, with an increasing number of schools wishing to establish schemes based upon the model created and supervised by the Reading and Language Service. Substantial gains have been noted; both the junior and secondary youngsters have made marked progress in terms of their reading and language skills, and in the case of the tutors their schools have noted an improved attitude, motivation and responsibility.

The junior school children involved in the project are those children who by the end of their time in the infant school are still non-readers, as identified by the County Top Infant Screening. The tutors from the secondary school are selected from among those young people who experienced similar difficulties and frustrations when they were younger and are, therefore, in a position to relate to the problems being experienced by the juniors and to bring a sympathetic understanding to the task which they were asked to perform.

In all of the literature available on the subject it was stated that the pre-planning of a cross-age tutoring scheme was important to its ultimate success, and a considerable amount of organisation and co-operation between the two schools to be involved was necessary before the project should be launched. Early discussions involved county advisers and educational psychologists, as well as the headteachers and their respective staffs. The parents of the youngsters had to be approached, and their approval sought. The meetings of the school staffs were particularly crucial. In the case of the junior school, all the staff were invited to a meeting, and in the case of the secondary school all the staff who might be directly involved in one way or another. Reaction varied from sceptical and dismissive to enthusiastic and welcoming; but both staffs were prepared to accept cross-age tutoring as an addition to their respective curricula.

Having gained the approval of both schools that the scheme should go ahead, the next priority was to select those pupils who would take part. Previous discussions with the schools' staffs had concluded that a maximum of eight pairs would be a viable figure for consideration. By sheer good fortune, the Infant Screening threw up a total of six children who quite clearly were encountering enormous difficulties with their reading and who lent themselves ideally to consideration for the project. Further good fortune accounted for the fact that the six were three boys and three girls. The average IQ of the group (as indicated by the Infant Screening) was 89; the average RQ was 78. To all intents and purposes they were non-readers.

In the case of the secondary school, discussion between the headteacher and staff of the Reading and Language Service resulted in criteria being arrived at for the selection of the tutors. They must be:

(a) Fourth-year secondary pupils (that is, not in their examination year).
(b) Not ex-pupils of the primary school involved. (The primary school staff felt certain reservations about welcoming back

into their school ex-pupils in an entirely different role – that is, as tutors. In fact, circumstances dictated that one tutor was an ex-pupil, but this proved to be in no way difficult or awkward.)
(c) Should possess an adequate basic verbal ability and expressive vocabulary level.
(d) Should be caring and sympathetic.
(e) Should have a history of 'failure'.

In addition, the headteachers felt that it would be more appropriate if girls were tutored by girls and boys by boys. Responsibility for identifying the tutors was left entirely to the staff of the secondary school. The project co-ordinator appointed by the Reading and Language Service specifically requested that he be given no information about the performance or background of the proposed tutors, thereby eliminating any prejudice.

During the final few weeks of the Summer term it was the task of the Project Co-ordinator to meet the proposed tutors and to explain what would be required of them in terms of role and commitment if they were to take on the task. In all earlier discussions with advisers, headteachers, the educational psychologist, staffs of both schools and the Reading and Language Service, there had been many reservations expressed about the ability or willingness of the tutors to remain committed to the project for the whole of the school year. The Project Co-ordinator took on the responsibility of ensuring this, and it was necessary, therefore, for him to establish at as early a stage as possible a relationship with the tutors which was clearly supportive. The importance of the task was emphasised and re-emphasised. It was also clearly pointed out that it was going to involve a considerable amount of hard work and application on their part; that it was not just a means of avoiding 'normal' lessons. It is, perhaps, worth pointing out that at no time during the ensuing year was there any hint of other than total commitment and responsibility by the tutors.

In the first week of the new school year it was important that the matching of the tutors should be done. There had been much discussion as to how the matching could best be achieved, but in reality it was done very simply. Within the agreed stipulation of boys-with-boys and girls-with-girls they were simply put together in a room containing books and games and left to sort themselves out into pairs. This was achieved without any difficulty, and the ensuing year demonstrated the success of the pairings. It is perhaps interesting to note that the little girl from the junior school who was extremely shy and introverted and who had a reputation for rarely speaking, was singled out by the one tutor who was equally shy and retiring and who rarely made any sort of verbal contribution without first being prompted. Equally, the most confident and forthcoming of the boy tutors found himself attracted to the most extrovert and outgoing of the youngsters.

The groups met for three half-hour sessions per week. At the earliest stages it was necessary for the Project Co-ordinator to monitor very closely the activities which were taking place, to direct the tutors in the work which they were doing, and to assist in planning and preparation. As the skills of the tutors developed and their relationships with the youngsters grew, they became more independent and able to function efficiently and productively without being totally reliant upon the Co-ordinator.

Throughout the year there were occasions when, because of illness or absence from school, it was necessary to temporarily change the pairings or for a tutor to assume responsibility for two youngsters. In this the tutors proved to be extremely flexible and responsible, and although the intention was that there was always one-to-one direct tuition there were many occasions where the formation of informal groupings was more appropriate to the needs of the young children or to the demands made by particular circumstances.

It was also the intention that the Project Co-ordinator would be present at every tutoring session in order to oversee the tutors' activities and to monitor events. However, there were a very few occasions when it was not possible for him to be present. Despite all previous reservations this proved to be no handicap whatsoever to the continuity of the project. The tutors developed an increasing responsibility and a much-enhanced self-confidence and self-esteem as the year progressed, and were able to function efficiently without supervision when required to do so.

Each tutoring session was followed by a 'de-briefing and preparation period' between the tutors and the Co-ordinator. These began as quite formal meetings held in a room set aside at the secondary school. They provided the opportunity to discuss the details of each tutor's contribution to the work of the junior children, and the establishing of an extremely positive relationship between the Co-ordinator and the tutors. This relationship was to prove a vital element in the success of the project. The tutors were constantly informed of observations made by visitors and staff members. They shared in the organisation and administration and were regularly placed in positions of decision-making and responsibility. As the year progressed the de-briefing sessions became less necessary and less organised. With growing skill and growing awareness, the tutors required less and less guidance; they were able to maintain the continuity of their work without the direction of the Co-ordinator, whose role became that of an observer rather than a controller or director.

As the personal relationship between the Co-ordinator and the tutors was vital, so too was that between the tutors and the youngsters. From the very beginning great emphasis was placed on the establishing of a relaxed and constructive atmosphere between the two members of each group. In this the tutors were brilliantly successful. They consistently demonstrated a very high degree of genuine care and concern both for their individual charges and for the group of youngsters as a whole. They found themselves in situations which were totally foreign to them and were expected to deal with them in an understanding and sympathetic way. It is doubtful whether anybody could have predicted the high level of maturity and straightforward common sense which was brought to the task by the tutors, and it proved to be both arrogant and insulting to think of these teenagers as 'failing' youngsters.

From the initial demands of simply sharing books with their young pupils, the tutors were guided into introducing individual programmes of learning, and activities which were considered appropriate to the needs of the junior children. It was emphasised that no single activity should last for more than ten minutes, and they were encouraged to include at least three or four elements in each tutoring session – reading, writing, spelling, drawing, discussing, playing games, sharing experiences, and so on. They were extremely successful in establishing good patterns of behaviour and work habits. They were always prepared for each session; work was ready for the youngsters and the tutors were 'in position' ten minutes before their charges came to the classroom which had been made available for their use. This meant that there was no delay, no settling-down period and no waste of time. It also served as a means of modifying behaviour, if necessary, and of establishing good work attitudes (for both tutors and tutored).

The gains made by the tutors were many. Their attitudes towards their peers, teachers, and each other have developed in a very positive way. They are aware of changes within themselves, and have spoken of 'being more responsible', 'working harder', 'not mucking about as much'. They are aware of the high esteem in which they have come to be regarded by the many adults involved to a greater or lesser degree in the project, and as a consequence their self-esteem has been greatly enhanced.

These tutors will be the parents of the not-too-distant future. The experience shared by them could prove significant when they have children of their own. Those engaged in educational research and development have often bemoaned the fact that many parents do not exhibit attitudes and skills which would ensure that their children became adept with language, and eager to read. School-leavers are prepared for parenthood in many ways, but there is no emphasis placed upon the importance of sharing spoken language and books with young children; or if there is, it is usually presented in such a theoretical way as to have little impact. Could it be that the current tutors will become quite different parents because of the experiences they have enjoyed together? They have displayed precisely those attitudes of care and concern, awareness and flexibility, understanding and support which we would like to see parents bring to their children in supporting the work of our schools. These teenagers are aware, through experience, of the importance of encouraging talk and positive attitudes to reading. More than this, they are now aware that they themselves can provide the help and support that is necessary to turn failure into success.

At the start of the project all the junior children taken into it could be regarded as non-readers, or at best as children who were finding enormous difficulty in coping with the demands of the classroom. Between September and July the gains in Reading Ages varied between 7 months and 27 months, with an average gain of 10 months. This measurable progress compares favourably with the gains made previously by children of similar age, ability and performance who had received small-group remedial help from a member of the Reading and Language Service staff. By receiving guided and individual tuition for short periods three times each week, the children have been put into a privileged position, have apparently recognised that fact, and have responded in a most positive manner. Their school appears well-pleased with the attitudes developed by the children and with their increased ability to cope.

In terms, therefore, of measurable and observed progress made by both tutors and tutored, cross-age tutoring can be regarded as having a significant part to play – being at least as effective as previously tried methods. It is intended that as a future development a small group of the young people who have been involved in cross-age tutoring should be given further experience in helping young children with early language development. The Reading and Language Service will be teaching parents of young children who are language retarded how to use talk effectively with them, and the tutors will be invited to work alongside the staff of the Reading and Language Service. The hope is that they will learn by direct experience the important part the parent has to play at this vital stage, and that this will carry over into their own parenthood.

Chapter 7

Children Choosing and Reading

Dina Thorpe

An assessment of the Family Reading Group as one way in which public libraries could encourage children to see reading as an acceptable leisure time activity was based on a group at Fleetville public library, St Albans. The gratification of the children as readers can be shown to be dependent on:

1. The way in which children are able to choose what they read.

2. The materials which are provided for their choice.

3. Factors of their use of leisure time which influence the way in which they read.

Observations and statistics relating to book borrowing from Family Reading Group meetings were augmented by interviews with children and their families to discuss attitudes to reading and libraries. 'After-school diaries' completed by 300 children in the Fleetville district provide a background of leisure-time activities of 9–11-year-old children.

In his novel *If on a winter's night a traveller* . . . (Calvino, 1981) he categorises 'Books You Haven't Read' as

>the Books You've Been Planning to Read For Ages
>the Books You've Been Hunting For Years Without Success
>the Books You Need to Go With Other Books On Your Shelves
>the Books Read Long Ago Which It's Now Time To Reread
>the Books You've Always Pretended to Have Read And Now It's Time To Sit Down And Really Read Them.

He then homes in on more specific reasons for choosing a book from amongst 'New Books Whose Author Or Subject Appeals To You', 'New Books By Authors Or On Subjects Not New . . . and New Books By Authors Or On Subjects Completely Unknown'.

This is indeed a process followed by an accomplished reader with an established pattern of reading! My study of the Family Reading Group as one way in which children could be encouraged to view reading as an acceptable alternative leisure time activity looked at 9–11-year-olds – children who, for the most part, were in the process of establishing a pattern of leisure time reading. How they chose their books, and how they approached reading them, showed how they benefited from consolidating their reading experiences.

The research project was based on the Family Reading Group held in Fleetville public library, St Albans. Ten meetings of families in the areas were observed over one year, and an analysis of book borrowing records, combined with informal monthly interviews with 14 of the children who came to the meetings, provided information on the way in which children choose their reading material – and the way in which they set about reading it once they are at home.

In addition, 300 children at four junior schools in the Fleetville area completed 'after-school diaries' for a two-week period before the first Family Reading Group meeting, and again one year later. In order to assess the way in which children could be encouraged to view reading as another recreational activity, it was necessary to chart what else they did in their spare time.

The correlation of the findings on these two strands – choosing and reading books – has implications for

(a) the range of material which needs to be offered to any specific age group
(b) the number of books which a child may be allowed to borrow from school or public library at any one time
(c) the length of time which a child may be allowed to retain a book which he has borrowed.

Choosing

Few surveys of children's reading have looked specifically at how children choose books, only at what they have chosen, or, at an even greater remove, how the librarian or teacher can choose for them. The Ingham/Clift Reading Record Form, used in Jennie Ingham's (1981) Bradford Book Flood survey, asked the children 'Where did you get this book from?' and 'Why did you choose this book?'. She concluded that 'In every case, a greater percentage of favourite books was chosen because the child already had some knowledge of the book.'

As part of the impact interviews which followed each of the first four Family Reading Group meetings at Fleetville, the children were asked what had influenced their choice of titles. These interviews took the form of informal discussion; because the answers were given in the course of conversation and not merely as written answers, it was possible for children to give more than one reason for the choice of a single title – for example, one boy said that he had *The Bagthorpe Saga* recommended to him by a friend, he had heard it discussed at school and had seen it on television. A cautious fiction reader, he needed to have his choice reinforced.

The following methods of choice were preferred by Family Reading Group members interviewed.

TABLE 7.1 *Methods of choice preferred by Family Reading Group members* (100 = 14)

Method	Percentage
Personal recommendation by friend/family at Family Reading Group	86
Book seen before (at school, TV, read before)	79
Book unseen, but author, series, subject recognised	71
Book unseen, but cover/blurb/title appealed	64

Personal recommendation

'If someone says "Gosh, this is fantastic, sit down and read it", you do,' said one of the children interviewed. In trying to make reading the 'in thing' to do, and to take advantage of the 'clubbable' nature of most 9–11-year-olds, the Family Reading Group relied on peer group recommendation of its bookstock. Comments such as 'We were looking for the Marmalade Atkins books, but everybody had got them' and 'I showed that one to Mary and then she read it, and then I found another one in the series and she read that as well' are examples of its success. The Family Reading Group also takes advantage of the increasing encouragement of parents to be involved with their children's reading lower down the age range. For the most part, even at junior school age, mum's advice does not yet bring on an urge to do exactly the opposite, and parental help with choosing books is welcomed: 'It is better if my mum comes, because, usually, while I am looking at one pile my mum looks at another pile and finds some books.'

Personal and group recommendations have the effect of broadening the range of reading possibilities. This point was stressed by both children and parents interviewed during the project: 'It has really broadened her reading, and it has broadened her approach to books – she is more prepared to take a whole bunch of books and look at them, and discount them if she doesn't like them.'

As well as broadening the range of books offered to the children, the Family Reading Group also extends parents' awareness of what is available: 'I am amazed at the number of interesting paperbacks that he brings back, and also there do seem to be books directed at his age group and with his range of interests, which I had thought never existed – I wouldn't observe them in my own searches round the library.'

The Family Reading Group aimed to make choosing books a positive experience, which would in turn encourage children to gain more satisfaction from their reading. The main factors of this policy were:

(a) the type of bookstock offered for choice
(b) children were allowed an unlimited choice of books
(c) children were given the opportunity to retain a book for 3–4 months, if necessary.

The bookstock

The Fleetville project was able to present children with a selection of material, from picture books to science fiction, and to monitor its use over a period of twelve months (ten meetings). The monitoring of use showed not only which books had been borrowed, but also which had been read, as children interviewed between meetings discussed the order in which they read their books, and also mentioned those which they only read in part, or did not read at all. The children of Fleetville would agree with Robert Leeson, when he says, 'The very survival of the literature, at any level, depends upon whether it can develop a broad popular appeal'. It is becoming clear that there needs to be a balance in collections of books for children between what adults think is 'worth reading' and what children enjoy.

A listing of Family Reading Group stock in order of popularity showed that the most popular titles were those which were instantly accessible because of:

(a) *presentation* – large print, the use of pictures inset into the text, short chapters
(b) *humour* – revolving around incredible situations rather than characterisation
(c) *wordplay* – of a sophisticated kind, in puns and 'in title' jokes or of a more obvious kind in rhymes.

Titles which naturally appeal to adults because they have a moral or a complex plot appear much lower down the list. It has been noted earlier in this chapter that personal recommendation played a large part in influencing children's choice of books. It is interesting to note from the Family Reading Group records, however, that even adult recommendation cannot raise the popularity rating of several 'literary' award-winning titles. Such books are rewarding to the 'practised' reader, but intimidating to the 'beginner', usually because of complexity of characterisation. Collections for children which are overweighted with such books, which, it must be agreed, are valid in their own right to practised readers, can prevent less practised readers from establishing the reading habit. This is because there may not be enough of the immediately accessible material in such a collection to give 'beginner' readers the opportunity to establish their skills.

Unlimited choice of books

The Family Reading Group had no restriction on the number of books which could be taken home, or the length of time which they could be retained. Meetings were at four- or five-week intervals, and although children were asked whether they still had a book at home each month, they were not told to return it immediately. The number of books which could be borrowed was one of the things which children commented on after the first meeting: 'Two of my friends went and they said it was really good, and they got hundreds of books – one of them got about twelve and another took about six.' The theory behind this was that once children had a wide selection of books at home to browse amongst, they would be better able to make a choice of a book suited to their mood or the time available for reading. This freedom brought out two salient points, one about a child's choice of books and the other concerned with how he reads them.

The unlimited number of books which the children were allowed to borrow meant that they could be somewhat flippant in their choice, and give in to whims and fancies – in other words, they could really begin to enjoy books in a light-hearted way. One boy took home twelve books from the first meeting, covering a wide range of reading ability and subject matter. Starting from the heavier end there was *The Hobbit* and Richmal Crompton's *William Again*, two titles from *The Bagthorpe Saga*, two in the Jesters series, one 'choose your own adventure' type story, two 'thick' comedies, *Mr Browser and the Comet Crisis* and Hildick's *The Great Rabbit*

Robbery, two quick reads and one near picture book. This is now he described his choice:

> I was being a bit silly when I took that one, I was just going round picking up everything I thought looked good, luckily I picked up ones which were good. These are the ones I picked up on purpose – *The Hobbit* and *William Again*, but the rest I just happened to pick up and that one is three books in one. I didn't pick that one *Adventures of the ABC Mob* because of the picture, but because of the author [Forrest Wilson]; these [Jesters] I read quite a lot of when I was a bit younger, and that one [Hildick] looked quite interesting. That one [*Mr. Browser and the Comet Crisis*] was on our booklist at school; that one, I read the bit on the back.

What was most notable was that, by the time he was interviewed the week after the Reading Group meeting, Andrew had read six out of his eleven books, and they were all those that he said he had picked up when he was 'being a bit silly'. The titles which were waiting their turn were the 'William' book, which his dad had recommended, *The Hobbit* and the two *Bagthorpe* titles, which he enthused about the following month. Had he only been allowed to borrow two books, the chances are that conformity of the school booklist would have had preference, and the excitement of rollicking through several 'fun' books would have been lost.

How long does it take to read a book?

The way in which reading group members developed a cumulative reading pattern, holding some books over, and part-reading them from month to month, whilst others are eagerly devoured or rejected outright, can be seen in the following record of books read, part read and rejected by children interviewed after the first five group meetings.

It can be seen that accomplished readers, such as Martin, Andrew, or even Ceri, have a far greater success rate in terms of finding the book that they take home readable than have beginner readers such as Louise or Lucy. Roger started

TABLE 7.2 *To show the pattern of books read (R), retained and part-read (PR) and retained and not read (NR) over a five-month period*

Child	Meeting 1 R	PR	NR	Meeting 2 R	PR	NR	Meeting 3 R	PR	NR	Meeting 4 R	PR	NR	Meeting 5 R	PR	NR	Totals R	PR	NR
Tom	—	—	—	4	5	5	9	5	3	9	2	4	7	2	5	29	14	17
Andrew	10	2	0	3	2	2	3	3	0	4	1	2	3	2	0	23	10	4
Ceri	—	—	—	4	2	0	5	1	0	4	4	1	5	2	0	18	9	1
Roger	3	2	2	5	1	1	2	1	0	5	2	1	—	—	—	15	6	4
Michael	4	0	2	5	0	1	2	0	4	3	4	2	—	—	—	14	4	9
Stuart	2	3	2	2	0	2	5	1	0	4	1	2	—	—	—	13	5	6
Louise	2	1	2	2	3	3	2	4	2	1	4	5	3	4	2	10	16	14
Stephen	4	0	1	2	0	1	1	2	1	—	—	—	2	2	0	9	6	3
Martin	4	0	0	0	1	0	2	1	0	—	—	—	2	0	0	8	2	0
Lucy	2	1	2	0	5	7	1	2	0	0	4	0	3	3	2	6	15	11
Jane	1	2	0	1	4	1	2	3	2	1	3	1	—	—	—	5	12	4
Nicola	0	3	1	2	4	0	1	2	2	0	3	0	—	—	—	3	12	3
John	1	1	1	1	0	1	—	1	1	—	—	—	—	—	—	2	1	2
Clare	—	—	—	0	2	3	1	2	3	0	3	1	—	—	—	1	7	7
																156	119	85

off as a slow and unwilling reader, but as all the books which he borrowed were well within his reading capabilities, and had some 'fun value' as well (*Dracula's Bedtime Storybook, Fungus the Bogeyman, The Great Smile Robbery*), he gained a sense of achievement through completing the books which he had taken home. The high figure for books which were 'part read' reflects the experimentation which readers were allowed by the unlimited loan system.

It was quite common for children to keep a book at home for two or even three months, and to mention it each time they were interviewed. They clearly did not see themselves as failures because they had failed to finish a book, nor did they view that book as a non-starter. They just read backwards and forwards amongst different types of books and at different reading levels, as these comments show:

> I read easier ones in the middle.
>
> When I read a book I can't finish, I start on another book; there is one book which I read twice.
>
> I leave it alone for a bit when I get bored with it, and go back to it when I want to have a read and don't know what to read.

This is a situation which most of us would recognise. Constraints at school and in the public library, which make children return one book before they are allowed to borrow another mitigate against this flexibility in reading.

Time to read

One girl, talking about her week, said, 'I have netball on Mondays after school, Tuesdays I have Brownies, on Wednesdays I have flute, on Thursdays I sometimes have Gym Club, on Fridays I don't have anything.' The social life of a 10-year-old with brothers, sisters, friends and relations is amazingly complex. Add to that the demands of homework and the television set, and it is surprising that they have any time to read at all!

So when did they read?

I read when I have some spare time – in the morning before going to school.

I read mostly in my room and mostly in the afternoons. You can't read when you are cold.

I read when I go to bed.

I read in the night when I wake up.

Once more, the after-school diaries complemented the children's comments on themselves during the interviews. The diaries gave the children the opportunity to clock the length of time which they spent on an activity between going home from school and going to bed. Although the use of the time clocks was not consistent enough for a complete record of the length of time spent reading, it does give some insight into how some children read, and their patterns of reading.

Lucy mentions reading only once in her 1984 diary, when she was in the third year at junior school. At that stage she was still forming a pattern of reading which shows more clearly in her diary a year later. Here, she often notes two or more books a day from the seven which she mentions over the two-week period. She seems to be reading from one heavy and one more lightweight book each day – during the first week alternating *The King of the Copper Mountain* with *The Little Vampire*, and during the second, with *Winnie the Pooh*. After the Reading Group meeting on the Thursday of the second week, she clearly 'dips' into titles which she has just borrowed, reading *The Thirteen Days of Christmas* for ten minutes on the next evening, the *The Great Piratical Rumbustification* for five minutes and *Oggy at Home* for fifty-five minutes on days in the following week. It is worth noting that *Oggy at Home*, which together with *The Little Vampire Moves In* she records reading for a far longer period of time, is, in fact, written at a lower reading level than the other titles which she records as reading for only ten or fifteen minutes at a time. She finishes the second week with a flourish: 'I finished reading *The King of the Copper Mountains*' – and then goes on to pick up *Winnie the Pooh* once more after tea. Like most children who completed diaries, she appears to read most consistently at bedtime and also at infill times:

whilst waiting to go out or between setting the table for tea and sitting down to eat it!

Tom, a more experienced reader, who gave as his favourite occupation in his 1984 fourth-year junior school diary: 'Reading, while drinking a very cold glass of un-fizzy lemonade' was one of the few children interviewed who read each day for several forty-five minute periods. He pauses only to have his tea, watch 'Dr Who' or to tell jokes to his dad! He usually reads after children's TV programmes have finished, except on Mondays, when he notes '4.35–5.15 read a book – TV is boring on Monday'. He reads from more than one book in a day, and the random element of choosing a book – mentioned by Andrew earlier in this chapter – appears again as Tom writes in his diary:

> 8.45 Started a domino rally with paperbacks, made another domino rally with paperbacks.
> 9.00 Found a paperback I wanted to read.

Or did he? At 9.15 he 'Gave up on one book, started a thick magazine'. The obsession of a really avid reader comes over well in the entry for Friday:

> 9.00 Got ready for bed.
> 9.20 Picked up my book again.
> 9.30 Told to get into bed.
> 9.30–9.40 Sneaked a few more minutes.

The Family Reading Group research project looked at particular aspects of a 9–11-year-old's lifestyle in Fleetville, and ways in which they could be turned to advantage in encouraging children to become confident readers. The after-school diaries showed that members were more likely to include reading amongst their spare time activities. The recorded borrowing patterns reflected a growing confidence in choice of materials, and the interviews with children demonstrated how they learnt to handle more complex concepts of character and reality in fiction as the year progressed.

In other words, they were on their way towards becoming 'readers' in Calvino's sense of the term! They were also enjoying reading. As one mother said, the group created '. . .

a situation where they can read, and not have it be something they do not admit to!'.

References

CALVINO, I. (1981) *If on a winter's night a traveller* . . . (London: Secker & Warburg).
INGHAM, J. (1981) *Books and reading development* (London: Heinemann).
LESSON, R. (1985) *Reading and righting* (London: Collins).

Details of children's titles mentioned in the text

AMBRUS, V., *Dracula's Bedtime Storybook* (OUP, 1981).
BIEGEL, P., *The King of the Copper Mountain* (London: J. M. Dent, 1968).
BODENBURG, A. S., *The Little Vampire* (London: Andersen Press, 1982).
BODENBURG, A. S., *The Little Vampire Moves In* (London: Andersen Press, 1982).
BRIGGS, R., *Fungus the Bogeyman* (London: Hamish Hamilton, 1977).
CRESSWELL, H., *The Bagthorpe Saga* (first four titles) (Harmondsworth: Penguin Books, 1980).
CROMPTON, R., *William Again* (London: Macmillan, 1983).
CURTIS, P., *Mr Browser and the Comet Crisis* (London: Andersen Press, 1981).
HILDICK, E. W., *The Case of the Great Rabbit Robbery* (Sevenoaks: Hodder & Stoughton, 1976).
LAURENCE, A., *Oggy at Home* (London: Gollancz, 1977).
MCGOUGH, R., *The Great Smile Robbery* (London: Kestrel, 1982).
MAHY, M., *The Great Piratical Rumbustification* (London: J. M. Dent, 1978).
MILNE, A. A., *Winnie the Pooh* (London: Methuen, 1926).
OVERTON, J., *The Thirteen Days of Christmas* (London: Faber & Faber, 1972).
TOLKIEN, J. R. R., *The Hobbit* (London: George Allen & Unwin, 1978).
WILSON, F., *The Adventures of the ABC Mob* (London: Pepper Press, 1983).

Chapter 8

Cross-Age Tutoring in the Primary School

Margaret Litchfield

An account of a project organised in four urban primary schools to examine the effect of regular book sharing between 10–11-year-olds and 6–8-year-old poor readers. Only non-scheme books were used and the project, though measuring performance, was also concerned with attitudes to reading and possible effects on the confidence and social skills of all the children involved. The teachers who were running the project had regular consultations with the organiser and were invited to give their views, both during and at the conclusion of the work.

Aims and objectives

1. To explore the possibility of structured, rather than coincidental, learning between cross-age children and to define, what, if anything, the paired children could offer each other.
2. To increase motivation, interest and performance in reading in those top infant/first-year junior children who were perceived by their teachers as children who would benefit from extra help.
3. To monitor the effect of using 'real' story books on attitude and performance.
4. To find out if a teacher-supervised, story method approach could be implemented by 10–11-year-olds.
5. To examine the reading performance and general social attitudes of fourth-year children after a sustained period of time as helpers.
6. To examine the practical application of the above points in terms of schools' organisation contexts.

Organisation

Two junior schools and two primary schools were approached and the aims of the project were explained to them. All four volunteered to take part. Two schools serve large council estates and two have an inner-city, multi-racial catchment. The schools were each asked to invite 12 fourth-year children to take part in the project, which was generally described as helping younger children with their reading. Although the fourth-years had to be able to read, the main criteria for choice were the ability to respond caringly to others, or a feeling on the part of their teachers that they might benefit from the sense of responsibility that being a helper demands. There was to be no coercion; the children were invited to volunteer. The schools were also asked to name 12 top infant/first-year junior children who might benefit from the extra reading practice the project offered.

All fourth-year children were tested at the beginning and end of the project using the Reading For Meaning section of the Hunter-Grundin Literacy Profiles. Tutors were also interviewed at the end of the project. All the younger children were pre- and post-tested using the Nelson Primary Reading Test and all were interviewed at the beginning of the project. The 'learners' were also interviewed at the end of the period. The teachers who were involved in the daily running of the work were also asked for their comments. All interview findings are described in the following sections, copies of the questionnaires are given in Appendix 3 and standardised test results in Appendix 2.

After initial screening, 6 couples in each school were allocated to the project and 6 were to act as controls, with the promise that they could take part the following term. The allocations were made in alternate descending score order to ensure a representative ability spread in both groups. The couples were to meet, under the supervision of a named teacher, for fifteen minutes per day, four times per week, for twelve weeks. Guidelines for helpers (see Appendix 1) were given out and explained to the fourth-years at an initial briefing session held by the teacher-in-charge. A video demonstrating this teaching method was also shown. All schools were loaned a selection of appropriate non-scheme books to use specifically for the project and the children were asked to keep a record of titles they shared.

Analysis of initial questionnaire administered to project and control younger children

All the children were learning to read with traditional schemes. Represented were Ginn 360, 1, 2, 3 And Away, Pirates, Laugh And Learn, Young Shorty, Gay Way, Racing To Read and Happy Venture. One child did not have a book as she was learning her words first.

Do you like listening to stories?

Ninety-four per cent of the children liked listening to stories. One child objected 'because you have to sit on the floor too long and it's hard'. An object lesson, perhaps, in classroom organisation.

Who reads to you?

All the sample said their teacher read to them and, gratifyingly, only 20 per cent said no one read to them at home. Mothers outnumbered fathers as story readers – 63 per cent compared to 27 per cent. Asian children more frequently mentioned their father. Interestingly, as a comment on the social fabric, there was only one mention of a grandparent. The ranked order was mother, father, sister, brother, aunt, cousin and grandmother. No one mentioned a friend. There was one rather sad, 'Mum did when I was littler'.

What's your favourite story? Can you read it, yet?

Favourite stories prove that tradition is very much alive. Fifty-six per cent of the children named fairy tales, with 'Jack And The Beanstalk' and 'Goldilocks' at the top. Only three children chose 'popularised' books ('He-Man' and

'Spiderman'). Only one child could not name a favourite story. Sixty per cent said they could not read their favourite and 16 per cent said they could read it 'a bit'.

Do you enjoy reading?

Only 10 per cent of the sample said they did not enjoy reading – a testimony to their endurance, perhaps, since all were considered to be having difficulty by their teachers. One response was a significant, 'I enjoy listening' and another, 'I enjoy reading at home – we have better books there, school books are boring'.

Is learning to read easy or hard? What's easy/hard about it?

Sadly, 67 per cent of the children thought learning to read was hard. By far the most common explanation for difficulty was 'hard words' or 'remembering the words'. The second most frequent reason was trouble with phonics, for example, 'I can't sound out words', 'I sound them out but I can't think. My mind gets stuck', and 'All the words you don't know, you have to sound them out every time'.

Is it important to be able to read?

Eighty-one per cent of the children thought it was important to be able to read. Of those who gave a negative response, one child stated that it wasn't important now but would be when he was grown up so that he could enjoy reading then. Reasons for a positive response were varied and many children gave more than one reason. The following were given and each answer formed from 4 to 25 per cent of total responses:
1. Enjoyment/pleasure (8 per cent).
2. To read hard/long books when you are older.
3. Reading is helpful in getting a job.
4. To read letters/messages.
5. To enable one to learn/to become clever.
6. To read to/to teach others.
7. For when you're grown up.

What do you do when you come to a word you don't know?

Again, responses to this question varied and some children offered more than one answer. An equal number – 65 per cent – mentioned both phonics and asking the teacher. Thirty-five per cent said they would miss the word out and come back to it but many thought this was 'cheating' or 'naughty'. Others mentioned 'writing it down', 'sit and think' or 'guess'.

Who helps you to read?

Some children mentioned more than one helper. Unlike the response to Question 2, only 71 per cent mentioned their teacher, but it may be that the others automatically assumed this. The mention of parents and relations mirrored the responses to Question 2. Again, no one mentioned a friend.

Analysis of final questionnaire administered to learners

Comparisons in this section are based on the pre- and post-interviews of project children only.

Do you like listening to stories? Who reads to you?

Responses to the first question were similar to the initial interview in that nearly all the children enjoyed listening to stories. Sixty-four per cent of the sample mentioned their tutor by name (often first) as someone who read to them.

What's your favourite story? Can you read it yet?

Favourite stories also followed initial findings – fairy stories predominated. This held for both sexes and for ethnic-minority children. Responses to the second question showed a marked reversal; originally, only 21 per cent of the project sample said they could read their favourite, but at the end of the project, 78 per cent said they could.

Is learning to read hard?

Responses to this question parallel the preceding one. The figures are:

	Yes	No	A bit hard
September	60.8%	17.4%	21.7%
December	39%	34%	26%

Is it important to be able to read?

All the children thought it was important to be able to read and reasons for this mirror initial responses, except that there was more mention of enjoyment.

Who helps you to read?

Sixty per cent of the children mentioned their tutor as someone who helped them and frequently this was the first person named. Other responses mirrored those of the initial questionnaire.

Have you enjoyed reading with X? Did you like the books you read?

Both these questions elicited an enthusiastic 100 per cent 'Yes'. The comments made are listed below, but the most frequent one was, 'It's great fun!'

1. You could choose your own books.
2. I liked the books.
3. It's really good.
4. She reads to me first.
5. I liked getting help.
6. I read all the books.
7. There were lots more pictures.
8. I kept on getting different books. I could take them home to read to my mum.

Which of the books did you like best?

Responses varied, but traditional stories still predominated over even such modern classics as *On Friday Something Funny Happened* and *The Bad-Tempered Ladybird*.

Do you prefer your class reading book or the books you read with X?

Eighty-four per cent said they preferred the books they read with their tutor. Reasons for this were:

1. They were good stories.
2. They had more interesting stories.
3. When I read them I get the words right and I enjoy them.
4. X tells me the words I don't know.
5. I can change my book when I want.
6. The pictures are better.
7. I've read more books. We read every afternoon.
8. My class book is too hard.
9. It's quieter when I read with X.

These comments are probably as indicative of method as they are of material. The sole reason given by those who preferred their class book was that it had more writing in it.

Are you a better reader now? Why?

One child was not sure if he was a better reader. All the rest were very definite that they were. Among the reasons given were:

1. I've had so much practice.
2. I can read more books.
3. I read to X every day.
4. I know lots more words.
5. The books seem easier.
6. I don't mix up so many words.
7. Every time I read to X I get the words right and when I'm at home I get the hard words right, too.
8. My teacher says I am.

Analysis of questionnaire administered to fourth-year junior tutors

Have you enjoyed helping X?

All the children said they had and were openly enthusiastic.

What have you liked/not liked about it?

There were no negative comments. Many responses stressed the pleasure elements. The following examples are representative:

1. I like helping.
2. It was good to see how the first-years read.
3. I liked being with younger children.
4. I liked watching X enjoy herself.
5. I liked watching X improve.
6. I liked the stories myself.

What have you learned from the experience?

This question elicited the most varied responses in the whole project. Included were:

1. I've learnt how to help.
2. I'm more patient.
3. I've learnt how to listen.
4. I've learnt that younger children need practice.
5. I've improved my reading. I think I read faster.
6. I've learnt when to ask the teacher for help.
7. I've learnt how people learn to read.
8. I've learnt how to talk to younger children.
9. I've learnt what it's like to be a teacher.

Do you think your reading has improved? How?

Eighty-six per cent thought their reading had improved and the rest thought their performance was about the same. Reasons given for improvement were:

1. I can read higher/harder/more books now.
2. I do more reading now.
3. I was very slow – now I get long words straight away.
4. Working with a first-year improved my reading as well as hers.
5. Practising every day makes it clearer for both of us.
6. Just a feeling.
7. My teacher says so.

Would you like to help someone else?

Even though it was pointed out that they had been working together for twelve weeks and were probably getting 'fed up' all the children responded firmly that they wanted to continue the project. Some said they would like to continue with the same child since they felt they really knew each other now. Others said they would like to help another child, either because their present learner had improved or because they felt others should have the opportunity to join in.

Analysis of teacher questionnaires

Have the tutors and learners enjoyed the project?

All four teachers answered 'Yes' to this. One pointed out that the learners were grumbling because the project had ended, and all confirmed that the tutors would like to continue.

Have the learners improved in (a) reading performance; (b) attitude to reading?

All reported observable gains in confidence and fluency and mentioned how eager the learners were now to read to anyone! They also reported more positive attitudes to books. All commented on affective improvements which are not demonstrable by standardised tests.

What do you think the tutors have gained/learned from the project?

There were no negative responses to this question. Points made included:

1. A better understanding of younger children.
2. Gains in confidence for the more introverted.
3. A sense of responsibility.
4. Improved self-esteem.
5. An understanding of the difficulty others can find with a task *they* find easy.
6. A sense of their own worth and reading ability.
7. Improved story-reading techniques.

What are your views on the use of non-scheme books for this project?

Responses to this question were very favourable, with comments such as:

1. They introduced children to the idea of reading 'any' books, not just *the* reading book.
2. The books often had 'harder' words in them, which encouraged children to use context and thus widen their cueing system.
3. They helped children who were 'non-goers' to start afresh.
4. They enabled a wider choice.

What are your views on the use of non-scheme books to teach reading?

Responses to this question were much more tentative. One teacher pointed out that they enabled the attitude of 'enjoyment' in reading to be caught more easily. Two of the schools were using an individualised approach with some story books included with the scheme but felt that both should be available rather than totally non-scheme books. One teacher stated that it made the teacher's role harder *vis-à-vis* grading policy.

Were there any organisational problems?

One school reported no difficulties at all. This was probably because the sessions took place in the lunch break and were called 'Reading Club'. The other three schools, partly because of industrial action, and partly because they felt the work should have the same status as any other curricular item, chose to run the project in school time. This meant they either relied on the headteacher for cover or supervised the project sessions alongside their own classes. All three felt more effective cover would have been useful and all stressed the importance of gaining the co-operation of other staff.

What advice would you give to another school which is considering initiating this project? Would you repeat the project?

All felt the work was well worth doing and would urge other schools to try it. Main advice was to make sure that the staff involved are really interested in making it work and to sort out organisational issues so that it will fit smoothly into school routine. All are repeating the work with the control groups, at their own volition, and all could see the work becoming a permanent part of the curriculum.

Are there any alterations you would like to make?

No one offered any changes to method or content. One teacher thought she might administer the work in six-week 'bursts' and one said she would like to undertake the project within her own vertically-grouped class of third- and fourth-year juniors. Two of the schools would also change their organisation for smoother running.

Book record forms

All pairs were asked to keep a record of the book titles they shared. The average number was sixteen and the range was from twelve to twenty-seven.

Conclusions

While the standardised test results (see Appendix 2) are not statistically significant, it is gratifying that both the tutors and the learners made greater average gains than did the control groups. The following points can be drawn from the questionnaires:

1. Young children have pronounced awareness of their reading ability, can articulate their difficulties and have formed concepts of the reading process, even if we, as teachers, were not wishing to convey their received impressions.
2. Young children's attitudes to reading and themselves as readers can be made more positive through the structured help of older children using 'real' books.
3. Children enjoy learning to read with 'real' books.
4. Cross-age tutoring is a two-way learning process with increased social skills as well as insight into how we learn being developed in the older children.
5. Young children are capable of monitoring their own progress and that of others. This has implications for the amount of trust we give children for their own learning and for how we can modify classroom organisation to facilitate shared learning.
6. Although there were organisational difficulties specific to the internal structure of individual schools, all the teachers found the benefits far outweighed these. All are continuing the work and all would recommend the project to other schools.

Appendix 1

Guidelines for helpers

Session 1 Talk through the two or three books given you by the teacher. You can discuss the pictures and what might be happening. Invite the child to choose one book. You read it aloud, as naturally as possible.

Session 2 As Session 1, but pause for the child to provide the next word or phrase. This will usually be at the end of the sentence or where there is a phrase which occurs often, for example,

>   Run, run, as fast as you can,
>   You can't catch me,
>   I'm ———

Session 3 Read the book aloud and ask the child to join in with you.

Session 4 Let the child attempt to read the book by himself. You tell him any words he doesn't know.

Any or all of these sessions can be repeated and some sessions, for example 2 and 3, can be joined together. Ask your teacher. After all sessions the child should take the book away with him, to share with others or to read alone.

Children should never be forced to continue with a book they find boring.

Appendix 2

STANDARDISED TESTS – WHOLE GROUP AVERAGES

First-year juniors and top infants – Primary Reading Test

Project groups		Sept.	Dec.	
		71.5	72.5	
		69.0	79.6	
		75.2	80.2	
		77.2	81.6	
	Average	73.2	78.5	+ 5.3
Control groups		Sept.	Dec.	
		70.5	70.5	
		68.0	76.5	
		72.6	73.0	
		76.5	79.6	
	Average	71.9	74.9	+ 3

Fourth-year groups – Hunter-Grundin Literacy Profile

Project groups		Sept.	Dec.	
		89.6	96.6	
		100.3	105.3	
		112.3	118.8	
		96.6	105.8	
	Average	99.7	106.6	+ 6.9
Control groups		Sept.	Dec.	
		87.8	91.3	
		108.2	114.5	
		102.5	107.1	
		100.3	105.3	
	Average	99.7	104.5	+ 4.8

Appendix 3

Initial questionnaire – first-years

1. Do you like listening to stories?
2. Who reads to you?
3. What's your favourite story?
4. Can you read it yet?
5. Do you enjoy reading?
6. Is learning to read easy/hard? What's easy/hard about it?
7. Is it important to be able to read? Why/why not?
8. What do you do when you come to a word you don't know?
9. Who helps you to read?

Final questionnaire – first-years

As 1 to 9 above plus:
10. Have you enjoyed reading with X? What did you like/not like about it?
11. Did you like the books you read?
12. Which of the books did you like best?
13. Do you prefer your class reading book or the books you read with X?
14. Do you think you are a better reader now? Why/why not?

Final questionnaire – fourth-years

1. Have you enjoyed helping X?
2. What have you liked/not liked about it?
3. What do you think you have learnt?
4. Do you think your reading has improved?
5. Would you like to carry on helping someone?

Teachers' questionnaire

1. Have the tutors and learners enjoyed the project?
2. Have the learners improved in (a) reading performance (b) attitude to reading?
3. What do you think the tutors have gained/learnt from the project?
4. What are your views of 'non-scheme' books in this project?
5. What are your views on the use of 'non-scheme' books to teach reading?
6. Were there any organisational problems?
7. What advice would you give to another school which is considering initiating the project?
8. Would you repeat the project?
9. Are there any alterations you would make?
10. Do you see a place for this kind of work in your normal school practice?

Chapter 9

Using Volunteer Helpers as Scribes

Brigid Smith

A description of using a language-experience approach with failed and failing secondary school pupils. Case studies of five readers and their scribes have been the basis of a research project which has set out to illuminate the process by which reading texts are produced and the progress in reading and linguistic development which took place in the readers. The language-experience approach capitalises on children's oral language abilities and drive to make narratives and meaning out of their experiences. The resulting texts are in the readers' own idiom and contextualised in their own life view. The texts have all the qualities of real reading texts — extending and reinforcing good reading practice. The readers are able to achieve immediate success in reading their own texts and this can overcome the resistance and negative attitudes of many failed secondary school readers.

A description of the practicalities of using this approach demonstrates that this is a positive way of using non-professional volunteers in the classroom. Training for volunteers includes a short video. A tutor pack has been produced, based on the research findings, to give maximum support to the volunteer scribes.

Further work being undertaken during 1985/6 will concentrate on the possibilities inherent in developing stories at deep structure level when reader/writers are given the opportunity of editing and revising their original dictated stories. Texts will be stored on disk and stories printed using the word processor to facilitate the editing.

Introduction

'A Local Habitation and a name': Shakespeare's description of the function of the poet and the teaching of reading to failing 11-year-olds may seem to be in uneasy juxtaposition. The view of the reader taken in this paper presupposes, however, that such readers are creative users of language; able to negotiate for meaning in words, able to create and understand the world of story. The narrative mode, the way we tell stories, would seem to be known to older non-readers but the means of articulating the stories they know is not easily available to them. The stories which we give them to read are often artificially constructed, with low readability levels achieved by using plenty of pronouns, but with a high processing load because of the need to link pronoun to referent as the text is being read. The content of such stories is frequently meaningless, patronising or plain boring. How can the secondary teacher help these pupils to learn to read competently and to enjoy reading, and also allow them to articulate and give form to the elusive 'airy nothing' in a way which will satisfy their need to read their own life story 'to find his interior fiction as part of a writer's intention' (Meek, 1980)?

Aims of the research

We accept that young learners and adult illiterates can often learn through reading their own transcribed narratives. Little evidence exists, however, to show what happens in the production of a dictated story, in the interaction taking place between scribe and author. In addition, a common reservation felt by classroom teachers is the time and effort involved in teaching pupils to read using this method. An initial pilot study convinced the researcher that this way of teaching older pupils to read *did* work; that the pupils were motivated to read, they read their own texts successfully first time and had stories to tell which were interesting and important to them (Smith, 1983).

In the course of the present research emphasis his been put on illuminating the process by which texts are produced, with the intention of standardising good practice so that a pack for training volunteer helpers could be produced. If it were possible for this method to be used successfully with non-professional volunteers then the reservation about teacher-time would be resolved – in addition, a more profitable and interesting way of 'helping' with reading might be described.

Description of the research undertaken to outline this method of learning to read

In order to illuminate the process and extrapolate pointers for standardising good practice, a case study was made of five 11-year-old readers learning to read by dictating their own stories and then using them as reading texts. The effectiveness of the method as a way of learning to read was to be judged by changes in the way in which the readers read their texts – through a miscue analysis of each reading session and by noting the number of self-corrections which readers made. In addition, some indication of the development of linguistic ability would be gained by looking at the complexity of sentences used in the dictation (McKenzie and Kernig, 1975) and at the basic structure of the dictated stories (Applebee, 1978).

Five poor readers were matched with five volunteer adults and eight sessions of 1 hour 20 minutes were tape-recorded. In addition, each reader was interviewed before the project began in an attempt to elicit from them the way in which they thought reading 'happened' and the strategies which they used when they found that they had difficulties in reading. Downing (1970) and Reid (1966) both found that pre-literate children had confused and incomplete ideas about what reading was: the five readers in this sample showed similar confusions. One thought she couldn't read because 'I don't try hard enough' another described the process as being 'trying to read because they don't understand the words. They've never seen words before'.

All the readers referred to 'spelling out', 'pronouncing' or 'sounding out' as a strategy for reading a word which was difficult. Only one referred to 'concentrating' and 'thinking' as part of the process of reading.

The initial training for the scribes

The initial training of the scribes was as non-directive as possible. The only clear instructions referred to the process of writing down/printing/reading/dictating (see Figure 9.1) and

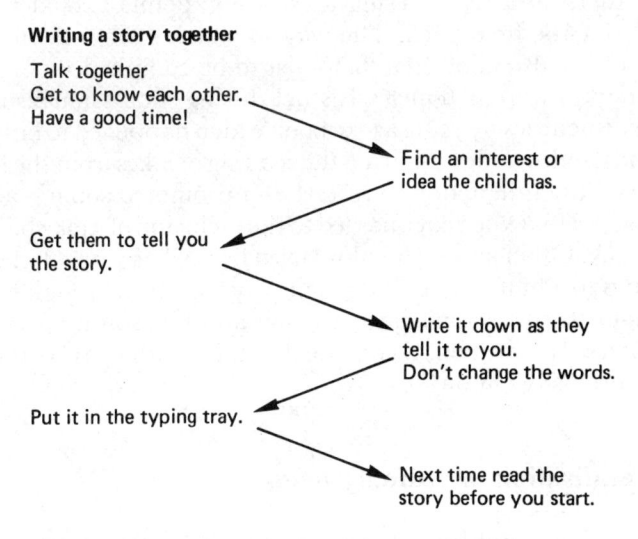

Writing a story together

Talk together
Get to know each other.
Have a good time!

Find an interest or idea the child has.

Get them to tell you the story.

Write it down as they tell it to you.
Don't change the words.

Put it in the typing tray.

Next time read the story before you start.

Don't forget to illustrate the book and decorate the cover. You can talk, look at books, visit the library to encourage the child in telling their story.

FIGURE 9.1 *Instructions to scribes*

to listening to the pupil read. It was felt that this was an important area to standardise and one in which expert advice should be made available. The model of listening to reading which was used was that devised by Glynn (1980) which is based on a behaviour modification model with praise as a reward. Scribes were introduced to the model in the form of a flowchart supported by cartoon substantiations. They were also shown a short video of the researcher listening to pupils reading.

Pattern of the dictating/reading sessions

A pattern for the sessions was suggested, although freedom was given to scribes to deviate from the pattern if necessary. In the event, starting a story was easier for some pairs than for others and as a result a 'starting points' booklet was made for the final pack. The way in which scribes dealt with difficulties also allowed a 'help' list to be compiled.

One pair who got hopelessly stuck during one session resolved their difficulties by using a joke book which happened to be lying on the window ledge. Sharing the reading of jokes from the book allowed the interaction to restart and promoted some reading activity. This experience has led to the inclusion of a joke book in the pack. Other successful ploys used by scribes when dictating ground to a halt were talking their way together through books without words, self-initiated writing and illustrating previous chapters. In addition, a good deal of talk, both conversational and serious, went on.

Generalisation to ordinary texts

The serious problem of generalising to ordinary texts was solved by one scribe who began to incorporate 'book' text into the dictated story, pleading ignorance of the technical nature of the book content (in this case, cars). One such text read:

> My Dad's got two cars: a Range Rover and an Avenger – that's me Mum's – it's orange.
> The Talbot Avenger is a two door or four-door saloon or estate with 1.3 or 1.6 litre engine. First introduced over ten years ago, but there are still plenty on the road.

This suggestion too was incorporated in the final booklet.

Observations and outcomes from this phase of the research

A close analysis of the sessions revealed that scribes and

author/readers had built up good relationships; in many cases distressed or disturbed pupils would use the opportunity of their reading session to talk. Over the eight-week period scribes listened and responded to anxieties about particular lessons and the demands made of the pupil within the lesson; difficulties with parents at home; anxieties about moving house; concern for the welfare of a friend and many other day-to-day concerns of the readers.

Both scribe and author showed a sense of pride and pleasure at the production of the story – particularly the first time it was returned to them as a printed text and was successfully read. Most authors also illustrated their books and made covers for them. For several of the readers it would seem that sustained, interested attention from an adult was a novel experience. The work of Lawrence (1973) would suggest that this was an important part of the success of the project. It may be that the lack of such talk pre-school is a contributory factor in some pupils' failure to learn to read (Wells, 1982).

The purpose of miscueing each reading session was to get an idea of the kind of cues which the readers might be using. No clear indication is given that there is a shift from dependence on one cueing system to another although comparison with cues used in a Neale Analysis Form A administered in the week before the research began shows a clear shift away from the use of grapho-phonemic cues without regard to meaning to the use of syntactical and semantic cues and grapho-phonemic cues that were semantically acceptable. There is, however, a clear indication that, as the sessions progressed, readers were becoming much more self-corrective – a measure of both increased confidence and of an intention to make sense of the text (Clay, 1973).

It may be that these readers, failing with ordinary texts, had been given less and less 'real' text to read (Smith, 1971). The success in reading their own stories would seem to have led to an increase in their ability to express their ideas in complex and interesting form. In particular Andrew, initially unable to be explicit about who was speaking in his story, began to give more shape and literary form to his stories. In Chapter One he wrote:

> Then the man heard that someone had called him a nasty name so he chased the bloke who had called him the name and was just going to hit him when 'big Daddy' came.

By Chapter Five his story is flowing more easily:

> When he got back to prison the prisoners started to sing to Spider. They clapped and cheered. One of them said, 'You're the "Big Daddy" now.'

In all cases the flow of the story and the increase in sentence complexity went alongside more confident and positive reading in which the readers began to take responsibility for correcting their mistakes.

The outcome from this first phase of research has been the production of a simple pack for teachers. It contains a booklet giving details of the method used to produce stories so that non-professional volunteers can be given a model for acting as a scribe, ways of helping if there are difficulties and a guide to generalising to ordinary texts.

In addition, a stock of dictated stories now exists as a library for readers and language exchanges with other schools have taken place. The texts are able to be used in school for other language-based purposes and some authors have recorded their stories to make a listening/reading package for younger children. Scribe/listeners have been consistent in their help – some are now in their third year of helping children in this way and they have ranged from 'drop-out' fifth-years to grandmothers.

Conclusion

This way of teaching reading allows the innate desire to communicate and to make narratives in order to construe the experiences which we have (Hardy, 1975) to be used in an effective way. Readers achieve immediate success in their reading, they read real texts which can be shared with others and which practise and extend the reading skills required for competent, reflective reading, they experience the 'common ground' which exists between writer and reader and so gain insight into both processes. Their reading behaviour began to be more independent with the emphasis in reading being on making sense of the text. As confidence and fluency grew increased use was made of syntactical and semantic cues and, when miscues occurred they tended not to impede the meaning in the text.

The next phase of this research intends to look at what happens when pupils are encouraged to go back to their texts and edit their original writing. Reciprocal gains in writing will also be monitored. Learning to be a reader by reading your own writing has important implications for the development of reflection, the organisation of textual language and the expression of ideas and feelings. It is a method which can be successfully used even in crowded classes and large institutions by utilising the vast untapped store of goodwill and desire to help which exists in the community.

References

APPLEBEE, A. W. (1978) *The Child's Concept of Story* (Chicago: University of Chicago Press).
CLAY, M. M. (1973) *The Early Detection of Reading Difficulties* (London: Heinemann Educational).
DOWNING, J. (1970) 'Children's Concepts of Language in Learning to Read', in *Educational Research*, vol. 12, pp. 106–112.
GLYNN, T. (1980) 'Parent–Child Interaction in Remedial Reading at Home', in M. Clark and T. Glynn (eds) *Reading and Writing for the Child with Difficulties* (Educational Review Occasional Publication no. 8, University of Birmingham).
HARDY, B. (1975) *Tellers and Listeners* (London: University of London, Athlone Press).
LAWRENCE, D. (1973) *Improved Reading through Counselling* (London: Ward Lock Educational).
MEEK, M. (1980) 'Prologomena for a Study of Children's Literature', in M. Benton (ed.) *Approaches to Children's Literature* (Southampton: University of Southampton Department of Education).
MCKENZIE, M. and KERNIG, W. (1975) *The Challenge of Informal Education* (London: Darton, Longman & Todd).
REID, J. (1966) 'Learning to Think about Reading', *Educational Research*, vol. 9, pp. 62–5.
SMITH, B. (1983) 'Silent Conversations: Observations of Secondary Pupils using a Language Approach to Reading', in B. Gillham (ed.) *Reading through the Curriculum* (London: Heinemann Educational for UKRA).

SMITH, F. (1971) *Understanding Reading* (New York: Holt, Rinehart & Winston).
WELLS, G. (1982) *Language, Learning and Education* (University of Bristol Centre for Study of Language and Communication).

Part II

Examples of Good Practice

Chapter 10

The Problem of Underachievement in School

Moira G. McKenzie

When we think of underachievement in school, particular youngsters come to mind – slow learners, those who score low on tests, the inattentive, the troublesome, and the inarticulate, many of whom are poor readers and writers. Their difficulties have been attributed to causes such as lack of experience, physical and health problems (the numbers seem to mount each year), linguistic and cultural diversity, and general discontinuity between school and home. A great deal of public concern and professional attention has been focused on making provision for many of these children.

My present concern extends beyond this recognised educational problem to include the concealed underachievement pervading classrooms and schools, that prevents too many children from achieving anything like their full potential as learners, and sometimes as human beings.

Many bright children find they can satisfy the requirements of the school with very little real effort. Average learners get by with repetitive preformulated learning, often verbally transmitted by the teacher and practised in work-books and exercises. Children who are slow to learn for whatever reason, and find reading and writing difficult, are most at risk in school. Their self-esteem and confidence in their ability to learn diminishes as they face increasing demands for reading and writing in areas of the curriculum. For them, as for many others, there is often little opportunity to learn through other non-literacy abilities or to develop their own special interests and talents.

Yet, we know that schools can and do make a difference in children's lives, in what they can learn and how they feel about learning. A most recent report *The Junior School Project* (1986), a four-year longitudinal study carried out by the Inner London Education Authority (ILEA), addressed the question of school effectiveness. The key questions were:

1. Are some schools or classes more effective than others when variation in the intake of pupils is taken into account?
2. Are some schools effective for particular groups of children?
3. If some schools are most effective than others, then what factors contribute to these positive effects?

Their findings stated emphatically that schools do make a difference, the difference is substantial and schools that were effective in promoting progress with one group of children tended to be effective for children in any other group.

Among the many factors that contributed to the greater effectiveness of schools were:

- where teachers provided a well-organised framework for learning yet allowed children freedom within this structure
- where the teaching was intellectually challenging.

These two factors have particular significance in that teachers recognise the value of allowing children some initiative in learning, and that the teachers involved had positive attitudes to children's ability to learn and offered them more than the obvious school routines. Many of us thinking back to our school days can pinpoint teachers who inspired and challenged us, and opened the way to learning and interests that have lasted throughout the years.

Many schools have endeavoured to help underachievers by increasing the range and quality of the experiences offered. Provision has been made for children with physical and health problems. Attention has been given to revising goals and procedures to facilitate the learning of children from diverse cultures and linguistic backgrounds. According to Gordon Wells (1986b) discontinuities between home and school are experienced to some extent by all children because of the special role of the school to educate. The differences are greater and more traumatic for those children whose home culture and language is furthest removed from the school.

A chief concern of school is literacy and it is in this area that children who are slower to learn are most vulnerable. What is meant by achievement in literacy? The concepts change over time. Traditionally, literacy in school meant reading and writing, often at minimal levels. Such low competence does not adequately serve young people in the modern world. Heath (1983), an anthropologist studying the growth and uses of literacy historically and culturally shows that successful literacy is rooted in culture and entails taking part in community life, that is, in literacy events that have purpose and meaning within the social/cultural group. Literacy flourishes where it has purpose and value for those who use it. This knowledge makes us pause and wonder whether some children in school fail in literacy because school reading and writing tasks often serve no real purpose that children can discern.

Since reading and writing are language is it useful to look at continuities between learning to talk and learning to read and write in some cultures. All children learn language, that is, they learn to make and receive meanings in their own cultural and linguistic communities. We know from the work of various researchers, that optimum conditions for developing language occur when children's initiatives are acknowledged and their interests shared with someone who listens and responds, who collaborates in making and negotiating meaning. In a social context, children learn to use language to organise, reflect on and communicate their thinking, their feelings and their experience:

> It is the art of formulating one's thoughts and feelings in order to communicate them to others that is the strongest spur to actively seeking to understand them.
> (Wells, 1986a, p. 107)

In other words, young learners construct their own knowledge, their own understandings, as they try to make sense of their experience in collaboration with those around them.

All children learn to talk, and *some* children learn to read before school. Most children in literate cultures have some knowledge of written language learned from the print in their environment and from any experiences they have had with books. There is real evidence of children's exploration of written language in the environment (Harste, Woodward, and Burke, 1984); how, in attempting to write their own messages, they explore ways of understanding the writing system (Ferreiro and Teberosky, 1982; Clay, 1975); and how, when they become aware of the alphabetic system they use whatever knowledge they have to invent their own spellings. Children, very much aware of the literate behaviours and events they see around them, make greetings cards, write letters, make books, shopping lists, messages, and so on before they can write in any conventional sense, and in doing so, demonstrate an understanding of the purpose of writing, and begin to learn how to do it.

Continuity in learning spoken and written language, and the most fundamental literacy learning is apparent in homes where parents share picture books and stories with their children. Through stories children become aware of the pleasures and satisfactions to be found in books. They experience the symbolic power of language to create real and imaginary worlds. They meet written language forms and vocabulary beyond the language in daily use. Stories offer a framework for reflecting on and understanding their own behaviour and feelings, their own inner worlds of emotion and self-awareness. It is no accident that stories such as *Where the Wild Things Are* (Sendak, 1963) are in such demand by children. Sendak's story reflects their own inner worlds of good and bad behaviour, impotence in dealing with adults, assumed power, anger and hate, and also secure love and reconciliation.

Holdaway (1979) sees such experience with picture story books as developing

> ... one of the primary linguistic skills [which] entails the ability to interpret symbols of the imagination in such a way as to accurately perceive the reality being represented. (p. 164)

Children's wide-ranging interaction with adults and picture books provides rich experience in creating and interpreting images of symbolic representation in words and pictures, hence they are a powerful entry to both literacy and learning.

The significance of these pre-school literary experiences in terms of achievement in literacy in school is increasingly being understood. Wells and Raban (1978) found in their study that children who on entry to school obtained higher scores in the knowledge-of-literacy test, knew a great deal about books and stories because they had been read to by their parents. They found that this test best predicted overall achievement at age 7 and even at age 10. The 5-year-old entrants showed real interest in the stories read to them, commenting and responding; they asked about the meaning of words, and displayed interest in some of the letters. They knew how to handle books. They were poised to learn more about reading and were coping well by the time they were 7–8 years old. By 10 years they were proficient readers, enjoying reading and generally able to be successful in other curriculum areas.

Conversely, youngsters entering school with little book experience had greater difficulty learning to read and write. Because learning to read is given such high priority in the early years of schooling, less successful youngsters are in danger of seeing themselves as poor learners with consequent loss to their self-esteem – and motivation to learn. Different cultures and groups within cultures have different values and uses for literacy. Heath's (1983) study describes in detail the very different ways in which three adjacent communities in North America engaged in literacy events. Since cultural practices are diverse there is likely to be some variations in the book experience children have on entry to school. But if we really understand the *potential* of stories and books for children's general and literacy learning, we would surely make this knowledge central in our early literacy programmes. We would link-in to the stories children bring from their homes, for few children fail to hear everyday stories to do with family lives, the neighbourhood, the church to which they belong and, of course, from television. Television is a common bond among the youngsters entering our schools. They play out Batman, the A-Team, Knight Rider, showing real understanding of the characters and the plots just as they do of favourite books.

There is no doubt that underachievement begins in the

earliest days in school if modes of teaching do not allow all children to find a way into literacy. What school can do for all children is to enable them to know and enjoy stories, to learn that stories and books are sources of pleasure and satisfaction, that they can read and handle books themselves, and make their own meanings. It is in sharing books with adults and talking about them as they read that children learn to bring the knowledge they have of the world to the meanings being made in text (Heath, 1983; Cochran-Smith, 1984; Dombey, 1983).

Just as children need to 'read' before they can read so they need opportunities to make their own meanings in writing – even before they can write. One of the great values of allowing children to invent writing and spelling on the way to learning to control written language is that the meanings they try to make are rooted in their own experience just as they are when talking. In other words, they are quite clear about what they are trying to do. They become aware of the purpose and function of written language in their own lives and in the life of the community.

It seems that, like talk, written texts grow out of stories, events in children's lives and the ongoing life of the classroom. They write about these events in ways similar to the way they talk about them. Holdaway (1986) reminds us that

> ... young children maintain cognitive clarity by an uncompromising closeness between concrete operations in the real world and their language development. Their style of learning is concrete and demands 'hands-on' interaction with the real world. Our task is to help them see a reflection of those forms of intelligence in the visual display of print. (p. 92)

This is more likely to happen in communities with their own significant purposes for reading and writing.

Early literacy in the school community

I said earlier that informed opinion suggests that problems of underachievement relate to lack of particular kinds of experience, discontinuity between school and home, and linguistic and cultural diversity. Since children enter school when they are 5 years old in Britain, and one or two years earlier if they go to nursery school, only the most pessimistic could think all was lost, that it was too late to prevent underachievement dogging some children's school lives. If children need to extend their experience in life – and what 5-year-old does not – then it's not beyond our wit to create school conditions that build in not only rich first-hand experience, but also the talk, the interaction, opportunities for play (including dramatic play) and the time and means for children to represent their experience in a variety of ways. For that is how real learning occurs and where literacy learning is most powerful.

Why can't the literacy programme for emergent readers be built around *stories*: hearing stories, telling stories, playing out stories, pretending to read stories (Holdaway's reading re-enactment), telling stories about their friends, their everyday lives, creating stories about anything under the sun. Wells (1986a) comments that 'making sense of experience is to a very great extent being able to construct a plausible story about it'. The stories read and told to children in turn make them better able to tell their own. Narrative is, according to Hardy (1968), 'a primary act of mind', the way we represent experience to ourselves.

Through literature children hear a variety of different kinds of discourse including stories, dialogue, description, play with words, rhymes and rhythms. They hear the 'tune' of language used in different ways. They become familiar with written dialect in oral form, with vocabulary to do with feelings, images, story characters such as kings and queens, witches and ogres, hens and foxes, poor heroes and rich villains. They become aware of the conventions of literature and expectations of the shared symbolism writers expect of their implied readers. In the intonation of the reader, which they take on themselves as they first 'read' and later *really* read, they get acquainted with the way words go together, the significance of how particular words are used, for example, sobbing *bitterly*; meeting the dragon *bravely*.

Children learning English as a second language begin to

use English to make meanings they know to be there. The repetition of stories, playing them out, the dialogue that accompanies story reading enables all children to learn to take meaning from written language. They become aware of cause and effect, behaviour and its consequence. They learn to predict both language and events in stories.

Children slower in learning to read and write may well not be slower learners – many of them are extremely competent in managing their own lives and affairs, just low on experience and understanding of books and all that means in terms of further literacy learning, and schools can certainly do something about that. Cultural and linguistic differences can be recognised and supported similarly. Stories from a variety of different cultures need to be part of *every* child's repertoire, and children from different cultures need to see themselves, their culture and the lives they are living reflected in the books they read. They too enjoy hearing stories many times, and make them their own through dramatic play and in a variety of art forms. We hear the influence of stories in their retellings, as in the following example of 6-year-old Yvonne who is Afro-Caribbean:

> Once upon a time there was a mother. She bore a beautiful baby. She used to call her baby but now she call her Snow-White.

And 7-year-old Deba, whose first language is Bengali:

> When Snow-white growed up she had nice mouth and everything.

And Mammun, also a Bengali speaker who was reading *Titch* (Hutchins, 1972), a story he knew well. He read:

> Peter had ——— big dig. [The text was, Pete had a big spade].

A week later he read:

> Peter had a big spade.

If we based our literacy programme on

- up-to-date knowledge of the processes involved in reading and writing, and

113

Using and developing the model in school.
Three stages in learning to read.

READING ALOUD TO CHILDREN
- Books, stories, rhymes, songs.
- Enabling children to HEAR and PARTICIPATE in stories repeatedly.
- Linking stories – books with everyday life and other stories.

BOOK CORNER
- Range of books and materials
- Display, organisation.
- Time, space, comfort.
- Links with read-aloud programme.
- Links with ongoing interests.
- Stories, poems, songs, recorded on audio and video tape.

SHARED READING
- Enlarged texts and stories, poems, songs.
- Notices, etc. in environment.

EMERGENT READING
- Children build up a repertoire of books and stories.
- Bridge spoken and written language.
- Explore environmental language.
- Develop concepts of print.
- Try 'reading' and 'writing' themselves.
- Get to know some words and letters.
- Develop a literacy set.

TACKLING PRINT
- Children get closer to the text when reading.
- Begin to build a sight vocabulary and a writing vocabulary.
- Begin to use the sound-symbol system.
- Begin to make generalisations and infer rules.

EARLY READING
- Children use a basic rule system.
- They predict and cross check their predictions against language and phonic cues.
- Their miscues generally make sense.
- They use self-correction strategies appropriately.

PERSONAL READING IN READABLE BOOKS
- Alone – to teacher – to parents
- Using book virtually to retell story.
- Approximation to text.
- Growing accuracy in reading because of growth of skills, e.g. directionality: 1-1 correspondence, sound-symbol correspondence.

EARLY WRITING
- Awareness of written language in the environment.
- The functions of writing.
- Time to write freely on own terms.
- Early spelling development.
- Contexts for writing.

SHARED WRITING
- Writing alongside a writer.
- Teacher and children compose – teacher scribes.
- Production of a variety of texts to be read.
- Feedback to personal writing.

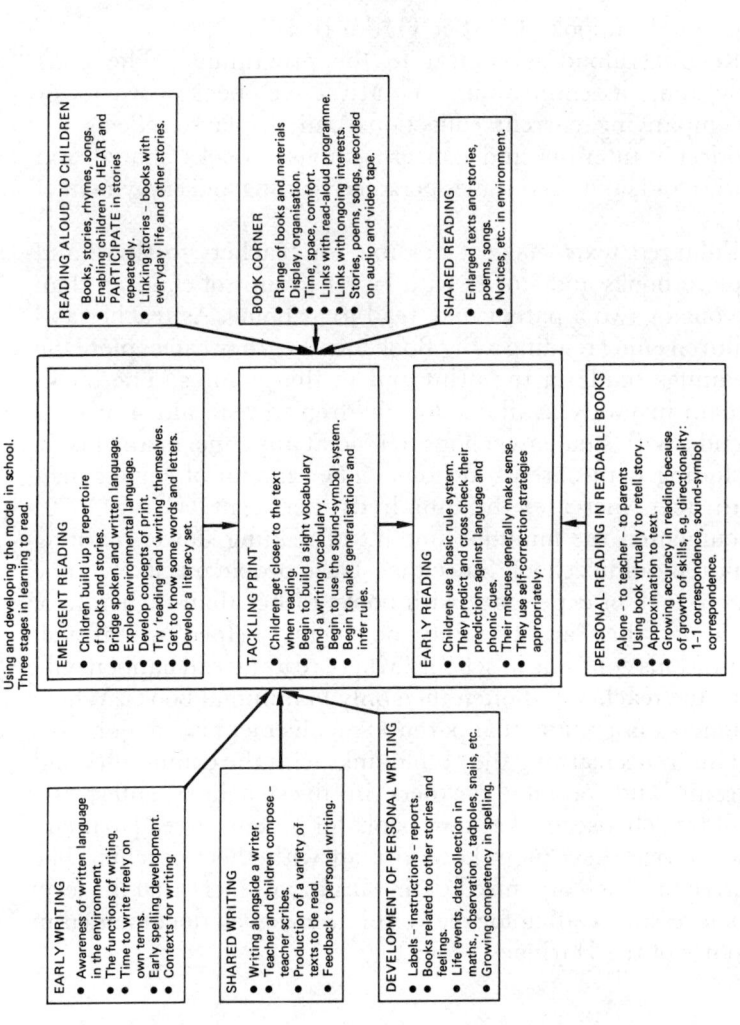

DEVELOPMENT OF PERSONAL WRITING
- Labels – instructions – reports.
- Books related to other stories and feelings.
- Life events, data collection in maths, observation – tadpoles, snails, etc.
- Growing competency in spelling.

FIGURE 10.1 *Model based on literacy events at home or nursery school*

- what we know of early literacy events that make a successful entry into reading and writing for many children

what might it look like? (See Figure 10.1.)

Reading aloud is central to the programme. The book provision, assembled in an attractive book corner, or accompanying current collections and displays, reflects the children's interests and concerns, houses books shared and stories told, and encourages personal reading and enjoyment of books.

Enlarged texts make it possible for teachers to share and explore books and stories with larger groups of children than the one or two a parent may read to at home. As teacher and children enjoy reading a Big Book together they can explore the meanings made in the print and in the pictures. The books remain instantly available for children to read alone or with friends, with smaller versions to read at any time, in any place, including with parents at home. The amount of engagement with text increases by hundreds per cent. Clay (1979) documented the minimal amount of reading slower-learning children did in school. Since their basic problem is likely to be due to lack of experience with books rather than their rate of learning, they are certainly not being helped when such limitations continue in schools, where reading can happen only with the teacher and often then only in minimal books. Where teachers understand that parental involvement is a major force in children's learning they build links with the community and parents and become partners in the teaching enterprise. Children choose to take home books for parents to read to them, and stories they know how to read with their parents. The degree to which organised parental support increased the level of successful reading for many children is well documented in reports of the Haringey project.

Writing

The model includes a number of text-making opportunities varying from the child's own attempts to children and teacher working together in collaborative shared writing to produce their own books. Each has its own possibilities and strengths which together add up to a rich experience of writing.

Individual writing

Children use written language functionally, just as they do spoken language. It serves their purposes for labelling, making lists (for example, shopping lists), giving instructions (for example, 'Don't touch' on their models), and 'Dear Mom, its your turn to clean up' on the fridge door. And for warnings: a child-written notice in one classroom reads, 'If you don't want a cross teacher you better push the coat trolley in!'

They make statements about important events in their lives at home and at school, for example, 'I went to the zoo'. Texts grow out of the ongoing life of the classroom, for example 'The snail has so much suction they stick to the sides and stay there'. Stories too are written, for example:

> Sarah and the snail was walking
> and they saw a witch and
> she cast a spell.
> Put in spiders legs
> Put in spiders head and
> Put in spiders eyeballs
> Put in spiders mouth
> And she stirred it up
> and it was stewed legs.

And from the same class of 5-year-olds in their first term in school, where riddles were in vogue, one child wrote:

> What am I?
> I've got two leaves
> And I have got lots of petals
> And I have got white petals
> And I am yellow in the middle
> What am I?

It seems that, like talk, written texts grow out of stories and events in children's lives, and the ongoing life of the

Curriculum-related writing

In a lively classroom, part of the dramatic play and activities reflect life in the community. Children create cafés, hospitals, job centres, home-corners, flower shops, and so on. They need writing to record patients, describe symptoms, display menus, advertise, and so on. In such dramatic play children take on roles, they use a range of spoken and written language, but writing is subsidiary to the main goal – running a successful café, keeping check of the patients, and so on. Speech comes and is gone. The assimilation of visual language into functions in use of written language, provides new and powerful ways of holding on to ideas, the possibility of referring back, of adding to information/ideas already expressed.

We should assume that a most fundamental aim of education is to raise the level of children's intellectual functioning and to enable them to interpret and reflect on first-hand experience. Winston's experience helped him to do this. In the following example, you can see how a group of 9-year-olds used the data relating to the classroom guinea pig, collected and recorded over a period of time, to predict the likely number and weight of the litter Miss Shaggy was due to produce.

> Miss Shaggy has had four litters in the past, the first litter she had was three Babies the second litter she had there was one baby the third litter she had 3 again and the fourth was still 3. The last litter Sally recorded and the weight of the first baby was 120 grams the weight of the second baby was 110 grams the weight of the third baby was 100 grams so it goes down in tens. If Miss Shaggy has three babies I think the first baby she has will weigh 150 grams and I think the second baby she has is going to weigh 160 grams and I think the third baby is going to weigh 170 grams. If we add up 150, 160 and 170 the answer is 480 the other 20 grams is I guess the weight of the fluid and milk which is food for the babies.
>
> (10 years)

(1)	31 1,400 1,270− 0,130 grams		Anthony hill weighed Miss Shaggy on Friday and she weighed 1,270 grams. I weighed her today and she weighed 1,400 grams so in four days she's increased by 130 grams

$$
\begin{array}{r}
31 \\
1{,}400 \\
1{,}270- \\ \hline
0{,}130 \text{ grams}
\end{array}
$$

Anthony hill weighed Miss Shaggy on Friday and she weighed 1,270 grams. I weighed her today and she weighed 1,400 grams so in four days she's increased by 130 grams

$$
\begin{array}{r}
1 \\
1{,}400 \\
900 \\ \hline
500 \text{ grams}
\end{array}
$$

I weighed miss Shaggy today and she weighed 1,400 grams. Her usual weight is 900 grams. So I took away 900 grams from 1,400 grams and the answer was 500 grams so she has increased 500 grams during pregnancy.

$$
3\,\overline{|500}\\
166\text{ r }2
$$

I took the number above, 500 and I divided it by 3 I divided it by three because miss Shaggy might have three babies and the answer is supposed to be the weight of the first baby.

The children explored the data, and then in words and mathematical notation worked out their predictions. They were delighted when the babies were born to find that their predictions were quite close, and then to add their findings to the already recorded data.

These are examples of what Wells (1986b) calls 'epistemic learning'. Wells argues for a reconceptualising of literacy, noting that much school learning, manifest in forms of writing, operates at lower rather than higher levels of thinking. Wells (1986b) identifies four levels:

1. *Performative*, that is, speech written down. The focus is on the code with little need for composing. Copying, filling in blanks would come into this category.
2. *Functional*, that is, being able to write preformulated types of writing such as reports, school essays, story-retelling. Much school writing is of this type. For example: 'I went to the zoo. We got on the bus. We saw elephants, tigers and monkeys. Then we went home and had our tea.'
3. *Instrumental*, that is, writing as transmission without much concern for transforming, putting together facts read or told in lesson.
4. *Epistemic*, that is, writing in which what is known is extended and reformulated. Critical thinking and evaluation are called for, and experience and thinking become knowledge owned by the learner. Writing and other forms of

representation through which children internalise learning come into this category.

Bereiter (c. 1972) sees these levels as developmental, but notes that some ways of teaching – helping children learn – allow *young* children to operate at an epistemic level. Wells (1986b) thinks that schools should take responsibility for enabling children to learn at an epistemic level throughout their school lives. The examples given above demonstrate how such learning is already happening in some schools. Helping children learn to read can also be done in ways that raise the level of their thinking and understanding of written language. We might take note of Donaldson's (1978) insights:

> Once the teaching of reading is begun, the manner in which it is taught may be of far-reaching significance . . . the PROCESS of becoming literate can have marked – but commonly unsuspected – effects on the growth of mind. It can do this by encouraging highly important forms of intellectual self-awareness and self-control. (p. 97)

Children's reflective awareness is enhanced by the feedback we give them, for example, when we respond first to the message in their writing, and, as appropriate, reflect back to them their growing knowledge of the orthography, the written language system itself.

Dramatising and playing out stories also enables children to make stories their own. They get enormous enjoyment from taking them further and sometimes turning the original on its head. This happened with *Mrs Wishy-Washy* (Melser and Cowley, 1980) a martinet of the farmyard who demanded that her animals should be clean. 'In the tub you go!' was her cry to the mud-caked animals in the farmyard.

In the new story created by the teacher and a group of 6–7-year-olds in shared writing sessions, Mrs Wishy-Washy scrubs the distinctive features off a number of animals – the crocodile lost his teeth, the skunk lost his smell – and so on. But what happened when she got to the elephant?

> Mrs Wishy-Washy saw a dirty elephant.
> She screamed, 'You dirty old elephant.

You need a bath. In the tub you go.'
The elephant tried to get in the tub
but. . .
He crushed it.
He filled his trunk with
dirty, muddy water and looked at
Mrs Wishy-Washy with his little eyes.
He lifted his trunk and waved it about.
He SPRAYED Mrs Wishy-Washy.
And all the animals said,
'In the tub you go!'

You can image the fun they had composing and illustrating this story and their delight in reading it over and over to anyone who would listen. Their teacher pointed out that the children drew on many experiences in writing the story, their knowledge of how such a story is organised and how it evolves, and their experiences with animals, real ones and those met in books and stories.

In all the examples given, children use what they know, extend and reformulate their knowledge in a variety of ways and so make it their own. This is 'accommodation', the forming of new schemes that will assimilate new learning.

Summary

Problems of underachievement in literacy could be tackled if we applied intelligently the knowledge we now have of

- the processes involved in reading and writing
- the kinds of early literacy experiences that seem to make for successful entry to literacy
- the value of intellectually challenging teaching at all levels.

If our concern for underachieving children is real we would set our minds to

- examine our practice at the beginnings of school and create conditions and programmes that allow a point of entry to children from different social, cultural and linguistic backgrounds

- move away from trivialising literacy by reducing it to skills learning, and improve the quality and the range of books and stories offered to children
- provide more opportunities for children to transform, extend and reformulate ideas and experience
- become aware of children who after a year's schooling have very little understanding of what is involved in reading, and find ways of helping them, for example, through Clay's Reading Recovery Programme (1985)
- create literate environments in school in which children use reading and writing for most crucial and significant purposes
    - to share the community life of the school and home
    - to enjoy the personal satisfaction and understanding that comes from experience with literature
- stimulate children to find language and literacy of real value to them for reflecting on, organising and reformulating experience, and making knowledge their own.

References

BEREITER, C. (C. 1972) *Integration of Skills System in the Development of Textual Writing Compensation* (Unpublished paper: Ontario Institute for Studies in Education).

COCHRAN-SMITH, M. (1984) *The Making of a Reader* (Norwood, New Jersey: Ablex Publishing Corporation).

CLAY, M. M. (1975) *What Did I Write?* (London: Heinemann Educational Books).

CLAY, M. M. (1979) *Reading: The Patterning of Complex Behaviour* (Auckland: Heinemann Educational Books).

CLAY, M. M. (1985) *The Early Detection of Reading Difficulties* (London: Heinemann Educational Books).

DOMBEY, H. (1983) 'Learning the Language of Books', in M. Meek (ed.) *Opening Moves* (Bedford Way Papers 17, Institute of Education, University of London).

DONALDSON, M. (1978) *Children's Minds* (London: Fontana/Collins).

FERREIRO, E. and TEBEROSKY, A. (1982) *Literacy Before Schooling* (Portsmouth, New Hampshire: Heinemann Educational Books).

HARDY, B. (1968) 'Narrative as a Primary Act of Mind', in M. Meek, A. Warlow and G. Barton (eds) *The Cool Web* (London: Bodley Head, 1977).

HARSTE, J. C., WOODWARD, V. A. and BURKE, C. L. (1984) *Language Stories and Literacy Lessons* (Portsmouth, New Hampshire: Heinemann Educational Books).

HEATH, S. B. (1983) *Ways with Words: Language, Life and Work in Communities and Classroom* (Cambridge: Cambridge University Press).

HEWISON, J. and TIZARD, J. (1980) 'Parental involvement and reading attainment', in *British Journal of Educational Psychology*, vol. 50, part 3, pp. 209–15.

HOLDAWAY, D. (1979) *The Foundations of Literacy* (Auckland, New Zealand: Ashton Scholastic).

HOLDAWAY, D. (1986) 'The Visual Face of Experience and Language: A Metalinguistic Excursion', in D. B. Yaden and S. Templeton (eds) *Metalinguistic Awareness and Beginning Literacy* (Portsmouth, New Hampshire: Heinemann Educational Books).

HUTCHINS, P. (1972) *Titch* (London: Bodley Head and Picture Puffin).

JUNIOR SCHOOL PROJECT (1986) (ILEA Research & Statistics Board).

MELSER, J. and COWLEY, J. (1980) *Mrs Wishy-Washy* (Leeds: Arnold-Wheaton).

SENDAK, M. (1963) *Where the Wild Things Are* (London: Bodley Head and Picture Puffin).

WELLS, G. and RABAN, B. (1978) *Children Learning to Read* (Final Report to the SSRC (UK)).

WELLS, G. (1986a) *The Meaning Makers: Children Learning Language and Using Language to Learn* (Portsmouth, New Hampshire: Heinemann Educational Books).

WELLS, G. (1986b) *Presentation at the Fourth International Conference on the Teaching of English* (Ottawa, Canada).

VYGOTSKY, L. (1978) in Cole, M., John-Steiner, V., Scribner, S. and Souberman, E. (eds) *Mind in Society* (Cambridge, Mass.: Harvard University Press).

Chapter 11

Play with Literacy: A Home–School Liaison Project to Support School Beginners

Helen C. Tite

In considering how the task of learning to read and write comes into sharp focus for the young child on entry to school, a review of current thinking about early literacy offers guidelines for a project supporting 4-year-old children and their parents in the term prior to school entry. The project takes into account the different perspectives of parent and teacher in the support offered to the children. Materials were developed to provide links between weekly play sessions in school and between school and home with the aim of supporting early literacy development as it was observed in play behaviour.

Learning and development are interrelated from the child's first days of life. To consider that learning comes into focus at 9 am or at statutory school age (Clark, 1976) precludes the development and the learning which has taken place within the family and with the child's first teachers, mother and father. I shall present the case for a home–school liaison which values the contributions of parent and teacher while encouraging the exploratory drive of young children in play to discover and find meaning in their experiences with storytelling and picture storybooks, drawing and writing materials. In prescribing such a liaison the aim is to provide an easy orientation to classroom life and in so doing to move more positively towards functional literacy with parental participation.

Observing children at play offers insight into their concerns and ideas while giving opportunities to make appraisals of their oral communication skills, (Tough, 1976). The range of materials we make available to children in play may open their understanding further. If we value the evidence of their play behaviour in their use of the materials of literacy such as books, printed matter, writing implements, we may have the opportunity to make appraisals of their understanding of written communication (Cohen and Stern, 1975). For the children observed in the project, the effect of drawing with pencils and other writing implements appeared to integrate their notions of the interrelationship between their pictures with their ascribed messages and a picture book with its ascribed story in illustration and the printed text. The play behaviour of pre-school children offers to their early educators the starting point to nurture beginning ideas for future learning.

The task of learning to read and write comes into sharp focus for the child when school begins. The pre-school experience of some will have already sharpened such a focus through enjoying stories and books with their parents and as Clark (1976) records in her study, some children will already be fluent readers when they begin school. For other children, as reported by Lomax (1979), their behaviour in a nursery setting which offers story and book experiences is one of lost opportunities as they do not value browsing through books. These differences underline the problems of the reception class teacher in the first year of formal schooling, who is expected to lead children into literacy. She finds those who can already read and have begun to write and those whose expectations for learning to read and write are not yet fully awakened. How does she begin?

On becoming a communicator

Lev Vygotsky (1978, p. 104) views the essence of play as a new relation created between situations in thought and real situations. Observations of children at play show them attempting to develop their understandings about oral and written language arising from their daily experiences. The evidence presented by Weir (1976) of her son Anthony at two-and-a-half years of age in his pre-sleep monologues playing and practising orally the forms of language for communication, has opened up our awareness of the exploratory drive young children demonstrate. The case studies presented by Butler (1979), Bissex (1980), Payton (1984) and van Lierop (1985) also provide evidence of the way in which very young children attempt to put meaning into their use of the tools of literacy – story books, picture books, other printed matter and writing materials. Downing (1985), in a review of research into how children learn to read, offers evidence from different countries which provides a focus on the child's reasoning about and understanding of the functions of communication in writing and reading. Clay (1982) in reviewing an earlier series of her research projects suggests that to be effective, teachers need to schedule time to observe exactly what their pupils are learning and to learn to put into words accounts of the behaviours they observe and what these might indicate (p. xi).

The evidence is there to be collected. The child in responding to the need to come to terms with demands, situations and expectations, finds that experiences need to be clarified and so in play creates an imaginary situation modelled on the reality experience. Vygotsky (1978) offers insight into play by noting that the young child in play behaves as though play is more a recollection of something that has actually happened, 'memory in action' (p. 103). This was observed in a nursery setting when two girls aged 4 years shared a storybook during a free play session. In reading the transcript we can note one child especially (Peer 1) moving towards a realisation of her purpose, to become a reader. Both children wore radio microphones.

> *Peer 1* returns to the book display and takes another book. She returns to where *Peer 2* is sitting cradling her 'baby' (a doll) opens the book and makes a series of nonsense sounds as she simulates reading intonation.
>
> *Peer 2* pushes the doll towards the book.
>
> *Peer 1* pulls the book away out of reach and starts to 'read' by responding to the pictures illustrating the story text.

'Can you just hold the baby? Otherwise I can't open the book can I!' (*Peer 2* adopts a listening posture with the doll placed on her knee and leaning towards the book.) 'All about Spring . . . Spring. One day Spring came. He asked . . . Winter came. One day Winter came . . . after she didn't know what to do so she went outside and played with the others. After, stepped in some . . . the puddles. Plish, splosh, splish, splosh. He went out for a long walk. Over . . .' (as she turned over the page).

Play is constrained by the rules of behaving in a particular way and using 'book language' as this non-reader demonstrates what she has learnt about the communication process involved in reading. In noting the interaction further we discover that Peer 2 is a reader but both are involved in creating an imaginary situation and using their play to create an opportunity to extend their understanding of the author's intention. The research by Sulzby and Otto (1982) underlines the relationship between children's understanding of texts and how they are related as a story by an author. The ability to compose their own stories appears to support children in their understanding of what it is to be an author and increases their awareness of the functions of literacy.

Peer 1: One day . . .
Peer 2: Spring! Spring!
Peer 1: Spring came and it was a lovely day outside. Over. What is this about?
Peer 2: And there's a robin and a cow and some birds.
Peer 1: Now what is this about?! Is it Spring or Summer?
Peer 2: Spring.
Peer 1: Spring? What is it about?!
Peer 2: Spring is . . . after winter, just before the summer time, brighter in the . . . (reading in text)
Peer 1: One day little girl went out and she got her little baby and put her in her own push-chair. It was raining suddenly when it was Spring and they all put their umbrellas up. Can't you see little one?

In using the picture storybook the girls are playing with a tool of literacy. Their use of the book in the nursery book corner and in employing a doll as a child listener to their parental role of reader offers the following understandings as they play:

- a story can be communicated by reader or teller
- you can use your own experiences to make a story
- a book is read in a particular way
- the illustrations support the reading of the story
- pages are turned over in sequence from the front to the back of the book
- the purpose of reading is to decode text
- the reader in creating the story from the text makes allowance for the listener's response to the story.

A realisation of how to communicate ideas through using the book is apparent. However, it is not just the use of the book to unlock the key to being a reader that the two girls are engaged in; they are also demonstrating what they understand as the process of communication from being an author in creating a story, to sharing it with others, to having it recorded in a symbolic form as a text. Vygotsky (1978) identifies it in the sense that 'a child is free to determine his own action but in another sense this is an illusory freedom for his actions are in fact subordinated to the meanings of things and he acts accordingly' (p. 103). If the child's environment contains the tools of literacy then the exploratory drive of the child as defined by Hutt (1971) is already effecting an engagement with them and the process of becoming literate has begun.

The focus provided by the child's attempts in explorative activity and play to unlock the process of literacy opens up a new perspective on reading and writing. The child as 'self teacher' (Bissex, 1980) will demonstrate their capability to perceive and abstract, reason and hypothesise, and move from one imaged eventuality to the next in making sense of their literacy experiences. This is echoed by Sue and Ron Scollon (1984) in their observations of son Tommy who, in using a computer gave evidence of understanding written communication before being able to read and write, as he recorded his game. The intriguing idea is promoted that children enter the communication system of the family, which naturally gives the child the opportunity to explore and investigate the phenomenon of literacy as the family experiences it.

Learning how to become an author of the story has been shown in the recording of two nursery children sharing a book. The first girl took the initiative as an emergent learner to create a story from the illustrations and her own experience of stories. The second girl demonstrated the power she already had over the printed text as an emergent reader. The ability to create a story and the link with beginning reading is an area which needs further investigation and teachers need to develop insights into how children comprehend the story/reading process (Tite, 1985). The research of Sulzby and Otto (1982) is supportive as it offers evidence of the emergent reading abilities of young children able to compose their own stories and act as authors. The link between reading and writing and the reciprocal gains has been recorded by Clay (1975, 1982) and it is speculated that children are also exploring these parallel strands of literacy in their play.

On becoming a writer

Goodman (1984) investigated the learning of young children in their development to become literate, 'children seem to work through the same problems that the adult inventors of written language historically have had to solve' (p. 108). She identifies these problems as which way to display letters, how to organise writing into units, how to balance graphic art with early writing attempts. As in the explorative activity and play with the artefacts of literacy, stories, picture books and writing materials, so evidence is available of young children's creative exploration of print and lettering in their drawings. Goodman (1984) draws attention to the syllabic principle about written language before the alphabet as a system emerges (p. 109). The observant teacher and parent will readily find children attempting to become writers through their drawings and scribblings. This higher level of abstract thinking underlines the experience of all children in approaching the task of writing, as Smith (1982) refers to it: 'orchestrating the writing act' (p. 139). It also highlights the teacher's problem of when to introduce formal instruction. Ferreiro and Teberosky (1983) in their investigations of writing before formal instruction begins in school noted that pre-school age children's responses led them to think that 'for these children, written language is a particular way of representing objects or, if one prefers, a particular way of drawing' (p. 129).

Behaviours which can be identified by teacher and parent offer insights into the appropriate skills and developing understandings to be nurtured. It is important to observe and identify the way in which each young child finds its way into the literacy game. Launching out into the unknown as an explorer of the learning behaviour of pre-school age children as they play can be exciting. Goodnow (1977) identifies young children's graphic solutions in drawing as 'visible thinking' (p. 154) involving all the features of problem-solving, notably thrift, organisation and sequence. She views children as investing a remarkable degree of time and effort in their observations of the world and the conclusions they are able to draw about it. In applying this view to the young child's thinking about stories and books and the medium of print, we should observe and value more the children's response in their drawings so that as teachers we may gain insights about their understanding of the process of written communication.

The idiosyncratic understandings, variety of skills and insights into their own capabilities as learners are as varied as the children in their physical presence in the classroom. What can unlock those differences is the way each child responds to the invitation to draw with pencil and paper. Drawing on the wealth of evidence provided by educational psychologists and researchers, teachers have at their disposal the means to support ongoing development and learning. When home and school share their insights and expectations for learning then learning for literacy can be a natural unfolding from oral communication to written communication.

Beginning school and literacy

The home-school link project 'Play with Literacy' was undertaken in two lower schools in an endeavour to involve parents of prospective entrants as participants in a programme to facilitate language development. The focus for designing the programme of language development was based on the following assumptions:

1. In facilitating language development in school we need the support of parents as active participants in their child's early learning.
2. The earlier such participation begins the easier it is for the child.
3. The process of communication begins in the oral language experience of the child and develops towards written communication.
4. Each child has accumulated understandings and skills which are idiosyncratic to their development of language and we need to observe before proceeding to begin instruction in reading and writing.
5. The child at play can be observed in their experimental approach to learning about literacy.
6. The disparity in the pre-school experience of children beginning school necessitates a play setting which enables the teacher to support individual needs.

The programme for 'Play with Literacy' began with an invitation by the headteacher to parents to share in play sessions with their children in the term prior to school entry. The weekly play sessions were held in the classroom to which the child would be coming in the new term. The pattern of the afternoon classes in the school was reorganised to allow the reception teacher to supervise the play session with the parents and children. Play provision was planned on a weekly basis to offer the opportunity for specific observations of the children with play materials. Play opportunities were promoted at home with play kits for the parents and their children. A set of three pamphlets to provide guidelines for discussion were introduced by the author as observer.

A questionnaire for the reception class teacher enquired

into the kind of behaviours, set tasks and skills that were expected of the children beginning school. A similar questionnaire for parents on their expectations about their children beginning school was administered. A checklist of developmental tasks identified as appropriate achievements for children of this age on beginning school was compiled by the teachers of each school. The checklist was used by the teachers informally for their own insights into each child's predisposition to communicate effectively and become learners in their new learning environment of the school.

At each play session the children were free to engage in play activities from the full range of play materials usually available in the classroom. At each weekly session, however, play materials were presented to elicit specific responses from the children as they played in accordance with the expectations of the particular reception class teacher to fulfil their own checklist. The activity which was consistently promoted at each session was drawing with a variety of drawing implements. For each child there was a collection made of drawings carried out during the school play sessions. A separate collection was kept of drawings brought from home in response to the pamphlets and play kits.

In making an appraisal of each child's collection of spontaneous drawings some interesting features were evident which have implications for the kind of support for beginning writing instruction when children enter school. The wide variation in children's ability to control their use of a pencil as well as to use drawing as a means of expression suggests that a longer period of orientation through play is necessary for some children before beginning formal instruction in reading and writing. The variations were:

- uncontrolled scribbling which indicated little experience of using drawing implements
- in contrast, very detailed representational drawings
- drawings with sequences which had accompanying storylines offered by the child
- drawings which filled the paper with strokes (intense effort)
- unrelated, scattered strokes (limited effort)
- individual letters scattered through drawings

- clusters of letters in word experimentation
- scribbles and tracing attempts over child's name and other words printed by adult.

For a small number of children the effect of drawing and the language experience approach encouraged by the parents' pamphlets appeared to support and integrate their notions of being a storyteller through their drawings. During the period of the summer term it was evident that the parents, aided by their discussions with the teachers, encouraged the children in their play and use of drawing materials and storybooks. All of the children benefited from the opportunities provided. There was a marked shift in their drawing skills from disordered to controlled scribbling and from controlled to representational drawing. This suggests that in their discovery of what they have done in developing their drawing skill, is an awareness of themselves as learners.

It would appear that experiences with stories and books before formal schooling begins may open up children's ideas naturally about the process of written communication, especially when drawing materials are readily available. The opportunity to express ideas spontaneously in play and drawing appears to provide the means becoming an author before becoming a reader for these children. This highlights the perspective offered by Vygotsky (1978) of the prehistory of written language (p. 111).

Implications for early education

The nursery curriculum needs to be extended to focus on the early engagement in literacy by some under-5-year-olds (Tite, 1985). Primary schools with an admission policy for 4-year-olds need also to consider carefully their procedures for admission to orientate the young child and parents to their expectations for learning. This concern is implicit in the study by Tizard and Hughes (1984) when concerns are expressed about the quality of the linguistic environment of young children at home or school in their early years of language development. Implicit in this is the establishment of a home–school liaison which values parents' participation in the early experience of their children's attempts to become literate.

An account of the 'Play With Literacy' project and the pamphlets for parents are available from:

Reading and Language Development Centre
Nene College
Moulton Park
Northampton NN2 7AL

References

BISSEX, G. L. (1980) *GNYS AT WRK: A Child Learns to Read and Write* (Cambridge, Mass.: Harvard University Press).
BUTLER, D. (1979) *Cushla and Her Books* (London: Hodder & Stoughton).
CLARK, M. M. (1976) *Young Fluent Readers* (London: Heinemann).
CLAY, M. M. (1975) *What did I write? A study of children's writing* (London: Heinemann).
CLAY, M. M. (1982) *Observing Young Readers. Selected Papers.* (London: Heinemann).
COHEN, D. H. and STERN, V. (1975) *Observing and Recording the Behaviour of Young Children.* (New York: Teachers College Press, Columbia University).
DOWNING, J. (1985) 'The child's understanding of the functions and processes of communication', in M. M. Clark (ed.) *New Directions in the Study of Reading* (London: Falmer Press), pp. 43–53.
FERREIRO, E. and TEBEROSKY, A. (1983) *Literacy Before Schooling* (London: Heinemann).
GOODNOW, J. (1977) *Children's Drawing* (London: Fontana/Open Books).
GOODMAN, Y. (1984) 'The Development of Initial Literacy', in H. Goelman, A. Oberg and F. Smith (eds) *Awakening To Literacy* (London: Heinemann), pp. 102–9.
HUTT, C. (1971) 'Exploration and Play in Children', in R. Herron and B. Sutton-Smith (eds) *Child's Play* (London: John Wiley & Sons), pp. 231–51.
LOMAX, C. (1979) 'Interest in Books and Stories', in M. M. Clark and W. M. Cheyne (eds) *Studies in Pre-School Education* (London: Hodder & Stoughton).
PAYTON, S. (1984) *Developing Awareness of Print: A Young Child's First Steps Towards Literacy* (Educational Review, Off-set Publication no. 2, University of Birmingham).
SCOLLON, S. and SCOLLON, R. (1984) '*Run Trilogy*: Can Tommy Read?' in H.

Goelman, A. Oberg and F. Smith (eds) *Awakening to Literacy* (London: Heinemann), pp. 131–40.
SMITH, F. (1982) *Writing and the Writer* (London: Heinemann).
SULZBY, E. and OTTO, B. (1982) '"Text" as an object of metalinguistic knowledge: a study in literacy development', *First Language*, vol. 3, pp. 181–99.
TITE, H. (1985) 'Storytelling and Beginning Reading: the use of a microcomputer to facilitate storytelling by nursery school children', in J. Ewing (ed.) *Reading and the New Technologies* (London: Heinemann), pp. 137–43.
TIZARD, B. and HUGHES, M. (1984) *Young Children Learning* (London: Fontana Paperbacks).
TOUGH, J. (1976) *Listening to Children Talking: A guide to the Appraisal of Children's Use of Language* (London: Ward Lock).
VAN LIEROP, M. (1985) 'Predisposing factors in early literacy: a case study', in M. M. Clark (ed.) *New Directions in the Study of Reading* (London: Falmer Press), pp. 64–80.
VYGOTSKY, L. (1978) *Mind in Society: The Development of Higher Psychological Processes* (transl. and ed. by M. Cole, V. John-Steiner, S. Scribner and E. Souberman) (London: Harvard University Press).
WEIR, R. (1976) 'Playing with Language', in J. S. Bruner, A. Jolly and K. Sylva (eds) *Play: Its Role in Development and Evolution* (Harmondsworth: Penguin Books), pp. 609–18.

Chapter 12

The Literate Home Corner

Nigel Hall, Elizabeth May, Janet Moores, Janette Shearer and Susan Williams

The 'home corner' in a nursery school was transferred from a non-literate environment to a literate environment by the incorporation of a wide range of home-related print. The results were filmed. It was found that the children, when given the opportunity to display their interest in and involvement with print, demonstrated: (a) a commitment to literacy; (b) an understanding of the purposes and uses of literacy; and (c) some understanding of how literacy works.

The world in which pre-school children live is extraordinarily rich in print. From birth to death people in Western societies are enveloped in print. It affects almost every aspect of our lives. Just as children are sensitive to many other aspects of the world they live in, so they are sensitive to, and responsive to, the print in their environment. Children see not only the print itself but, more importantly, the way people use it and in turn are used by it. It would appear somewhat strange if children living in this print-rich world learnt nothing from it. And yet, in essence, that appears to be the implication of several pieces of research.

During the 1960s and 1970s Downing (1970) carried out a number of investigations which suggested that children starting formal schooling at the age of 5 years do not know much, if anything, about literacy. He felt able to declare that: 'Young beginners have serious difficulty in understanding the purpose of written language' (p. 8). There is considerable additional evidence that children starting school often have limited notions of literacy. Yaden (1984) reviewed over one hundred studies in this area and came to the conclusion: 'Beginning readers are largely unaware of the overriding structure of the writing system as well as their own speech. They have disparate notions as to what behaviour comprises the act of reading and the necessary steps they must take in getting ready to become a reader' (p. 34).

The unfortunate consequence of such findings was the perpetuation of the view that children know virtually nothing about literacy. Yet why should it be the case that children respond differently to the print-world than to all other aspects of their environment? Ferreiro and Teberosky (1983) put this problem into perspective when they said:

> We have searched unsuccessfully in this literature for reference to children themselves, thinking children who seek knowledge, children we have discovered through Piagetian theory. The children we know are learners who actively try to understand the world around them, to answer questions the world poses ... it is absurd to imagine that four or five year old children growing up in an urban environment that displays print everywhere (on toys, on billboards and road signs, on their clothes, on TV) do not develop any ideas about this cultural object until they find themselves sitting in front of a teacher. (p. 12)

There is now a considerable body of evidence (reviewed in Hall, 1987) that children are much more attentive to this world than was implied by Downing's (1970) work. By using more naturalistic techniques, investigators have been able to show that many, if not most, children are developing very subtle understandings of the way literacy operates. The work of Goodman (1980), Ferreiro and Teberosky (1983), Harste, Woodward and Burke (1984), Heath (1983), Read (1970), Sulzby (1985) and many others, reveals an often complex and sophisticated set of strategies employed by children to make sense of the phenomenon that we label literacy.

But where are these thinking children in nursery or reception classes? They are often, apparently, invisible. Too often we visited nursery classes where the only concessions to literacy were a book corner and story-reading sessions. Such provision is, of course, vital, but it represents only a narrow sample of the whole range of literacy events experienced by children outside school.

We wondered whether it would be possible to create a context in school which would allow children to use, and to display, some of this knowledge about print that they had developed outside school. Harste, Woodward and Burke (1984) reported that they tried to create such an environment: 'We brought the book corner out to the center of the room, added a writing table with different kinds of paper, writing instruments, envelopes, and stamps, put a pad of notepaper for taking messages by the play telephone in the home area, initiated a "Sign-In" activity whereby children kept their own attendance, and in general tried to accent and highlight reading and writing activities' (p. 43). They claimed that the data they collected suggested that the children spent, on those activities, from three to ten times the amount of time they had normally spent in the formal reading and writing activities that had been going on in the classroom.

A similar kind of provision was created by Conway (1985) for hearing impaired kindergarteners. He created a writing area with a wide range of materials. He found that writing became a regular free-choice activity of the children and suggested that the writing in that classroom 'was a meaningful activity and the children engaged in writing because it fulfilled personal and social purposes' (p. 95). He claimed that such free experiences give children 'The opportunities to explore, experiment, discover, consolidate and refine their understanding of writing as a mode of communication' (p. 105).

In both the above examples the provision was, in general, fairly arbitrary with respect to the world of print outside the school. In Conway's classroom the provision was simply a space and materials with which to write. The Harste, Woodward and Burke room did relate some of the provision, for example the supply of a notepad by the phone, but most appears, from their description, to be simply the provision of general resources for writing and reading.

It was decided to attempt to create a print environment which did relate, in as many ways as possible, to the real world of print outside of school and to see what use was made of it by the children.

The nearest equivalent to a home in a nursery school is, inevitably, the 'home corner' or 'Wendy house' as it used to be called. Such an area was of interest for two principal reasons. Firstly, because such areas often contain a range of resources designed to encourage home-based play, and secondly, because such areas are on the whole the province of the children rather than the teacher. Children are usually left to play in the ways that they decide are appropriate. Adults may sometimes join in with the play but such adult behaviour is usually in the context of the 'rules' for the play generated by the children. The home area seemed thus to be an ideal place to create, as far as was possible, a print-rich area in which the children would be free to use, in any way they wished, the materials provided. The choices were, once the initial provision had been made, entirely theirs. The question was, would the 3- and 4-year-olds use the area to 'explore, experiment, discover, consolidate, refine and display' their literacy knowledge, or would they ignore it because they were essentially ignorant of the nature and purpose of literacy?

The classroom and the provision

The classroom was a nursery classroom in a primary school. The school was situated in an urban area and the children came from a range of economic and ethnic backgrounds. The building was about one hundred years old. The classroom was, principally, one large room, although there were additional small play areas in corridor space just outside the classroom. There were also outdoor play areas. There was good overall nursery provision in the classroom and there was an exceptionally close and warm relationship between the children and the staff. It was a very busy, very happy class. The room contained a well-used library area and several story-reading sessions were held each day. The nursery staff said that the only writing the children ever did was to sometimes put their names on a drawing or when there was some kind of formal card-making, usually at Christmas. Although there were some labels on displays, in general the children did not have much opportunity to use materials related to literacy beyond those already mentioned.

The 'home corner' of the classroom contained a 'toy' cooker, a phone, tables and chairs, and several other pieces of equipment associated with the notion of 'home'. It was a classroom rule that only four children were allowed to use the area at any one time. In general, the staff reported that they did not interfere or influence the play in the 'home corner' except sometimes to quieten it down.

For this investigation the 'home corner' was subject to a 'print-flood'. By the cooker were placed cookery books, recipe pads, a recipe note book and writing utensils. Similarly, throughout the home corner related and appropriate literacy materials were provided. It was felt important that a wide range of print-related resources were provided, particularly with the writing utensils. Harste, Woodward and Burke (1984) reported that 'Children at three know that usually pens are used for writing and crayons for drawing. In fact when Joan asked one of her three year olds to write with a crayon, her young sophisticate said, quite matter-of-factly, "No I need a pen"' (p. 84). It was felt that if the children in this study had any sense of appropriateness they might fail to display some literacy behaviours if given only crayons or pencils.

The 'home corner' also received a desk area with paper, envelopes and writing utensils. Newspapers and letters were pushed through the door before each session. In addition, diaries, planners, telephone directories, books, catalogues and other print material were placed in strategic places. The results were videoed unobtrusively although the children were free to come round the back and watch the monitor while recording was in progress. In addition, notes were made while the play was in progress.

In order that the results could be interpreted simply and easily it was decided to consider the children's behaviour through three fairly straightforward categories: (a) the children's commitment to literacy; (b) the children's understanding of the purposes of literacy; and (c) the children's understanding of how literacy works.

The children's commitment to literacy

Prior to our intervention the children in this class did not appear to have a commitment to literacy. By this we mean that they did not elect to act in literate ways out of free choice. Prior to the intervention, when asked if they could write, most of the children said 'No, I can't write'.

However, when confronted with the resources available in the modified 'home corner' the behaviour manifested by the children certainly did demonstrate a commitment to literacy. During the four days that we recorded we noted 290 events in which literacy-related behaviour was exhibited. These ranged from fleeting bits of engagement to highly organised and sustained episodes of play in which literacy was a consistently embedded feature.

When faced with writing utensils, and space and time in which to write, the children did not avoid writing or claim they could not write. They used writing in a whole range of ways without any hesitation. They simply 'set to' and wrote. The children also incorporated the reading items into their play. Sometimes the items were absorbed within other play and sometimes the reading items provoked certain types of play. On occasion the children seemed to be exploring the materials in very personal, non-play ways. In one event a young boy was told by one of the girls, involved in some family play, to read the newspaper. There then followed a five-minute solo engagement (the girl had gone away) in which the boy manipulated and manoeuvred the paper until he had sorted it round to the correct orientation and then he sat and gave it the most intense scrutiny. It was as if he was not only exploring the orientation of the newspaper (which, being the *Guardian*, was a large object for him to handle), but also exploring the role of being a newspaper reader.

If commitment can be measured, even crudely, by the number of engagements, their variety, intensity, and duration, then these 3- and 4-year-old children were very committed to the idea of using, and enjoying using, print, and were committed to the creation of meaning-laden marks.

The children's understanding of the purposes of literacy

The way children use print and print-related items is an important piece of evidence about children's understanding of the purpose of print. Kammler (1984) gives a good example of this. She wrote: 'At age four, Shaun changed his name to Ponch, asked for a black wig and began playing CHIPS (California Highway Patrol). This involved zooming around on his two wheeler with a pencil and pad tucked in his back pocket. Like his macho, motor cycle riding TV hero my son Ponch issued hundreds of tickets to the law abiding citizens of Wagga over the next few years' (p. 61). The use of print made by Ponch was not simple. It was embedded in his understanding not simply of the making of marks but of how print played a role in policing, parking and speeding offences, control, power, and the rules of law of his country. Without his knowledge of these wider issues his play would have been unlikely to occur as it is these wider issues which give meaning to the print event.

In the same way the children in the nursery school demonstrated not only a knowledge of some of the purposes of print but also knowledge of the social contexts in which these purposes were embedded. Inevitably the range of understandings displayed was limited, but it is clear that there are a range of functions which are quite comprehensible to the children. Mostly these relate to experiences that they are likely to have had rather than those that have just been talked about.

In one morning session the children started playing within a restaurant context. They next created a French café (and used various accents to complement the play). Children later created a bank followed by school play and ending up with a session at MacDonald's. These play sessions involved different children at different times. Within these play sessions the children incorporated print-related behaviour in many appropriate ways. They showed menus, took orders, read packets and wrote on memo boards. The use of any of these behaviours was not as a single event but as an incorporated part of the more general context of the play. Thus the print-related behaviour was always used appropriately within the context of the play situation being generated.

There were many events associated with letter writing. This was often accompanied by the reading of letters or acting out post-person roles. The letters were often delivered within the classroom. In one event the child wrote a letter which he said was to tell people about work. The boy put the letter in an envelope, took it to someone else, opened it and said it tells you to go to work and that you must put a tie on. The note pads were used frequently, particularly those by the telephone.

These children still had many things to learn about print but it was nevertheless clear that the children had some knowledge of a range of purposes for print. In many respects this is not really surprising as there are many situations where written language use is not difficult to understand. Children do experience greetings cards, thank-you cards and letters, lists to Father Christmas, menus, advertisements for favourite products, packets with familiar foods, shopping lists and, of course, stories.

The children's understanding of how literacy works

The primary means of discovering what the children knew about how literacy works was to examine the kinds of visible marks they made when attempting to write. The children in this nursery school, when given the appropriate resources, wrote constantly. They filled several hundred sheets of paper, envelopes and pages in diaries, books and cards. They also wrote on calendars, memo pads, in the air, on notice boards and on telephone pads.

The first thing to note is that the children almost always used the correct terminology. They used 'draw' when they wanted to draw a picture, and 'write' when they wanted to write messages of any kind (and by message is meant any intended meaning conveying marks). There did not appear to be any confusion in the discrimination between the two activities. In schools, ambiguity is frequently created by teachers when they combine drawing with writing. We believe that it is probably the case that when children have access to appropriate context their use of the terminology is invariably correct.

The children displayed a very wide range of mark-making intended as writing. It was clear that the experience of the children in using print was quite varied. For some children the merest of lines or squiggles was sufficient to count as writing whereas for others there were intricate mixes of learned elements and created elements. It is, however, always possible that these differences were not simply due to inequality of experience but caused by the children 'reading' the requirements of the situations differently.

The children's writing manifested many of the characteristics identified by Clay (1975). Some were still at the 'sign concept' level; they were happy that any marks they made could be held to represent anything they liked. Most, if not all, understood the 'message concept', that marks could be made to convey meanings and messages. The more complex uses of marks utilised, in varying ways, the 'recurring principle', 'directional principles', and 'copying principles'. There were a number of pieces of work which appeared to represent what Clay calls the 'inventory principle', where the child lists most of what it knows in an effort to take stock of what it knows or to demonstrate what it knows. None of the children were writing in what might be termed 'conventional' ways; they all still had much to learn. It was, however, clear that many of the children were interested in how literacy worked and were busy using what they knew of how literacy worked. The results were often unconventional but were nevertheless a demonstration of how much had been learned already; a demonstration that would have been impossible without the appropriate resources and the opportunity for display.

Conclusion

Children in their non-school lives are surrounded not only by print but by people using it, and, frequently, people talking about it. Children take an interest in this print-world just as they take an interest in many other aspects of their world. For young children most of their print experiences are either within the home or within a family situation such as shopping. In school there are often very few opportunities for them to display and use their knowledge of these events. Teachers have long understood the necessity to provide home-related objects both within and outside 'home corners'. Thus most nursery classrooms are richly provided with a whole range of resources such as cookers, vacuum cleaners, telephones, beds, prams, and so on. However, the full use of many of these, and many other home-related items can be sensibly extended by the provision of home-related print. When given such resources it is clear that children use them with enthusiasm and insight. For the teacher the advantage is the chance to see children using literacy knowledge and skills in a much wider range of ways than would normally be evident within a classroom. For the children the experience is useful because it acts as a link between the world outside school and the world inside school; it helps them understand that literacy, in all its manifestations, is valued by both home and school.

The children in this nursery group were exploring the use of written language to establish ownership and identity, to build relationships, to remember or recall, to request information, to record information, to fantasise or pretend, and to declare. Those children were not waiting for formal schooling to use literacy but they had been waiting for the opportunity to display their use of it.

References

CLAY, N. (1975) *What Did I Write?* (London: Heinemann Educational Books).

CONWAY, D. (1985) 'Children (re)creating writing: a preliminary look at the purposes of free choice writing of hearing-impaired kindergarteners', *Volta Review*, vol. 87(5), pp. 91–107.

DOWNING, J. (1970) 'Relevance versus ritual in learning to read', *Reading*, vol. 4(2), pp. 4–12.

FERREIRO, E. and TEBEROSKY, A. (1983) *Literacy before schooling* (London: Heinemann Educational Books).

GOODMAN, Y. (1980) 'The roots of literacy', in Douglass, M. P. (ed.) *Reading: a humanising experience* (Claremont: Claremont Graduate School).

HALL, N. (1987) *The emergence of literacy: young children's developing understanding of reading and writing* (London: Hodder & Stoughton).

HARSTE, J., WOODWARD, V. and BURKE, C. (1984) *Language stories and literacy lessons* (New Hampshire: Heinemann Educational Books).

HEATH, S. B. (1983) *Ways with words: language, life and work in communities and classrooms* (Cambridge: Cambridge University Press).

KAMMLER, B. (1984) 'Ponch writes again: a child at play', *Australian Journal of Reading*, vol. 7(2), pp. 61–70.

READ, C. (1970) 'Pre-school children's knowledge of English phonology', *Harvard Educational Review*, vol. 41(1), pp. 1–34.

SULZBY, E. (1985) 'Kindergarteners as writers and readers', in Farr, M. (ed.) *Children's early writing development* (New Jersey: Ablex).

YADEN, D. (1984) 'Reading research in metalinguistic awareness: findings, problems, and classroom applications', *Visible Language*, vol. 18(1), pp. 5–47.

Chapter 13

Intonation in Early Reading

Elizabeth Goodacre

Teachers often comment on the lack of expression in children's early attempts at reading, referring to the style as 'word-by-word' or 'one word at a time' reading, 'word calling' or 'barking at print'. This paper describes two studies which sought evidence on the amount and type of intonation in children's early oral reading. Although there was evidence of children using stress to emphasise individual words and syllables, they used a variety of intonation patterns which seemed to fulfil different functions. The writer concludes by discussing a number of issues which emerge from the studies, including whether teachers and parents need to have explicit knowledge of the functions of intonation to help children learn to read.

Crystal (1980) describes 'intonation' as a term used in the study of suprasegmental phonology, which refers to the distinctive use of patterns of pitch. We are familiar as listeners with the rise and fall of the sounds of spoken language. Pitch sequences can vary in regard to range, height and direction. The word 'contour' can be used to describe the melodic aspect of this rise and fall. Stress is the prominence given to specific syllables or words in such patterns and is usually due to an increase in loudness or change of pitch. In popular usage, stress is usually equated with the idea of emphasis, denoting relevant importance to the particular syllable or word. There will also be the effects related to juncture – the contrasts produced by the use of silence – commonly recognised as pauses or hesitations. In speech, intonation with its variations in pitch and use of juncture is an important signal of grammatical structures, performing a role similar to punctuation in writing, but involving more contrasts. Also, intonation has a secondary role in communicating information about personal attitudes. We can usually recognise when a speaker wants to convey anger or sarcasm by their tone of voice, although ascribing such intentions may be related to our familiarity with the particular language and knowledge of the speaker's culture and social habits.

When a reader reads aloud the listener is likely to expect the reader to make use of intonation, but as Warham (1981) has pointed out, this may be an unfair assumption to make about children learning to read. She thinks 'beginning readers need to be made aware that the rise and fall in the voice, the various pitch levels, and the structural parts of the text are all part of reading'. She does not suggest how beginners should be made aware of such features. However, one would expect that this is often done by the listener or 'hearer' supplying a model of appropriate intonation; that is, showing how the phrase or sentence should be read. Hannon et al. (1986) in their comparative study of the hearing strategies used by teachers and parents, made use of a coding category 'providing a reading model': 'This occurred either before the child attempted a passage or after hesitant reading. The adult's intention in providing a fluent reading of the text may also have been to stimulate interest, to emphasise the meaning of the text (sometimes by stressing words the child had miscued) or to consolidate previous learning.' Teachers made use of this type of 'move' significantly more often than did parents.

Teachers and researchers seem familiar with the lack of intonation in the reading aloud of beginners and this is often described as a characteristic feature of the early stage of reading acquisition. In my reading I have come across references to such behaviour which has been variously described as:

word-by-word reading;
one word at a time reading;
word calling; and
'barking at print'.

Clay (1972), describing the behavioural records of children

who succeeded in learning to read, observed that finger-pointing at words and word-by-word reading (features usually considered symptomatic of poor readers) were useful actions for the beginning reader being taught by a language-experience approach: 'Part of the learner's task under these instructional conditions is to isolate word units in his speech and in the printed text, and match the two. . . . Word by word reading is not to be hurriedly trained out unless the teacher is certain that the child is visually locating the words he is saying.' Clay saw word-by-word reading as the way in which the beginner learns to match the spoken word to the printed word.

Two studies of children's intonation in reading aloud

The writer carried out a three-year project 'Phonological Segmentation and Teaching Reading' in English schools during the period 1978–81. Towards the latter part of the investigation, two small studies involved young readers' use of intonation in oral reading. The first study concerned thirty children (both good and poor readers) aged 7 to 11 years reading unseen, complete, one-page stories of increasing reading difficulty. It was soon discovered that there was very little data on the development of children's intonation patterns in spontaneous speech, let alone on children or adults reading aloud (Brazil *et al.*, 1980; Warham, 1981).

As Chapman (1983) has commented, 'a component of language that has been taken for granted and not received enough attention over the years is the development of children's ability to fully master pitch or intonation, that quality of speech that conveys meaning . . .'. Another problem was which transcript system to use, particularly in regard to the sensitivity of coding systems to different intonational features, and the reliability of subsequent scoring. Although there is need for caution in the interpretation of the study's observations, mainly on the basis of reliability, it was found that the younger and slower-progressing children tended to make use of a falling nuclear tone which gave emphasis to individual words (and sometimes syllables and phonemes). However, few consistently read in what could be identified as a 'one word at a time' style.

Indeed, it was common to find three or four styles of intonation operating:

(a) An automatic style Making use of rising and falling tones, with varying emphasis upon individual words within the written sentences. In the younger readers, emphasis could often correspond to each word, because the child was usually finger-pointing each word and 'mapping' the spoken word on to the printed word. However, most of the words in the beginning books and primers tended to be one-syllable words which facilitated this approach. Where a word had more than one syllable, the initial syllable was most likely to be emphasised, for example:

It is fun in the water (pronounced as 'war/ter')

However, sometimes individual phonemes were stressed as in:

Pat likes the water. (emphasis upon consonants 't' and 's' at the end of 'Pat' and 'likes').

(b) A dramatic reading with exaggerated contours This has some similarities with 'motherese' or the speech adopted by children to younger siblings where the function is to gain and hold the listener's attention. Such speech emphasises prosodic features, being characterised by raised pitch, vowel lengthening, exaggerated intonation and stress patterns, and greater overall variation in intonation contours (Farwell, 1973). In this type of reading the young reader seems to have sufficient attention to spare – from word recognition and semantic/syntactic strategies – to be able to consider the needs of the listener and how to gain and retain their attention.

(c) A 'minimal' style In which the reader adopts a neutral or level tone often making little use of loudness or intensity of pitch: often characterised by listeners as 'reading to him/herself'. Frequently in the 'reading to someone' situation, this would give way to

(d) A questioning or rising intonation, the function of which is to gain 'feedback' from the listener or 'hearer' about the accuracy of word recognition attempts, for example:

$$\underline{\quad\underset{\text{Have}\ |\ \text{a}}{\textcircled{R}}\underset{\text{look.}}{\_}}\ \overset{\rightarrow}{\text{Have}}\ \overset{\rightarrow}{\text{l/oo/k//}}\overset{\rightarrow}{\text{look}}\ (\text{sigh})$$

$$\underset{\overset{\rightarrow}{\text{Here}}}{\textcircled{T}}$$

Child read 'Here', which had occurred on the previous page, for the beginning word 'Have' in a neutral tone. Repeated it with a rising tone which prompted his teacher to interrupt and prompt with the correct word 'Have' given in a rising tone. The child continued reading, lengthening the vowel in 'look' and giving it a rising tone. When despite a pause this did not produce any response from the 'hearer', he repeated the word without the lengthened medial vowel and giving the word a falling nuclear tone, which was immediately followed by a long-drawn-out sigh! Playing this tape to various teacher groups this last paralinguistic feature is interpreted as indicating boredom, confusion or dejection.

The second study was concerned with the extent to which beginners demonstrated evidence of 'mapping' spoken words on to the words in printed text. We particularly wanted to see whether readers at the finger-pointing stage consistently used a nuclear falling tone on each word or, depending on the number of syllables in the word, used different tone contrasts stressing different segments of individual words. As in the above example, phonemic information about graphemes might be generalised by children at different levels – single phonemes, morphemes, syllables, familiar letter clusters, and so on. To return to Clay's (1972) observational studies, she has referred to 'voice pointing' taking over from finger-pointing but has not offered any further description of the characteristic features of such 'voice pointing'. Forty children aged between 5 and 6 years, identified by their teachers as at the finger-pointing stage of beginning reading, were studied over a term, reading from the normal reading material provided by their teachers. In fact, disappointingly, this study provided little reliable data. There was an enormous problem in obtaining 'good' tape-recordings in the naturalistic settings. Also, the children were often observed to silently rehearse appropriate articulations, no evidence of which appeared on the recordings! Occasionally these articulation attempts could be heard as semi-subvocalisations, which proved far too difficult to analyse and code reliably. Unfortunately, funding came to an end, or a further study, possibly using video, would have been considered.

Conclusions and implications

Although in many ways these two studies were exploratory, raising more questions than they answered, they suggest some interesting discussion points:

1. Beginners and slow readers tended to emphasise, by the use of different stress patterns, various segments in the sentences they read. They were also able to use different intonation styles which seemed to fulfil different functions, varying from the often observed word-by-word reading (possibly facilitating word recognition strategies) to the socially interactive questioning style seeking 'feedback' from the listener, usually in regard to the effectiveness of the word recognition strategies. 'Fluent' or 'expressive' reading appeared to be related to the familiarity of the grammatical structures, the number of times the words or phrases had been read aloud by the reader, or the reader's confidence or dependence on their 'hearer' for effective 'feedback'.

2. Parental involvement schemes have increased which provide different types of advice and information for parents as to how they can help their children. Few if any of these schemes seem to refer to intonation directly. For example, should parents be alerted to the rising, questioning tone as indication of 'feedback' being requested? Is this a reliable cue in the hearing situation? Does the E2L (English as a Second Language) speaker for example, consistently make use of this particular strategy?

3. In 'paired' or 'echo' reading, the adult or competent reader reads alongside the learner, allowing the child to indicate when he or she no longer requires such support. Although some video demonstration material exists, there is little systematic information available about how intonation functions in this type of learning situation.

4. There has been interest during the last decade in 'repeated reading' (Chomsky, 1978; Samuels, 1979; Lauritzen, 1982). The learner attempts a first reading, works on any difficulties, and reads it again until the result is 'fluent' or 'smooth'. Dahl (1979) evaluated this method, reporting that errors were cut in half and speed increased by 50 per cent, although improvements in comprehension were smaller. Again, it would be useful to know the type of intonation patterns which emerge in 'repeated reading' as the reader 'improves', and if this were possible, at what cost, if any, to other aspects of the reading acquisition process. For example, although oral reading errors on the particular passage decrease, is the rate of acquisition of phoneme/grapheme knowledge affected?

5. In the development of writing there has been gradual acceptance that learners should be allowed to separate the creative and editing stages, and that 'drafting' is an acceptable aspect of the writing process. Perhaps we should also allow this to happen in reading that it is acceptable for the reader to reread the sentence for meaning. Children who are encouraged to read their own writing to others or to read aloud to entertain others are likely to realise for themselves the importance and the functions of intonation for holding a listener's attention.

6. Using taped material of teachers and parents hearing children read aloud with teacher groups, it is apparent that teachers vary in their awareness of intonation 'cues' and their attributions to metalinguistic behaviours such as sniffs and sighs. In analysing tapes, most find they can 'hear' pauses and hesitations, and recognise rising and falling tones, but finer elements of analysis such as stress and more complex intonation patterns, particularly intonation contours in phrases and individual words, are far more difficult to

recognise. An individual's ability to recognise pitch patterns and awareness of rhythm and tempo in spoken-aloud text would be likely to be related to the individual's hearing acuity, auditory discrimination ability and musical skills. Much of the awareness of intonation must be based on implicit knowledge. What isn't clear is whether making such information explicit, by, for example, analysing examples of intonational features in young readers' oral reading, would help adults to be more effective facilitators of young readers' progress.

The writer would like to acknowledge the help in the collection of data and the invaluable discussion of ideas which were provided by Peter Brennan, who acted as research assistant for the three-year project referred to in this chapter.

References

BRAZIL, D., COULTHARD, M., JOHNS, C. (1980) *Discourse Intonation and Language Teaching* (London: Longman).
CHAPMAN, T. (1983) *Reading Development and Cohesion* (London and Exeter: Heinemann Educational Books).
CHOMSKY, C. (1978) 'When you still can't read in third grade: After decoding, who?', in S. J. Samuels (ed.) *What research has to say about reading instruction* (Neward, Delaware: International Reading Association).
CLAY, M. M. (1972) *Reading: The Patterning of Complex Behaviour* (London: Heinemann Educational Books).
CRYSTAL, D. (1980) *A First Dictionary of Linguistics and Phonetics* (London: Andre Deutsch).
DAHL, P. R. (1979) 'An experimental program for teaching high speed word recognition and comprehension skills', in J. J. E. Button, T. C. Lovitt and T. D. Rowland (eds) *Communications Research in Learning Disabilities and Mental Retardation* (Baltimore: University Park Press).
FARWELL, C. B. (1973) 'The language spoken to children', *Papers and Reports on Children's Language Development*, Stanford University, vol. 5, pp. 31–62.
HANNON, P., JACKSON, A. and WEINBERGER, J. (1986) 'Parents' and Teachers' Strategies in hearing young children read', *Research Papers in Education*, vol. 1(1), March.
LAURITZEN, C. (1982) 'A modification of repeated readings for group instruction', *The Reading Teacher*, vol. 35, pp. 456–8.
SAMUELS, S. (1979) 'The method of repeated readings', *The Reading Teacher*, vol. 32, pp. 403–8.

WARHAM, S. (1981) 'Discourse and text: a linguistic perspective on reading skills', in L. Chapman (ed.) *The Reader and the Text*, 17th UKRA Conference (London: Heinemann Educational Books) pp. 91–8.

Chapter 14

Letterland: Changing the Language of Reading Instruction

Lyn Wendon

From the perspective of a child the alphabet is initially a set of signs without significance. Although the letters are designed to signal and to signify they cannot – until the child has been initiated into the workings of the symbol system.

From the perspective of the teacher the instruction language available to explain our symbol system is a problem in its own right, because it is full of technical terms which are also without significance to young children.

Until we can pull them into this adult frame of reference, terms such as 'vowels', 'consonants', 'double consonants' – even terms such as 'words', 'alphabet names' and 'letter sounds' – the children cannot take in the instruction. Letterland captures children's interest in the technical features of written language and provides mnemonics to aid understanding and retention.

Parents who try to take up a teaching role at home often discover a similar communication barrier. They cannot find the language to explain the mechanics of reading at a child's level of understanding.

This communication barrier has always been with us, perplexing both teachers and parents and in response to this problem, many experts currently recommend dispensing with formal instruction altogether, in favour of 'learning to read by reading':

'Leave language intact!' they say.

'Don't chop it up, or analyse the bits, and then make

children struggle to put it together again. Wait until they *can* already read.'

'To concentrate on the medium first is to kill the message.'

I agree with these views . . . in so far as they are a reaction to *traditional* methods of phonic instruction. These have never been very efficient. But then, universal literacy has never been as important as it is today. However, to throw out unsatisfactory methods of instruction is not to make the problem go away.

If traditional phonic instruction can kill the message, so unfortunately, can an exclusive stress on sight-reading, and sentence units for those millions of children who cannot recognise whole-word shapes beyond a ceiling of a few hundred words. For them the strategies of the psycholinguists turn them into insecure guessers, not confident readers. Children who cannot cope with global strategies need to start with smaller units, the building blocks which make the words, which make the messages. By reading many good, 'real' books to them, and with them, they may realise that books *can* give pleasure.

When we teach them to 'behave like readers' they do it just as well as all the others, at first. But gradually they fall behind, because their visual memories cannot hold the expanding load of whole-word shapes. They cannot make the internal parts of similar-looking words *signify* when contextual clues fail. This is also where their dislike of reading usually begins, and for too many the dislike will last for a lifetime.

None of us can afford to align ourselves at one end of the spectrum of teaching strategies, whether it be 'learning to read by reading', or by teaching the nuts and bolts first. We must be experts in all methods to meet the needs of every type of child. Furthermore, ALL children need information about the medium *early on* to develop their own *writing* skills. When children fail to learn to read and WRITE, or fail to ENJOY learning to read and write, this is OUR failure as professionals, and this is why I set out, well over ten years ago, to try to find ways to change phonic instruction – to make it more fit for the purpose of teaching beginner readers – ideally *before* any child can fail.

Working with 'special needs' children who had already failed was a big eye-opener. Studying their confusions made me find fault with many traditional practices. The first was our dreary rule language, so alien to young children's ears. The second was our use of the terms 'Aee, Bee, Cee, etc.'. We usually teach these time-honoured alphabet names for two ostensible reasons:

1. So that we can talk about the letters; and
2. So that we can use the names to teach the sounds.

But if we look closely, the 'Aee, Bee, Cee' is a very flawed set of terms. How many teachers – or parents, who often teach the alphabet names to their pre-schoolers – are aware of the following facts:

- The 21 consonant names are *never* used in reading;
- Therefore any child who is taught them first, either at home or at school, is learning something as irrelevant to *reading* as, for example, the names of Sanscrit symbols?

A close look at the consonant names shows that:

- 8 have their sounds at the *start* of their names: *b, d, j, k, p, t, v, z;*
- 6 have their sounds at the *end: f, l, m, n, s, x*; and
- 7 have their sound at *neither end: c, g, h, q, r, w, y.*

Is it surprising that many children take a year or more to sort out where the clues may (or may not) be for remembering the sounds?

But that is not all. How many of us are aware that:

- 15 of the consonant names, that is, almost 75 per cent, actually *begin* with another letter's *sound*?

Here are the offenders:

- *c*–see, *f*–ef, *g*–jee, *h*–aitch, *j*–geay, *k*–cay, *l*–el, *m*–em, *n*–en, *q*–cue, *r*–are, *s*–ess, *w*–double-u, *x*–ex and *y*–why.

Furthermore:

- 12 of the consonant names, that is, 57 per cent, *end* with another letter's alphabet *name*: bee, cee, dee, gee, jay(a), kay(a), pee, cue(u), tee, vee, double-u, and why(i).
  These facts may account for much typical confusion among young children between two other important instruction words, the terms 'sounds' and 'names'.

To add to the confusion:

- the 5 vowel *names* 'Aee, Ee, Iee, Oh and You' give children no clue to their 5 *sounds*;
- Conversely their 5 *sounds* give no clue to their 5 *names*. Yet in traditional instruction language we teach spelling by alphabet *name* as soon as possible, even when we are talking about the short vowel sounds.

This minefield is no place for children.

But how else can we talk about letters? Call them 'the ah, the buh, and the cuh'? When a child spontaneously writes m-u-m-e for Mummy, are we comfortable saying: 'You have left out your second "muh", dear, and actually *Mummy* doesn't end with an "e". It ends with a "yuh" '? This is a very artificial manner of speaking. It can also be dangerous, when teachers pronounce all too many letters with an accompanying 'uh' sound: muh, nuh, tuh, suh, vuh, thereby distorting their real sounds. When teachers introduce this distortion it is entirely predictable that the children will find it difficult to blend sounds. Can we blame the child who sounds out 'puh-lah-ah-nuh' and decides the word is 'Pollyanna'?

So the 'ah, buh, cuh' tradition has its own minefields.

A solution: change the language about the signs

I decided to replace both the 'Aee, Bee, Cee' and the 'Ah Buh, Cuh' terms with *alliterative* character names – as a transition stage which could last two years, one year, or less, just long enough to ensure that no child need be injured in any of these minefields.

First I designed Pictogram letter characters by fusing pictures right into the letters. These Pictograms are a set of shape-associated mnemonics, devised to improve first, childrens' perception of each abstract letter shape, and second, their access to each sound (always reliably at the START of the alliterative names). Then, because these mnemonics turned out to be surprisingly effective, and because I needed to keep the learning load light for my special needs children, I re-used the same 31 characters to illustrate *changes* in sound.

I invited the children to follow the letter characters *into words* and to study their *behaviour* right there: letters interacting with each other as 'characters'. Drawn from already familiar objects, these mnemonics have made it possible to create an imaginary world called 'Letterland' where teachers can explain, at a child's level, how letters constantly (or inconstantly) interact.

To avoid the communication barriers built into our traditional instruction language the Letterland teacher adopts a story language instead. For example:

> Sammy Snake loves to hiss so he hisses a lot. There aren't many hisses he misses!
> The Hairy Hat Man hates noise, so he never speaks above a whisper in words. Sometimes he makes no sound at all.
> But whenever you see Sammy Snake next to the Hairy Hat Man in a word, DON'T expect each of them to be making his usual sound.
> We know the Hat Man hates noise, so what does he do whenever he finds Sammy Snake slithering up behind him saying 'sss'?
> He turns back to Sammy Snake and says 'SH'!
> That's why we always hear the 'SH' sound instead whenever we see Sammy and the Hat Man next to each other in a word.

From this little example it will be seen how the introduction of Pictogram characters and the concept of 'Letterland' change the teacher's instruction language. Instead of handing out facts and rules, and then demanding to have them back,

159

the teacher NARRATES. The narration turns dreary facts and rules into little anecdotes which, as they entertain, also happen to teach.

The ideas are childish, if you like. This is because they are designed for children. Some of them actually were originated by my special needs children. Their learning difficulties, I discovered, did not prevent them from thinking imaginatively, once they were given scope to use their imaginations to explain the idiosyncrasies of their own written language.

An important result of this new, narrative form of instruction, springing in the first instance from children, is that from the outset *they can speak the instruction language themselves*. They are freed from a merely passive role of receiving instruction. Simply by sharing with each other the latest story, or reminding a friend of an earlier one, they can even instruct each other! Teachers in hundreds of British schools report that their children *do* talk about 'Sammy Snake' and the 'Hairy Hat Man', and all their other new-found Letterland friends in the playground and at home. How many children have ever gone home and spontaneously told their parents a traditional phonic rule?

These findings demonstrate how Letterland teachers are developing a very special, exciting relationship between themselves, the children and their parents. The advice to teachers and parents currently is to join hands in partnership, an emphasis which I heartily endorse. (Why did we fail for so long to adopt this common-sense approach?) There is a new potential in this partnership, which becomes possible in the context of Letterland. Teachers are now in a position to strengthen the dynamics of the partnership by turning it into a triangle.

The first model, which we all endorse, combines the teaching energies of both teachers and parents for the benefit of the child:

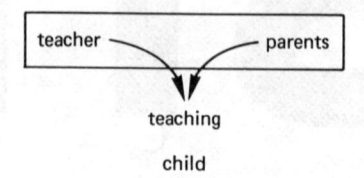

teacher ⟶ ⟵ parents
teaching
child

But notice how the child is continuously the receiver of adult input.

The second model gives the *children* a special role in the transaction, and ensures that the language of instruction is *theirs too*, from the start.

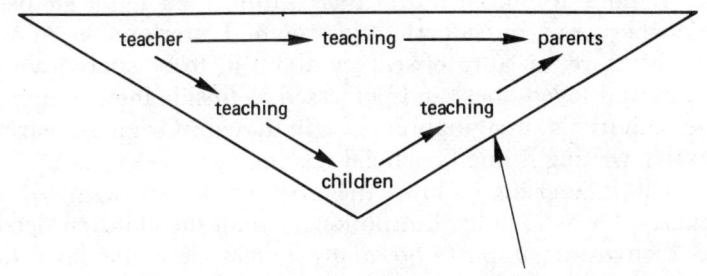

```
teacher ──────▶ teaching ──────▶ parents
         teaching          teaching
                 children
```

Here is where the dynamics change in the child's favour.

Every teacher has experienced how the need to *teach* any new subject *galvanises their own learning* of any subject. Letterland enables teachers and parents working together to give children this same beneficial experience. This is how it works:

1. The teacher briefs the parents, in gradual stages, about the Letterland characters and interconnecting stories. The parents go home – not to teach what they have learnt – but to let the CHILDREN TEACH THEM. The PARENTS, lending a willing ear and maintaining good eye-contact, RESPOND AS LEARNERS.

2. Each child goes home each day with a little something to tell Mum or Dad about Letterland: 'who is who', how to animate each letter, to tell any relevant story details, or share a little Letterland rhyme or song.

The role reversal of the 'child in the know' and the parent as 'the willing learner' does wonders for a child's self-esteem and the parent provides a good role model by demonstrating, daily, *an interested learning attitude, at the child's hands*. The child's oral language skills – so often atrophied by the TV age they live in – are expanded instead.

In what other ways does the Letterland approach meet the

needs of teachers and parents working together to make their children literate?

1. The special nature of the Letterland characters: seen on the Letterland frieze and Picture Code Cards and in Letterland storybooks, but *invisible* within their letter shapes everywhere else outside the classroom. Letterland learning has, therefore, an aura of secrecy about it, to be shared with friends and loved ones, and possessed as 'inside information'. The children's imagination is stimulated. Original, early creative writing is one beneficial result.

2. Each Pictogram endows the abstract letters with *object constancy*, for as long as, but no longer than the children need the Pictogram support. So many letters defy the laws of object constancy (*b/d/p/q*, *n/u*, *f/t*, *s/z*, *M/W/N/Z*, *h/y*, etc.), leaving both teachers and parents, in *plain* letter teaching, with no role except as correctors of mistakes.

3. Animating letters has a unique effect on children. Even 3-, 4- and 5-year-olds can do it all by themselves. Thousands of pre-school siblings have already proved that they can master the abstract symbols as easily as their older brothers and sisters, just by scribbling the Pictogram character details on to the letters written boldly for them.

4. Rhyme, rhythm and song accompanies *every* letter (to teach *handwriting* as well as sounds). Here is another good area for parent participation.

5. The system generates original artwork. This 6-year-old 'architect' has designed a jigsaw house for Jumping Jim. There is ample scope for all kinds of arts and crafts: puppetry, modelling, map-making, even embroidery, in the Letterland context (see page 163).

6. The use of play-acting enables children to speedily identify letters by identifying with them. When you have play-acted *being* a letter, you do not forget how it behaves in words. The imitation pattern creates the memory pattern. The play-acting easily leads to Letterland assemblies and drama: another good opportunity for involving parents as costume and prop makers and audience.

7. The teacher repeats him/herself less. Each little story anecdote is an ideational recall-route, far easier to remember

than the bare facts. So there is an economy in both the teaching and the learning time.

8. A further economy is built into the stories: revision. Note how the SH story actually *revises* the original sounds of S and H while creating the logic to explain the new sound.

9. The mystery and complexity of English spelling is often as mysterious to the teacher and parents as to the child! These mysteries are dispelled as each story 'reason' clarifies why this or that word, or whole group of words, is spelt just so. Yes, the reasons are only fictions, but they provide logic and context, where mindless memorising does not.

Summary

In summary, the purpose of the Letterland approach to reading is to reinstate, for the benefit of teachers and parents *and* children, the teaching of word structure in a form which is sufficiently palatable, sufficiently interesting and relevant, sufficiently vivid, logical and explainable that no school need defer such instruction until their children have become readers – or have experienced failure and dislike reading.

The shift into narrative language makes this difficult area 'user-friendly'. Both teachers and parents team up to turn the instruction both figuratively and literally into child's play.

The result in terms of 'progress', out there right now in

over 6000 British schools, will one day deserve a systematic statistical report. All the indications are that teachers find it much easier to make the signs signify. The evidence:

- Letterland classrooms usually achieve alphabet fluency (both *small* and *capital* letter *shapes* and *sounds*) within the first term of the reception year (or 2 terms, if the teacher is new to Letterland and therefore is used to expecting less).
- The children take pleasure in learning about the structure of the English language.
- Fewer top infants in Letterland schools need remedial help when they reach the junior stages.
- Creative writing develops swiftly, and with it a *thoughtful* approach to spelling. (Every remedial teacher knows how difficult it is to eradicate habitual spelling errors, once they have become automatic!)
- Experiments with different reading schemes, before and after introducing Letterland, show that a separate but parallel introduction to words through Letterland makes for swifter progress through *any* reading scheme. Alternatively, it enables schools which prefer only non-scheme books to launch their children safely on them.

Finally I would like to acknowledge the strengths of the British educational system which have made the development and growth of 'Letterland' possible. It could not have happened, first, without the children's input, and second, without those many creative British teachers who have enriched it, working in a primary educational system where curriculum decisions are theirs, and resourceful and inventive uses of published material is encouraged.

Chapter 15

Parents and the Writing Process

Roger Beard

This paper will examine the implications of recent research into the nature of the writing process for the potential involvement of parents in children's writing development. Drawing parallels with the ways in which parents have been involved successfully in children's reading development, the paper will identify some of the key similarities and differences in these two aspects of collaboration in early literacy.

One of the most notable features of British research and publication in reading studies during the first half of the 1980s has been the attention paid to parental involvement in children's early reading development. The great catalyst in this was the so-called 'Haringey project' (Tizard *et al.*, 1982) which indicated that parents hearing 6–7-year-old children read at home on a regular basis over a two-year period appeared to have a highly significant effect on children's reading attainment over the whole ability range. The increase in attainment compared with parallel classes (some of which were given additional, small-group teaching in reading) was maintained a year after the main experiment was ended.

Other similar findings have been reported from Rochdale, in the so-called 'Belfield Project' (Jackson and Hannon, 1981) and from Derbyshire (Bushell *et al.*, 1982), although both these studies were less rigorous, in that they did not involve the use of control groups. Also in the 1980s there have been reports from many parts of the country on the increased use of 'paired' and 'shared' reading involving parents. Paired reading, which was first reported by Morgan (1976) and Morgan and Lyon (1979), involves parent and child reading aloud simultaneously from a book in which the child has shown interest and which is compatible with the child's chronological age. If the child wishes to read independently, he or she taps on the table and continues alone until substantial delays lead to a resumption of simultaneous reading. It was an approach first developed for use with children who were experiencing difficulties in learning to read.

'Shared reading' is a derivative of 'paired reading' (Greening and Spencely, 1984) in which the child and adult (or more able child) read in partnership and the adult pays no attention to the child's errors or miscues, providing instead sympathetic continuity in reading aloud the text.

Many local projects have been set up across the country (for example, Widlake and McLeod, 1984) which have been influenced by these and other related studies, arousing a considerable amount of interest and in some cases a good deal of rhetoric on how parents might be brought more directly into children's reading development. The whole field is well covered in a collection of papers edited by Topping and Wolfendale (1985). In this chapter, I am going to take a closer look at some of the assumptions behind these studies and draw from them some tentative thoughts about the possibilities for involving parents in children's *writing* development. Firstly, drawing upon material from a forthcoming book on reading (Beard, 1987), I want to take a closer look at some of the outcomes from the studies on parental involvement in children's reading, concentrating on the what, the how, the who and the why.

What is the evidence on the benefits of parental involvement in reading?

The Haringey study was an appropriate catalyst in this movement, for it was a carefully designed experiment with due regard for control groups and statistical analysis of results although, as Bryant and Bradley (1985, p. 19) point out, the study might have been improved by the control group having as much contact over books with their parents as the experimental group had. Otherwise, it is not easy to be absolutely sure that it is actually the experience of reading to the parent which benefited the children in the experimental group.

However, a distinguishing feature of the other research studies mentioned above is their lack of control groups. Therefore, the reported increases in measured reading attainment could be attributable to factors other than parental involvement, or indeed, might have happened by chance. Even if parental involvement is taken to be an important influence in improved reading performance, it is still not clear which dimensions of involvement are most productive.

How do we explain the positive results?

Clearly practice, supportive and sympathetic circumstances and enhanced self-concept may play an important part in explaining the positive outcomes from studies such as those outlined above. But a more detailed look at involvement in the *process of reading itself* reveals the possibility of conflicting explanations. For example, Morgan (1985) explains the apparent effectiveness of paired reading by using a behaviourist approach which emphasises modelled and reinforced responses to the printed word. Yet it could be argued that paired or shared reading provides a very thorough experience of the reading process in action, so that the learner can begin to construct an appreciation and understanding of the way the system works, an approach more akin to humanistic approaches in the psychology of learning and a psycholinguistic view of reading, as Morgan has recently acknowledged.

Who is involved in parental involvement in early reading?

Despite the upsurge of interest, there are some chastening findings about the limited spread of interest in this area of reading. Hannon and Cuckle (1984), for example, report a survey of practices in sixteen infant and first schools in one LEA. Only six headteachers and three top infant teachers of the twenty interviewed allowed books from school to be taken home without expressing reservations about the practice. Attitudes and practices *may* be changing on a large scale, but specific evidence is still only accumulating slowly.

Why involve parents in early reading?

As Johnson (1980) suggests, research into home–school links has tended to assume one or more of three rather distinct frames of reference: parental rights; educational disadvantage; and reciprocal roles between parents and teachers. Obviously the Education Acts of 1980 and 1981 played a part in changing the climate surrounding parental involvement with schools generally, both in governing them and choosing between them. But much of the research into reading involvement seems to have been in the second of the frames of reference: dealing with children with difficulties in reading or children from disadvantaged backgrounds, or both.

It is a little unfortunate that parental involvement in the reading 'movement' has not built upon the clear-cut findings of what sympathetic and supportive home circumstances can provide for children in language and reading development. Wells (1985) offers a major source of evidence on the legacy which homes bequeath: experience of constructing a shared reality of the world through talk; insights and awareness about the conventions of print; the experience of being read to frequently. Similarly Clark (1976) highlights some key features which were associated with children who were reading fluently on entry to school: parental interest in and value of education, parents setting the credible example of reading silently themselves in front of the children, children's regular use of a local library, parents and grandparents reading to and talking with children. With findings such as these, even the most dedicated and successful teacher has to acknowledge that a considerable amount of a child's early achievements in language and literacy are due to at least the reciprocal influences of home and school.

First thoughts on parental involvement in children's writing

With the above cautious thoughts in mind, we can now explore some initial thoughts on similar parental involvement in children's writing. Immediately, we have to face up to the fact that a simple transfer of ideas and principles is not appropriate. Reading involves decoding written language; writing involves *encoding* it and therein hangs a mighty tale, which for many can be a mighty task. In many ways a book creates its own context. Casually picking up a story from a shelf can almost immediately involve you into another vicarious world created by the author. Adults can quickly take on the role as facilitators in creating the relationship between author and child-reader.

Writing is altogether different, depending as it does upon the overall context in which, and for which, the written word is brought into being. The role of the adult is now much different and in some ways more demanding, for the adult has to be sensitive to and ready to realise the context in which writing is produced, by adult or child. It seems to be that this central difference between the nature of decoding and encoding language means that it is less likely that parental involvement will be as immediately and even unconsciously effective as it seems to have been in children's reading. Such effectiveness is likely to depend on several major factors including purposes, process and practice.

Recognising the role of purpose in writing

Much writing in everyday adult life is taken for granted and its educational value underrated. Much writing in schools is artifically contrived, comprising dummy-run exercises or unconvincing teacher stimulation (see, for example, the successive reports from HMI surveys of schools), nicely parodied by Owen (1985).

Any collaboration between home and school on writing is likely to need to take account of the range of purposes for which we write. My own work on this topic has identified the various aims or purposes which lie within the so-called communication triangle (Beard, 1984).

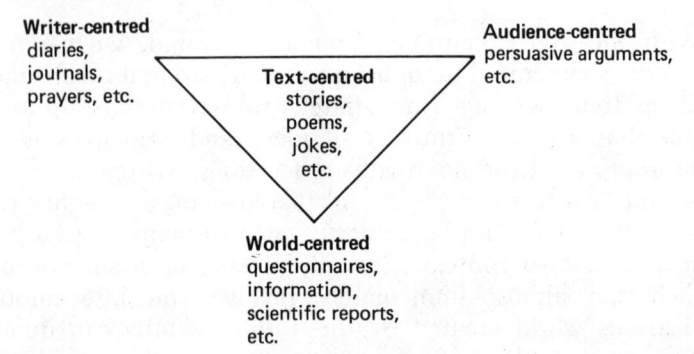

```
      Writer-centred                                Audience-centred
      diaries,                                      persuasive arguments,
      journals,         Text-centred                etc.
      prayers, etc.      stories,
                         poems,
                         jokes,
                         etc.

                       World-centred
                       questionnaires,
                       information,
                       scientific reports,
                       etc.
```

Frameworks such as this help indicate the variations in emphasis in writing and the underlying criteria which influence the success of these variations such as the following:

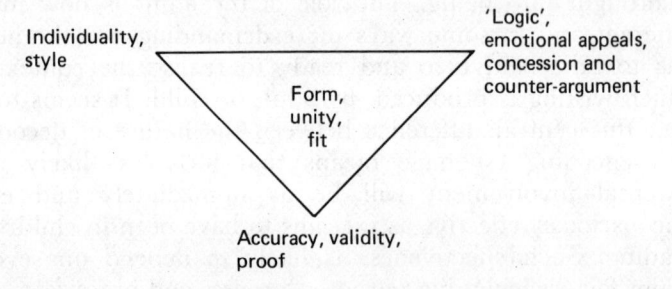

```
                                                    'Logic',
      Individuality,                                emotional appeals,
      style                                         concession and
                          Form,                     counter-argument
                          unity,
                          fit


                      Accuracy, validity,
                      proof
```

Thinking about the underlying process of writing

If these kinds of purposes are properly realised, then it is only a short step towards thinking about the underlying process which makes them possible. To avoid the kind of narrowness which may have blinkered Morgan's early work on paired reading, there is much to be gained from the instigators of parental involvement in writing, making explicit their own assumptions on what is involved in writing. Many will find it useful to distinguish between

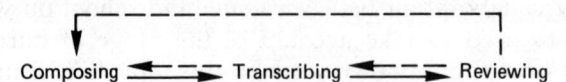

Composing ⇌ Transcribing ⇌ Reviewing

Each of these involves highly *patterned* behaviour, in composing, searching the mind for *content* knowledge (what to say) and *discourse* knowledge (how to say it) according to Bereiter and Scardamalia (1985), to avoid the rambling, 'knowledge-telling' approach which children fall back on. Transcribing involves a complex tapestry of the three *structures* of language: grammar, vocabulary and spelling. Reviewing involves trying to read in a peculiarly detached way, yet with a writer's alertness to technique, and redrafting as necessary. And all this has to be related to the parameters of *aim* and *audience* as well as the awareness of available *content* and the appropriate *modes* of writing (Beard, 1986).

Realising the practices of writing

This kind of framework offers a considerable richness for exploitation by parents and teachers in helping children. To indicate just a few: the use of a double-page spread, with the left-hand page used for various *composing* strategies – word lists, points in an argument, steps for instructions, brainstorming; specific techniques to help with the patterns of English *spelling*, finger tracing, word lists which share the same letter strings, (whether or not they sound the same) the look-cover-write-check sequence; the use of some kind of agreed notation for *review*, revision and rewriting, (circles, underlining, arrows, dotted lines, brackets and margin notes).

Kinds of parental involvement

With these prospects and possibilities in mind, what *roles* can parents play? Three basic ones might be summarised as *demonstration*, *collaboration* and *facilitation*. It is clear from research that parents can play a crucial role in showing children 'print in action' so that they develop what Downing (1979) calls 'cognitive clarity' – attending to the techniques and functions of the tasks undertaken by the skilled performer. This seems particularly feasible in 'world-based', functional writing. Writing captions in family photograph albums, notes for the milkman or letters to granny can all play a part in introducing children to the 'literacy club' (Smith, 1984).

Collaboration may be especially valuable when children are attempting something which is especially demanding and where the children are at the threshold of their performance. For younger ones this may be the extended story, for older children the extended argument. It may seem excessive to reallocate 'school-based' work to the home in this way, but some attempt to plan, organise and sustain writing over several days can be a realistic way of providing children with a kind of writing experience which will prepare them for the demands of later years far more than the short-burst writing which characterises many classrooms.

The parent can be facilitator too: providing opportunities for children to keep the reflective, introspective kinds of journal or diary to which the Adrian Mole books (Townsend, 1983) may have given a fillip. Here, of course, the stream of consciousness should be given the respect and privacy it behoves. The crowning glory of this facilitative role can be in the buying, borrowing and reading aloud the children's literature which has so distinguished the past thirty years or so in Britain. To increase a sensitivity to the charms and secrets of poetic language what more could parents do than read Alan Ahlberg's delightful *Please Mrs Butler* (Puffin), Michael Rosen's mischievous *Wouldn't You Like to Know?* (Puffin), eloquent anthologies such as *A Puffin Quartet of Poets*, or perhaps the finest of all, Charles Causley's subtle and secretive *Figgie Hobbin* (Puffin)? As Smith (1982) reminds us, we learn to write by reading. Parents will welcome being told about what is best to read to their children.

Parents, process, school and community

In this chapter I have given some tentative indications of how the current trends in parental involvement in schools may be extended to writing. Such indications assume that some parents may need to make adjustments in their home life-style to accommodate them. Some parents will reject them, but it seems unjust to those whose children might benefit not to encourage collaboration where it is possible. My indications also assume that some schools may need to make adjustments to their patterns of communication: telling parents more about the school's curriculum and their overall teaching intentions so that the parental role can be developed in good time – and telling them this much *earlier* in the school year than is often the case.

Finally, if we turn to the four questions I used earlier when discussing reading, the question *why* can now be given the priority it deserves. If the broader reciprocal frame of reference is adopted, then teachers will have to concede that some parents will have more experience and knowledge of writing than they do. The shopkeeper, the journalist, the clerk, the foreman, the housewife or house-husband may all provide insights into what it is to have one's occupational and domestic existence bound up with the use of the written word, whether on paper or computer screen.

Should a school parents' meeting turn its attention to parental involvement in writing, it would be wise to take into account the views of professional writers, too, and those professional writers and academics who write so engagingly about writing, such as Smith (1982) and Wilkinson (1986). Frank Smith now swears by his word processor, whereas Iris Murdoch won't depart from her fountain pen (Walsh, 1985) and I have to confess to being wedded to a set of three yellow plastic propelling pencils, with erasers attached which cost me a total of 75p. Together with A4 lined paper and inevitable use of double-page spread (left-hand for notes), these pencils have produced 200 000 words of dissertation and publication over the past six years.

It is considerations such as these which will help give parental involvement in children's writing development the realistic perspective which it deserves.

References

BEARD, R. (1984) *Children's Writing in the Primary School* (Sevenoaks: Hodder & Stoughton Educational).
BEARD, R. (1986) 'Reading Resources and Children's Writing', in Root, B. (ed.) *Resources for Reading; Does Quality Count?* (London: Macmillan).

BEARD, R. (1987) *Developing Reading 3–13* (Sevenoaks: Hodder & Stoughton Educational).

BEREITER, C. and SCARDAMALIA, M. (1985) 'Children's Difficulties in Learning to Compose', in Wells, G. and Nicholls, J. (eds) *Language and Learning: An International Perspective* (Lewes: The Falmer Press) pp. 95–105.

BRYANT, P. and BRADLEY, L. (1985) *Children's Reading Problems* (Oxford: Basil Blackwell).

BUSHELL, R. et al. (1982) 'Parents as Remedial Teachers', *Journal of the Association of Educational Psychologists*, vol. 5(9) pp. 7–13.

CLARK, M. M. (1976) *Young Fluent Readers* (London: Heinemann Educational).

DOWNING, J. (1979) *Reading and Reasoning* (Edinburgh: Chambers).

GREENING, M. and SPENCELEY, J. (1984) 'Paired Reading Made Easy', *Psychology: Journal of Cleveland County Psychological Service*, Spring.

HANNON, P. and CUCKLE, P. (1984) 'Involving Parents In The Teaching of Reading: A Study of Current School Practice', *Educational Research*, vol. 26, pp. 7–13.

JACKSON, A. and HANNON, P. (1981) *The Belfield Reading Project* (Rochdale: Belfield Community Council).

JOHNSON, D. (1980) 'Home/School Relations', in Cohen, L. (ed.) *Educational Research and Development in Britain 1970–80* (NFER–Nelson) pp. 459–72.

MORGAN, R. T. T. (1976) ' "Paired Reading" Tuition: A Preliminary Report on a Technique for Cases of Reading Deficit', *Child Care, Health And Development*, vol. 2, pp. 13–38.

MORGAN, R. T. T. (1985) 'Paired Reading: Origins and Future', in Topping, K. and Wolfendale, S. (eds) *Parental Involvement in Children's Reading* (London: Croom Helm) pp. 115–18.

MORGAN, R. T. T. and LYON, E. (1979) ' "Paired Reading" – A Preliminary Report On A Technique For Parental Tuition of Reading-Retarded Children', *Journal of Child Psychology and Psychiatry*, vol. 20, pp. 151–60.

OWEN, G. (1985) *Song of the City* (London: Fontana Lions).

SMITH, F. (1982) *Writing and the Writer* (London: Heinemann Educational).

SMITH, F. (1984) *Joining the Literacy Club* (Reading: Reading and Language Information Centre).

TIZARD, J. et al. (1982) 'Collaboration between Teachers and Parents in Assisting Children's Reading', *British Journal of Educational Psychology*, vol. 52, pp. 1–15.

TOPPING, K. and WOLFENDALE, S. (eds) (1985) *Parental Involvement In Children's Reading* (London: Croom Helm).

TOWNSEND, S. (1983) *The Secret Diary of Adrian Mole aged 13¾* (London: Methuen).

WALSH, J. (1985) 'Monstrous Regimens: The Art of Writing', in *Books and Bookmen*, December, pp. 6–7.

WELLS, G. (1985) *Language Development in the Pre-School Years* (Cambridge: Cambridge University Press).

WIDLAKE, P. and MCLEOD, F. (1984) *Raising Standards* (Coventry: Community Education Development Centre).

WILKINSON, A. (1986) *The Quality of Writing* (Milton Keynes: Open University Press).

Chapter 16

Teaching the Catching of Spelling

Margaret L. Peters

It is in the early years that spelling is 'caught' and parental behaviour determines this. Catching spelling depends upon parents and teachers knowing what is to be caught, in the sense of their knowing the nature of the orthography. It arises from their directing of children's attention to, and sensitising them to, serial probability within the spelling system. In developing a kind of imagery and increasing the span of apprehension through the shared activity of daily life, and through intentional communication with children in speech and writing, parents and teachers together are teaching the catching of the skill within the language process.

Teaching the catching of spelling

In the annals of spelling research, the 'catching' of spelling has an interesting history. Since the late nineteenth century, when the teaching of spelling was standard practice in schools, there have been constant rumblings about whether spelling needed to be taught at all. In other words, the idea of children just 'catching' spelling has acquired some respectability. We know that for some children spelling is no problem. They do just 'catch' it.

Though spelling is caught by some children, there are very strong reasons why it should be caught by all in the cause of communication, and courtesy. It may be a worthwhile status symbol, but it is in the freedom it gives one to express what one wants to say precisely that it is most valuable. This is not to say that spelling is taught as an isolated skill. It is taught within the process in order to develop the product, which is purposeful writing.

To say it is 'caught' does not imply that this is through maturation or some kind of spelling acquisition device. Even if it were, there would be outside influences at work. 'Caught' means that it is picked up in certain favourable circumstances in the context of concerned and perceiving adults. It is in the early years that the catching of spelling occurs and it is parental behaviour that determines it, just as in the school years it is teaching behaviour that determines good spelling.

Before examining those aspects of parental behaviour that help children to catch spelling, it is worth eliminating those factors that do not help children to catch it.

It is not merely within that nexus of warm and stimulating linguistic experience that is the heritage of the favoured child that it is caught. If it were, all linguistically favoured children would be good spellers, and we know this is not so. It is not caught through listening, since the English spelling system can have more than one spelling for any one sound, for example, cup, done, does, blood, tough, and more than one sound for any one spelling, for example, does, goes, canoes. It is interesting that attempts by use of a computer to generate the spelling of a word from sound alone have not been of practical value. As Smith (1985) observes, 'children who spell by ear are the worst spellers' (p. 163).

It is worth remembering that it is not caught just through reading, for we do not look at every word we read. Indeed, there is a population of highly intelligent and literate adult readers who are poor spellers, simply because they have never needed to look closely at individual word structure. If one asks these people how they learned to read, they will usually say they can't remember, or at their mother's knee or by what used to be called learning to read by 'Look and Say,' an approach, as Dean (1968) observed, which is unlikely to promote close examination of words. Their poor spelling stems from their just not having needed to look closely at words as they read, anticipating rather than reacting to the print. These intelligent and literate adults also report that they read very fast, so as adults they still do not look at the internal structure of words.

What is our spelling system like?

First, it is too easy to ignore the question as to what is being caught. If we know what spelling is like, if we can describe our model of spelling, we can then appreciate the extent to which such catching can be facilitated in the early years by parents as well as teachers.

Far from being the unsystematic, unpredictable collection of words handed down from a muddled and motley collection of etymological sources, spelling is an example of what is known as the stochastic process, which is any process governed by the laws of probability. In the case of the language process the expected probability of occurrence of any single element or sequence from the point of view of the reader or listener is governed by the immediate context and his previous personal experience of similar kinds of context. We are accustomed to this process in the case of words or sequences of words in speech and writing, for we know which words it is possible to use next in sequence as we speak or write. We do not say 'I am going into the . . . fork', or the 'said' or the 'yellow'. We can say 'I am going into the garden' or the 'possibility' or even the 'red'. Such word sequences are obviously greatly affected by meaning. Even so each word is on a scale of probability of occurrence from acceptable to wholly unacceptable, and this applies to every word in turn. It is what happens as we predict the forthcoming word or words, and as we make swift preliminary forays ahead, in our reading and listening as well as in our speaking and writing.

It is the same with spelling except that the probability is with letter sequences not word sequences. It is the probability of letters that can occur in sequence – that is to say, letters that can stick together – that determines whether a word is spelt acceptably or not.

Spelling is a kind of grammar for letter sequences that generates permissible combinations without regard to sound (Gibson and Levin, 1975). As in word sequences (grammar) there is a scale of probability-range from letters that can occur in sequence to those that cannot occur, that is, from highly probable to highly improbable, and even impossible letter sequences. We must remember, of course, that although this is a kind of grammar for letter sequences within a word, the spelling can be affected by grammatical and meaningful constraints, as in the case of homophones, where, for example, the spelling of 'mist' or 'missed' depends on the context.

It is not a matter of whether a word is regular or irregular. There have been repeated studies into the proportion of regularity in the orthography. One of the most recent investigations, by Flesch (1983), of a computerised list of decodable words put it at 97.4 per cent exactly! Words which are not decodable, that is, grapho-phonetically regular, are still made up in a sequentially probable manner. Such a sequence CAN happen, and we know it can happen because it 'looks right'. After all, we show this when we do not know how to spell a word and we 'write it down to see if it looks right'. As humans, sight is our preferred sense, and this is a reliable check to spelling, but it is not so much the visual appearance that informs us, as the knowledge of letter by letter structure (Frith, 1980), which we call letter patterns or letter strings in the context of serial or sequential probability.

Knowledge of the spelling system

The parent or teacher may be aware of serial probability as a result of playing games like Scrabble or Countdown, or doing crosswords or just by being intrigued by word structure. If he or she is, likenesses will be noticed within words, and he or she will be in a position to point out letter strings. The fact that the parent or teacher is aware of them and interested in them will motivate the directing of children's attention to them. With a selection of varied and efficient internal lexicons available (Underwood and Underwood, 1986) a rich resource in interrelated knowledge of orthographic analyses and word meanings will be provided for the whole linguistic development of the child.

In the writer's research, it was interesting to note that of the children who neither catch nor learn spelling very early, those who are favourably placed in family order (that is, the oldest or the youngest) do, in fact, tend to progress well, since they are inevitably more accustomed to variable, exploratory and mutually satisfying talk, reading and attending to words than do children in the middle of a family (Peters, 1985a).

Catching the code

This is where the parent as well as the teacher is able to promote the catching of spelling. Children who have caught spelling are familiar with letter sequences in the world around them. They have become sensitised to the coding of English in a benign social context where parents and teachers are reviewing, commenting on and predicting events in the child's day, for example, shared activities which are registered by the child in speech and writing.

Many children seem to catch spelling as they catch other linguistic skills – 'To him that hath shall be given'. These are favoured children who have experienced something more than just their parents' care and concern in the pre-school years. Some parents have done something else as well as talking and reading to their children. While reading stories, while shopping, while watching television, and so on, these parents have not only pointed out words they meet, but have lightly and incidentally indicated the internal structure of the words they come up against. 'That bit's like a bit in your name,' says his parent to Martin as he eats his Smarties or his Mars bar, and he is being helped very neatly in the catching of spelling. The child who said, 'She's in me because she's Anna and I'm Joanna,' had learned to look with interest at the internal structure of words, catching spelling by becoming sensitised to the coding system of our orthography. It is the interested parent who initiates looking with interest at words.

The directing of attention

It is by directing children's attention to looking at words within words, and at interesting letter patterns or letter strings that are within the child's name or like the name of a sweet or detergent or other product that appears in the child's vicinity. We do not 'look with intent' unless we have a reason for doing so. In the case of spelling this is to reproduce a word. This involves an intention on the part of the parent or teacher that the child should look closely at the word before writing it, pointing out the interesting features and expecting the child to be able to reproduce it without copying. The resource is in the parent or teacher who knows the nature of the orthography. For others who do not, and who wish to use published materials, such resources have been described and evaluated (Cripps and Peters, 1986).

Developing a kind of imagery and increasing the span of apprehension

It is the interested and perceptive parent who discusses with the pre-school child the experiences of the day, reviewing these serially: 'First we went to Granny's . . . then we went to the supermarket'. This is the way into extending the child's imaging, another important contribution to the catching of spelling. And while developing the child's imagery, the parent is increasing the serial span of apprehension, both very important sub-skills for the child who is learning the catching of spelling.

Intentional communication

The roots of literacy are in shared activity. The talk, the reading, the directing of attention, the reviewing of and predicting of joint activities, are all the ground from which literacy grows. And from the very earliest stages it is 'intentional communication' with another person that is central to language development (McShane, 1980). Not only is the child directing and regulating parents orally, but very soon directing them in writing by leaving messages, not only to parents but to munificent beings such as teeth angels (Peters, 1985b). It is the accepting, the responding, the encouraging and the seizing of opportunities such as these for spoken and written communication that is so promising for literacy.

The evidence for this is in the quality of such purposeful writing, for notes and letters written as 'intentional communication' are more legible and the spelling nearer the conventional English orthography than in other contexts. This is necessarily so, since for the child, the message is important and must be clear enough to be read; the message must get across. We remember what care we take as adults when writing letters of application for posts, that spelling is correct and handwriting is legible. So in school, also, we respond to, we encourage, and we devise opportunities for purposeful writing and rejoice in it as 'intentional communication', for we, as teachers are a privileged audience. Durell is quoted by Graves (1978) as saying, 'We have known for years the child's first urge is to write and not read and we haven't taken advantage of this fact. We have underestimated the power of the output languages like speaking and writing.'

Facilitating the catching of spelling in the early years frees children to communicate in writing so effectively that their readers attend entirely to the content of what they are reading and are not distracted by bizarre spelling. This facilitation occurs incidentally, in a low key. It is teaching the skill within the process, through the directing of attention by the perceiving parent, a parent who not only knows what the spelling system is like, but rejoices in the intentional communication in speech and writing, that is at the root of literacy.

References

CRIPPS, C. and PETERS, M. L. (1986) *Resources for Spelling* (Reading and Language Information Centre, University of Reading School of Education).
DEAN, J. (1968) *Reading, Writing and Talking* (London: A. & C. Black).
FLESCH, R. (1983) *Why Johnny Still Can't Read* (New York: Harper & Row).
FRITH, U. (1980) 'Unexpected Spelling Problems', in Frith, U. (ed.) *Cognitive Processes in Spelling* (London: Academic Press).

GIBSON, E. J. and LEVIN, H. (1975) *The Psychology of Reading* (Cambridge, Mass.: MIT Press).

GRAVES, D. H. (1978) *Balance the Basics*. Paper on Research about Learning (Ford Foundation).

MCSHANE, J. (1980) *Learning to Talk* (Cambridge: Cambridge University Press).

PETERS, M. L. (1985a) *Spelling: Caught or Taught? A New Look* (London: Routledge & Kegan Paul).

PETERS, M. L. (1985b) 'Purposeful writing', in Raban, B. (ed.) *Practical Ways to Teach Writing* (London: Ward Lock Educational).

SMITH, F. (1985) *Reading*, rev. edn (Cambridge: Cambridge University Press).

UNDERWOOD, B. and UNDERWOOD, J. (1986) 'Cognitive Processes in Reading and Spelling', in Cashdan, A. (ed.) *Literacy, Teaching and Learning Language Skills* (Oxford: Basil Blackwell).

Chapter 17

Adult Attitudes to Children's Handwriting

Peter Smith

Over the past fifteen years much attention has been given to the problems involved in developing children's writing. There are indications that attitudes may be as important as abilities. This brief chapter is offered in the conviction that children's attitudes to writing will only be healthy if those of the adults with whom they interact are similarly helpful. Unless parents understand and support the changes in approach currently being introduced, their possibly contrary and even negative attitudes may mitigate against the efforts of teachers.

Introduction

In Chapter 15 Dr Roger Beard surveyed recent developments and current thinking about many aspects of the writing process, but had relatively little space in his chapter to discuss two key elements that are known to concern parents greatly, these two topics being spelling and handwriting.

The issues involved in spelling are authoritatively dealt with by Margaret Peters in her excellent chapter in this volume entitled 'Teaching the Catching of Spelling'. To ensure that a balanced picture of all aspects of the writing process is presented I am including here some comments on the skills of handwriting. There is, of course, a strong link between spelling and handwriting. As Peters (1985) says:

> Quality of handwriting is highly correlated with spelling attainment, so also is speed of handwriting, for it is a myth that the slow writer is the careful writer and vice versa. The slow writer is often one who is uncertain of

letter formation, who is faced with a decision every time he comes to a fresh letter and, as often as not, makes a random attempt at the letter he is writing. The swift writer is one who is certain of letter formation and, as a bonus, is certain of letter sequences so that he can make a reasonable attempt at a word he may never have written before. (p. 55)

In line with current thinking, Dr Beard distinguishes between the composing, transcribing and reviewing aspects of the writing process. Similarly, Smith (1982) talks of composition and transcription as two different aspects of writing, where the first may be carried out by the author and the second by a secretary, although frequently both aspects are done by the same person. Clearly, both Roger Beard and Frank Smith agree with Graves (1983) that a consideration of the two aspects of the writing process encourages the act of drafting which is so important to the achievement of many purposes.

An attitude to children's writing which thus allows a proper consideration of 'process' rather than concentrating totally on 'end product' requires, perhaps, a reappraisal of traditional attitudes to the skill of handwriting. Many parents and some teachers still seem to expect precise and careful handwriting at all times even though such an emphasis is likely to be detrimental to the quality of the content of the writing. A more sensible attitude to the whole question of standards of handwriting would appear to be one which takes into account different stages in children's development and different purposes for their writing. It is sometimes suggested that there is need to think of (at least) three standards which may be helpfully described as:

1. *A formal best*. This may be careful manuscipt or a cursive style. It is likely to be used when writing out a piece for display or when concentrating on skills during formal handwriting lessons. For some purposes, for example, making notices, capital letters may be used.

2. *A swift but easily legible style*. This is likely to be used when writing to friends or in examinations.

3. *A fast personal writing* for making private notes and for writing quick messages.

This concept of a continuum of standards within a basic style is fully discussed in *Developing Handwriting* (Smith, 1977, ch. 6) and again in the *New Nelson Handwriting Teachers' Manual* (Smith, 1984). Indeed, the *New Nelson Handwriting Pupil's Books* (Smith, 1984) are designed to support teachers in achieving a school policy which aims to teach a basic swift, legible hand to all pupils which has the potential to be developed into a set calligraphic hand as appropriate while still remaining legible, even at high speed.

It is clearly necessary for all schools to develop a sensible, realistic policy for handwriting and to ensure that parents are acquainted with the policy so that they can support the work of the school when opportunities occur in the home, as they inevitably will. Most schools do have such a policy, which usually includes at least one set of published materials. A range of available schemes is discussed in Smith (1977) but additional schemes have become available since.

The principles underlying most available schemes are (a) acceptance that the skill of handwriting remains an essential acquisition for every child even in the age of the word-processor; and (b) that the emphasis should be on the process of writing rather than on the end-product. This second principle is important in two ways. On the one hand, the content of writing is generally considered to be more important than the presentation. On the other hand, when learning the skill of handwriting it is more important that letters are formed correctly than it is for them to look right. In other words, teachers and parents should try to help children commence letters in the right place and make them with correct directional movements. The recent research into children's awareness of literacy before school by Ferreiro and Teberosky (1983) and others reminds us of the enormous challenge facing teachers of young children. Observation of the children in any class of infant-aged children shows a wide range of levels of understanding and skill and thus makes great demands on teachers who have to decide when and how to intervene with guidance and instruction. Undue emphasis on precision in the early stages can be inhibiting and counter-productive, but incorrect movement and unhelpful pencil grips, for example, can become ingrained habits which impede later progress in the development of fluent legibility.

Teachers devise and utilise a wide range of teaching techniques and devices including mnemonics but there is a general acceptance that work on writing patterns is helpful for most children. Lower case letters can profitably be studied in groups relating to the relevant basic pattern. A variety of teaching techniques together with organisational strategies to enable teachers to play their role effectively in catering for the needs of individuals, groups and/or whole classes are described in Smith (1977) and Smith (1984).

References

FERREIRO, E. and TEBEROSKY, A. (1983) *Literacy Before Schooling* (London: Heinemann Educational Books).

GRAVES, D. (1983) *Writing: Teachers and Children at Work* (London: Heinemann Educational Books).

PETERS, M. L. (1985) *Spelling: Caught or Taught? A New Look* (London: Routledge and Kegan Paul).

SMITH, F. (1982) *Writing and the Writer* (London: Heinemann Educational Books).

SMITH, P. (1977) *Developing Handwriting* (London: Macmillan Education).

SMITH, P. (1984) *New Nelson Handwriting Teacher's Manual* (Sunbury-on-Thames: Thomas Nelson).

SMITH, P. (1984) *New Nelson Handwriting Pupil Books A, B, 1, 2, 3 & 4* and *Infant and Junior Spirit Masters*.

Chapter 18

Individualised Spelling: The Spellbank Project

Frank Potter

By making use of purpose-designed software, the Spellbank project aims to: individualise the learning process; assist with classroom organisation; and help children to become more independent.

Each child has his or her own database of words they frequently misspell. This database, or spelling bank, can then be used in different ways. One program uses it to correct children's 'guesstimates'. For example, if a child types in becos, bekoz or other variants the computer responds:

Is it   because?
Clue to meaning   Why? Because . . .

Another program can search through this individual database for the words most commonly misspelled by that particular child. The search can be confined to words with a common letter pattern (for example, all words with the pattern ie, such as field). These words can either simply be printed out, or they can automatically be inserted into a look-cover-write-check spelling program – which includes a focus on the meaning of the word.

The spelling correction program avoids the problem of children queueing up for correct spellings. This problem has been documented at junior and infant level by the Extending Beginning Reading Project *and in* The Quality of Pupil Learning Experiences.

The database search program ensures that children practise spelling words they need to learn – thereby individualising the learning process. Because the children use the programs with a high degree of independence, Spellbank *is the very type of software that could profitably be taken home, and not only for the children to use. No matter how good we are, we all need to check some spellings!*

Independence

We think it only natural that painters should stand back and review their work, to see if it is turning out the way they had intended – and then make any necessary changes, but in the past it has not been natural to think of children doing the same with their writing. Yet it is only by giving children control over their writing that they can learn whether what they have written is turning out the way they intended, and it is this element of control that makes redrafting so tremendously valuable in developing children's writing. It is no coincidence that Richard Binns (1978), who has so strongly advocated systematic redrafting, was originally an artist.

One of the aims of the Spellbank project is to give children more control over learning to spell.

Classroom organisation

Giving children more independence has the added advantage of helping classroom organisation. One problem in the primary classroom is the seemingly endless queue of children waiting for correct spellings. This has been documented at junior and infant level by Southgate *et al.* (1981) and Bennett *et al.* (1984): if children were more independent, then teachers could be more efficient and effective.

Individualisation

Peters (1985) makes a useful distinction between the 'how' and the 'what' of teaching spelling. The 'how' includes whether one should teach phonics, spelling rules, morphemic regularities, the look-cover-write-check routine, and so on. Whatever one's view about the 'how', it is still necessary to decide 'what' words to use.

We certainly do not want formal word lists. Good reasons why not are given by Peters (1985): she mentions one list which contained the words 'bissextile', 'decennial', 'chimerical', and 'chalybeate'! Even though this is an extreme example, many lists have been prepared using sources remote from children's writing needs, including words which they may well not need until they are adult. Peters (1985) quotes Fernald (1943, p. 210) as saying: 'Formal word lists will always fail to supply the particular word a person should learn at a particular time' (p. 69). Peters goes no to point out that nearly half of the authors of spelling materials do not present any rationale for word selection (p. 84).

If we want the 'what' to be useful and productive, we should choose words

1. Which children want to learn;
2. Which they frequently misspell;
3. Placed in groups which *look the same* – that is, words containing a common letter string (for example, *ie*).

It is obviously almost impossible for the busy classroom teacher to individualise the learning in such a manner. It would involve making a note of all the children's misspellings and how frequently each occurred. This would be time-consuming enough, but the words would then have to be placed in groups containing common letter strings – always bearing in mind that a word might appear in more than one group (for example, *neighbour* might appear in the *ei*, *gh* and *ou* groups). This in itself would be a full-time job for the classroom teacher.

Spellbank solves one of the problems by having individualised databases or dictionaries – or what we call *spelling banks*. Each child has his or her own individual disk, on which are stored the words he or she frequently misspells, together with a clue to the meaning and a frequency count reflecting the number of times he or she has misspelt the word.

Using the *database search* program, a search can be made for the most frequently misspelt words containing a particular letter string – for example, the most frequently misspelt words containing the letter string *ie*. The search can also be limited to words beginning or ending with a certain letter string. This enables the search to be confined to words containing *ed* endings or the prefix *mis*, and so on. When the search is complete the words can be printed out and/or a file created. This file can then be used with a rather sophisticated look-cover-write-check program.

However, all this would still not provide sufficient additional help if the teacher had to update all the individual databases and the updating procedure is where *Spellbank* is unique. Not only does it make little or no demands on the teacher, it actually helps with classroom organisation and enables children to become more independent. Two programs, a spelling correction program and an updating program, are used in the following manner.

First the children are taught to adopt a variant of Binns's (1978) convention for when they do not know how to spell a word (or think they do not know). Rather than break off in the middle of writing, the children simply make a phonic attempt and put brackets round it. When they have finished writing they check all their attempts, not by going to the teacher but by using the spelling correction program. For example, a child might write (*bekoz*) and (*beautifull*). Instead of joining a queue for the teacher's attention the child would enter *bekoz* into the computer, which might respond:

Is it   because?
Clue to meaning   Why? Because . . .
(Press Y for Yes or N for No)

The child responds in the affirmative and the computer increases the frequency count of that entry by one.

The program will correct a wide variety of misspellings. For example, *becos, becoz, bekos* and many other attempts will be trapped. The main algorithm in the program ignores vowels completely and will trap most phonic variations, which is why the children are encouraged to make phonic attempts (incidentally, this also makes it easier to decipher the children's misspellings).

Sometimes a misspelling will not be trapped because the word is not in the child's database. Suppose that *beautiful* is one such word. When the child enters *beautifull* the computer reports that the word cannot be found and records it on disk. The child then has to find the correct spelling *beautiful* and devise his or her own clue to the meaning – perhaps *opposite of ugly*. Note that it is only a *clue* to the meaning and not a definition. Occasionally this clue is essential – for example, to distinguish between the words *sun* and *son*. Even when it is not essential it is still desirable, to make sure that the child focuses on meaning.

The child then uses the updating program, entering the spelling *beautiful* and the clue to the meaning *opposite of ugly*. The next time that child uses the spelling correction program *beautifull* will be trapped, along with numerous other misspellings of *beautiful*.

Classroom experiences

The project is still in progress but it seems to be achieving its aims. The spelling correction program does stop children asking the teacher for spellings, but with only one computer in the classroom queues do form in front of the computer!

The children seem to become more independent quite naturally. They have no problem updating the database themselves, and all the teacher need do is to check that the children have not updated the database with any misspellings!

The locus of control

We have already found the spelling correction and updating programs give children a significant degree of independence, but we think that they could profitably be given some control over the use of the other programs. The teacher would provide the child with a list of letter strings to choose from, and the child would then use the *database search* and *look-cover-write-check* programs independently. The teacher would, of course, need to help the child to evaluate his or her progress.

'Spinoffs'

Spellbank has also been found to be helpful in ways not originally envisaged:

1. It encourages children to use a dictionary to find the correct spellings and help devise the clues to the meanings.
2. Much valuable discussion about the meanings of words ensues when children are trying to think of the clues.
3. It encourages children to be precise and concise. The maximum length of the clue is about 25–30 letters and spaces.
4. It helps the learning of metalanguage. For example, in one classroom the children were told not to include proper names in the database. The teacher remarked how quickly they learned what a proper name was, in contrast to her experience with equivalent classes in previous years.
5. In another class the children adopted the tactic of entering hyphens when they were uncertain of the vowels. For example, *believe* might be entered *bel--ve*. They found this helpful and the spelling correction program works just as well (it ignores all the vowels as these make up the majority of mistakes). The teacher concerned liked this practice. She had always been worried that every time a child spelt a word incorrectly this misspelling was reinforced. They have now adopted this as a general practice and use hyphens whenever they are uncertain of a spelling – on or off computer. This is yet another refinement to Binns's convention mentioned earlier.

The author's view of the teaching of spelling

Clearly influenced by the work of Peters (1985) work, the author's view of the 'how' of spelling is presented below. *Spellbank* has obviously been shaped by this view though it should be made clear that it is only part of a total programme of teaching spelling. However, *Spellbank* will be useful to any teacher, no matter what their view on the 'how' of spelling.

The author's view is:

1. That children should learn the morphemic regularities in our spelling system. In *cats*, *dogs* and *horses* the final letter *s* is regular in that it is a plural marker, even though it is pronounced differently. *Disappeared* has only one *s* because

the word is formed by the prefix *dis* being added to the word *appeared*. *Spellbank* helps here by enabling a search to be made of words with the same prefixes, suffixes or inflectional endings.
2. That children should learn words together that look the same (no matter how they sound) – *Spellbank*, or course, enables such lists to be created in the best possible way.
3. That there is little value in children learning spelling 'rules' (such as *i* before *e* except after *c*).
4. That the main value of learning phonics for spelling is to enable children to write something recognisable when they are uncertain of how to spell a word (and for checking that their attempt is a reasonable phonic alternative) – *Spellbank* encourages children to make phonic attempts, because of the way that the spelling correction program works.
5. That children should learn to use the look-cover-write-check strategy, paying attention to the visual, kinaesthetic, semantic and acoustic representations of the words – *Spellbank*'s look-cover-write-check program focuses children's attention on meaning by including the clue to the meaning as well as the word itself. To the author's knowledge it is the only such program to do this. Work is currently being undertaken to include acoustic and kinaesthetic dimensions in the program.

A home–school link

Because the children use the programs with a high degree of independence, *Spellbank* is the very type of software that could profitably be taken home, and not only for the children to use. No matter how good we are at spelling, we all need to check our spellings sometimes!

Acknowledgements

The author would like to thank Jacky Parry and Dorothy Benbow for their help in this project.

References

BENNETT, N., DESFORGES, C., COCKBURN, A. and WILKINSON, B. (1984) *The Quality of Pupil Learning Experiences* (Hillsdale, New Jersey: Lawrence Erlbaum Associates).

BINNS, R. (1978) *From Speech to Writing* (CITE, Moray House College of Education).

FERNALD, G. M. (1943) *Remedial Techniques in Basic School Subjects* (New York: McGraw-Hill).

PETERS, M. L. (1985) *Spelling: Caught or Taught?* (London: Routledge & Kegan Paul).

SOUTHGATE, V., ARNOLD, H. and JOHNSON, S. (1981) *Extending Beginning Reading* (London: Heinemann Educational).

Software

SPELLBANK is published by Questlar, 139 Eastbourne Road, Southport, PR8 4EB.

Chapter 19

Computer Essentials for Home and School

David Wray

This chapter considers the need for teachers and parents to collaborate in the use of the computer for educational purposes, as they have begun to do successfully in other areas of the teaching of reading. It puts forward several criteria by which teachers and parents can evaluate educational computer software, and goes on to argue that there are a limited number of types of computer program that are really essential for children to have experience of. These 'computer essentials' are described and their educational value briefly discussed.

Introduction

The mid-1980s will probably be remembered as the era of the 'computer explosion'. The microcomputer has begun to make its mark on our everyday life in a whole variety of ways, but what is perhaps most remarkable is the degree to which it has penetrated our home lives. Evidence suggests that the United Kingdom has the highest proportion of homes possessing a microcomputer of any country in the world (Obrist, 1983). This would seem to indicate a high degree of computer awareness in British home life, although it must be admitted that the greatest proportion of these home computers are used simply as games-playing machines (Obrist, 1985).

Running alongside this growth in computer ownership, however, there has also been a growing interest in the educational potential of the microcomputer. Many families acquired a computer for the use of their children, hoping thereby to improve their educational chances. By virtue of a very forward-looking government-sponsored scheme, virtually every primary school in the country now has at least one microcomputer, and many have more than one. The presence of this vast market for educational software has ensured an enormous growth in the quantity of software available, mostly specifically aimed at schools, but significant amounts of it aimed at the home market. Much of this software has been designed to assist in the development of reading and language, which are clearly perceived as areas of major importance in the education of primary school children.

Unfortunately, much of the software which has been produced, especially for home use, has often seemed to encourage inappropriate ideas about children's learning of reading and language and its use appears likely to undo some of the advances which have been made in the last decade or so in the ways schools set about developing these vital skills. There is a clear need for teachers to set about educating the parents of their children in the kinds of computer experiences which would be most beneficial and which would best develop the experiences the children will be getting in their school computer use. It has been shown that the approach of parents towards the reading instruction of their children can be influenced by carefully planned schemes for involving them, (Hewison, 1982) and the use of the computer would seem to be an important area for developments of this nature.

Before this can be done, of course, teachers themselves need to decide their priorities in terms of computer use, and this task is unfortunately not made easier by the sheer quantity of educational software available, and the questionable nature of much of it. To sort through this software is a mammoth task. It is hoped that this chapter might help in this task by first suggesting a set of criteria by which useful software might be judged, and secondly by suggesting that, in fact, the amount of software which both schools and parents actually need, to develop reading and language at least, is limited to around five types of program.

Judging good software

By applying insights from the teaching of other areas of the language and reading curriculum it is possible to arrive at five criteria by which good software for developing reading and language can be judged.

Openness

Open-endedness is a well established criterion by which most good educational materials can be judged, and software is no exception. 'Open' software is often recommended in the literature, yet there does seem to be some confusion over the meaning of this term. In fact, the term can be interpreted in either of two ways: 'open' can imply software in which there is no predetermined content and which simply operates as a tool (Anderson, 1984) upon content which is chosen by children or teacher, or it can imply software which is open-ended in the directions in which it might lead. In the first category we might place programs such as word-processors or data-handling programs, in which the choice of content is determined by the children or the teacher. An adventure game would fit into the second category because, even though its content will be predetermined, it can be used as a stimulus for a wide variety of activities, according to children's interests (Wray, 1985).

Stimulates creativity and problem-solving

Any good reading and language material should cause children to think, rather than merely call for a series of rote responses. Educational software has been particularly bad at this, and the majority of programs produced are still at the 'drill and practice' level. What is needed is software which stimulates problem-solving, either posing problems itself, like an adventure or a simulation, or acting as a tool for solving them, like a data-handling program.

Can be used across the curriculum

It is established wisdom now that language development

does not just occur in English lessons, and good software should encourage this across-the-curriculum language work. Open software is much more likely to enable this to happen as is software which operates as a tool rather than as a delimiter of content. A word-processor can, for example, be used to write about any subject, and a good adventure game can stimulate work in areas ranging from science to creative arts (Wray, 1985).

Flexibility

With software, as with any teaching material, the acid test of usefulness is whether the material is flexible enough to be used in whatever way is seen as appropriate by the people using it. Teachers have, hopefully, by now realised that there is no such thing as a set of materials which will do all their teaching for them, and educating parents to realise this would seem a high priority for any home–school linking programme. A danger inherent in drill and practice software is precisely that it encourages its users in the mistaken belief that all that is necessary for learning to take place is to put the learner in front of the screen and allow the program to get on with the teaching. This is especially unfortunate in view of the fact that there is no lack of possibilities for the use of flexible software as Anderson's (1984) list of suggestions for the uses of the 'computer as tool' testifies.

Encourages co-operation

One of the most significant ways in which our knowledge about language development has advanced in recent years has been in the recognition we now give to the place of co-operation and discussion. It would seem highly desirable that educational software be seen by teachers and parents as a suitable context in which this discussion can flourish. It has been demonstrated that there are arrangements the teacher can make to maximise pupil discussion (Potter and Walker, 1985), but no amount of organisational manipulation will make up for the poor stimulus for discussion provided by some commercially available software.

Essential pieces of software

There seem to be at least five types of software which meet the above criteria and would seem essential for every primary classroom to have available, and clearly will be beneficial if children have experience of these types of programs at home as well as at school. Accordingly, the list can also be used as a set of guidelines for schools to pass on to interested parents.

Adventure games/simulations

The power of the adventure game and of the simulation in stimulating discussion and problem-solving in children has been well documented (Bleach, 1985). There are several case-studies now available of classroom work with adventure games involving fantasy (Potter and Wray, 1985) and with simulations based upon realistic situations (Whittington, 1984). These programs put great emphasis upon the ability to read the screen very carefully, and often to make inferences on the basis of that reading (Wray, 1985). It has also been suggested (Hart, 1984) that there is a great deal of potential in encouraging children to devise and program their own adventure games. There are now available several 'write your own adventure' programs, which seem to fit perfectly the criteria of openness and stimulus for thinking which were established earlier. What a useful home–school activity it would be for children to collaborate with their parents in devising at home an adventure game, which could subsequently be used by their classmates at school.

Word-processing

Recent work on children's writing stresses the encouragement of reworking and redrafting (Graves, 1983). The problem with this is, of course, the sheer physical drudgery of writing and rewriting (Wray and Gallimore, 1986). A word-processor takes away the physical problems of writing and can genuinely free children to concentrate on composition and enhancement of quality. Studies have begun to be reported which suggest the success of word-processors in junior schools

(Broderick and Trushell, 1985), and with very young children (High and Fox, 1984). A not insignificant benefit of the word-processor is the ease it provides of producing multiple copies of a piece of writing. This means that copies of children's writing can be sent home with them as a matter of course, and children can carry on editing and redrafting with the help of their parents. Home–school co-operation can thus take place even if there is no computer in the home. Clearly though, if there is a computer with word-processing facility available at home, then children will appreciate all the sooner the usefulness of it as a tool for writing, and more rapidly acquire some of the techniques for exploiting it.

Data-handling

Handling information is already part of most children's experience in schools, even if limited only to the project on themselves in which they collect information and display it as a series of graphs of children's heights, weights, spans, and so on. Again, the computer is ideally suited to tasks of this nature, and can allow children to handle data in quantities and with results that they could not otherwise manage. The adaptation of the 'ourselves' project to the computer has been described by Johnson (1984), and Ross (1984) has demonstrated that the computer can make possible the analysis by children of complex collections of data which would otherwise be beyond them.

Data-handling is the application of the computer which is most familiar in the everyday world, although many people view with some concern the proliferation of computerised data-bases containing all manner of personal details. Much of this concern is justified, although a significant proportion must stem from simple ignorance of the way computers work. Giving children experience in school and at home in data manipulation and analysis, and even more usefully in designing and constructing their own databases, might be a way to alleviate some of this fear in future.

Information presentation

As well as gaining practice in the design, construction and manipulation of collections of information, children should also become familiar with computerised means of presenting information, that is, with the tools of information technology, such as Teletext and Viewdata. Use of these systems will gain in importance as time goes on, and their use is already an essential feature in many walks of life. Many homes which do not have access to a computer will have a television set capable of receiving Teletext, and children will often be very skilful in the operation of such sets. Having a computer available, however, allows use of such systems to go beyond such essential, but fairly passive, activities. 'Teletext emulation' systems, of which there are several now available, allow children to design and present their own 'pages' of information and use them in the compilation of school magazines, project reports, and as a vehicle for information exchange between schools, and between home and school. There are many possibilities for development here, not least being the presentation for parents' evenings of a rolling, on-screen class or school magazine.

Planning logical procedures

It is becoming clear that, as well as being taught by, or learning through, the computer, children should also be given the chance to *teach* the computer to do things in a logical manner. Anderson (1984) characterises this as 'computer as tutee'. There are several possible computer environments, or 'microworlds' (Papert, 1981) in which this is possible, although possibly the most famous of these involve the use of the computer language, LOGO. A great deal has been written describing the possibilities of this language as a vehicle for problem-solving and for developing a healthy attitude towards mistakes. It has been suggested that the use of LOGO with children can 'promote language interaction among children' (Marshall, 1984), and it is this aspect which assures its inclusion in this list of five essential types of software for developing language and reading.

Conclusion

This chapter has attempted to do two things: it has first outlined a set of criteria which, it is hoped, may be found useful by teachers and parents alike in selecting and evaluating educational software from the vast range which is now available, and particularly that which purports to develop language and reading. Secondly, it has put forward the idea that there is, in fact, a limited range of software that is really essential for use with children. It is felt that the five types described here meet the requirements of providing an adequate introduction for children of the range of uses of the computer in the world outside school, and also of facilitating valuable reading and language activities in their own right. A child who gained experience in these five areas at home and at school really would begin to be prepared for the world of new technologies into which he must venture.

References

ANDERSON, J. (1984) 'The computer as tutor, tutee, tool in reading and language', *Reading*, vol. 18(2), pp. 67–78.

BLEACH, P. (1985) 'Using Magic Adventure in the classroom', in Potter, F. and Wray, D. (eds) *Micro-Explorations (1)* (Ormskirk: UKRA).

BRODERICK, C. and TRUSHELL, J. (1985) 'Word processing in the primary classroom', in Ewing, J. (ed.) *Reading and the New Technologies* (London: Heinemann).

EWING, J. (ed.) (1985) *Reading and the New Technologies* (London: Heinemann).

GRAVES, D. (1983) *Writing: Teachers and Children at Work* (London: Heinemann).

HART, R. (1984) 'The tombs of Arkenstone', in Open University *Micros in Action in the Classroom* (Milton Keynes: Open University Press).

HEWISON, J. (1982) 'Parental involvement in the teaching of reading', *Remedial Education*, vol. 14(4).

HIGH, J. and FOX, C. (1984) 'Seven-year-olds discover microwriters', *English in Education*, vol. 18(2).

JOHNSON, J. (1984) 'Using the computer for data-handling', in Open University *Micros in Action in the Classroom* (Milton Keynes: Open University Press).

MARSHALL, P. (1984) 'Logo at Clitterhouse', in Open University *Micros in Action in the Classroom* (Milton Keynes: Open University Press).

OBRIST, A. (1983) *The Microcomputer and the Primary School* (Sevenoaks: Hodder & Stoughton).

OBRIST, A. (1985) 'The microcomputer in home and school', in Ewing, J. (ed.) *Reading and the New Technologies* (London: Heinemann).
PAPERT, S. (1980) *Mindstorms: Children, Computers and Powerful Ideas* (Brighton: Harvester Press).
POTTER, F. and WALKER, S. (1985) 'Organising group work with a micro', in Ewing, J. (ed.) *Reading and the New Technologies* (London: Heinemann).
POTTER, F. and WRAY, D. (eds) (1985) *Micro-Explorations (1)* (Ormskirk: UKRA).
ROSS, A. (1984) 'The strongest conker in the world', in Open University *Micros in Action in the Classroom* (Milton Keynes: Open University Press).
WHITTINGTON, I. (1984) 'Ponies, adventures and archaeological investigations', in Open University *Micros in Action in the Classroom* (Milton Keynes: Open University Press).
WRAY, D. (1985) 'The adventurous way to use the computer', in Ewing, J. (ed.) *Reading and the New Technologies* (London: Heinemann).
WRAY, D. and GALLIMORE, J. (1986) Drafting in the classroom, *Primary Teaching Studies*, vol. 1(3).

Chapter 20

The Personal Computer as a Vehicle of Home–School Liaison

Jonathan Anderson

If we think of new technologies as new ways of doing things, we might list among educational technologies to have impinged on schools the following: language laboratories, instructional television, i.t.a., words in colour. To this list could be added programmed instruction, teaching machines, Cuisenaire, reading laboratories, reading rate controllers. . . . These were all new ways of doing things, new ways of teaching, new ways of learning languages, new ways of teaching maths, of learning to read, and so on.

A question that occurs is whether the current enthusiasm for computers will wane as it has for these other technologies. These technologies each generated an enthusiastic band of followers. But where are they now, these educational innovations of yesteryear? And will computers follow the same path, to be replaced in turn by newer 'gee-whiz' technologies and, like these previous innovations, be relegated to back-room cupboards in schools?

Why do so few educational technologies survive? None of these previous technologies have lasted. In fact, almost the only technologies to have survived are books, chalk boards and ballpoint pens. Until the early part of this decade, and perhaps even to the present in a majority of schools, the technologies of teaching, with the exceptions noted, have changed little from what they have always been. Chalk and talk still characterise the majority of teaching situations.

In the answer to these questions are pointers to the importance of the personal computer as a vehicle for home–school liaison.

Computers at home and at work

One explanation to have been advanced, in answer to this

series of questions, is that the enthusiasm for most of the innovations listed – those which have had little impact – has come from *within* education; in the case of computers, the pressure to innovate has come from outside. Schools have been very much the reluctant partner. The real pressure has come from professional computer associations, from computer companies and vendors, from the government and Departments of Industry and Trade, and, not least, from parent bodies. Education systems, schools and teachers have needed to be pushed into the computer age, often rather unwillingly.

A second hypothesis for the acceptance of new technologies by schools has been put forward by Pogrow (1983). He argues (p. 22) that two criteria must be present if any technology is going to have a major impact on instruction:

1. The technology has become cultural, by which is understood that it is found in a large number of homes.
2. The technology is widely used as a tool in the world of work.

It is rather easy to see how computers differ from, say, Cuisenaire or i.t.a., on these two criteria. Neither of these two technologies could remotely be described as cultural in that they are found in many homes; nor are they encountered as work tools anywhere in industry or commerce. Despite the enthusiastic support of followers, the public at large remained puzzled about the new maths in general and about Cuisenaire in particular, and very few heard enough about i.t.a. even to be puzzled.

How do computers fare on Pogrow's criteria? According to a report in *The Times* a little while ago, about 11 per cent of homes in England had some kind of computer. The figure is probably higher today. In the United States, the number of homes with computers is said to be about 15 per cent. A South Australian study (Aherran, 1986) concluded that for the state as a whole about one in five primary-aged children have access to some kind of computer at home. Young children in Australian kindergartens are quite familiar too with computer paper, which they use for art and other work, and this is yet another cultural aspect of computers.

In the workplace, there is hardly a business or industry that has not been affected by this all-purpose general tool – the computer. This was recognised by *Time* magazine when in 1983 it broke sixty years of tradition by naming a machine, the computer, as major newsmaker of the year. Another writer (Wellington, 1985) states emphatically that 'computers are fundamentally, qualitatively different from other pieces of educational technology. Quite simply: computers pervade society' (p. viii).

The need for school–home liaison

Schools, therefore, appear to be caught in a pincer movement. On the one hand, the technology of computers is cultural, to use Pogrow's phrase, and has invaded the home; and, on the other hand, it is a pervasive tool in the workplace. If Pogrow's thesis has validity, the home plays a key role in whether a technology lasts in schools. In the case of computers, the home contains members who are in the workforce and, as well, the home predominantly shapes the child's cultural environment.

There is a major cause of concern, however. It is clear that society today depends heavily on computer-based technologies and will continue increasingly to do so. As the chairman of one of the world's major airlines recently noted: 'By bits and bytes over the last 40 years, the world has become computerized . . . In only four decades, the incredible computer has become the indispensable computer' (Ferris, 1985, p. 3). There may be questioning in certain quarters about this over-reliance on computer-based technologies but society as we know it could not operate without our chips and bits and bytes.

In contrast to what has happened in society, not all teachers and educational administrators have been persuaded by the promise of computers in the classroom, and already there can be detected something of a backlash. At least three reasons might be advanced for the reluctance on the part of some educators. Perhaps it it because computers are still relatively new – it is worth remembering that the very first microcomputer made its appearance only in 1975, and then just in kit form and, after all, it took thirty-six years for the printing press to reach England from Germany. A second reason for reluctance may be because of teachers' unfamiliarity with the technology (most teachers' education is 'BC', that is, before the widespread use of computers). Or perhaps, as already noted, many teachers remember similar enthusiasm for programmed learning, for teaching machines, for language laboratories and other educational technologies.

Whatever the reason, the possibility of a backlash against computers by schools, is the greatest challenge of the chip, since it runs the risk of putting schools out of step with what is happening in the rest of society. It is for this reason, especially, that there should be liaison and co-operation between home and school regarding computers.

Problems ahead

Apart from the potential backlash against computers by educators, of which there are already signs, there are other problems ahead. One of these is the possibility for tension between schools and home, especially if homes are thought to be encroaching on the schools' educational role. In this new area of computer education, parents represent a vast, largely untapped reservoir of knowledge about computers. Further, there are frequently more computers in students' homes than there are in schools attended by these same students. Schools, however, are still coming to terms with differences between learning about computers and learning with, from and through computers; and many teachers are inadequately prepared for using computers across the curriculum. Thus there is an understandable reluctance on the part of schools to utilise this pool of talent in their communities; and often schools do not even enquire whether students have computers at home.

Many parents encourage a learning environment at home, and the advertisements of computer companies, often directed to parents, boldly claim better opportunities and higher grades for students who have their own computers. Of course, as most people know, computers without software are useless bits of machinery, and the quality of much commercially available software produced for the home market is sadly lacking. But here is the bind for schools. Should they encourage homes to buy similar computer equipment to that used in schools, and should educationally produced software be made available to parents at the same price as it is to schools? In other words, does computer education extend beyond students, to parents? And is there a risk that students might be bored at school if they have access to the same kinds of software at home? Parents are seeking help about hardware and about software, and sometimes see schools as uncooperative, even protective, about the educational uses of computers.

Other parents are urging schools to include computer programming as part of the curriculum. In so far as this wish is based on the belief that students who can program will be better prepared for the work-force, parents may be mistaken, since the indicators are that the number of positions for programmers will be limited. This is not to say that all students ought not to be familiar with computers, but misapprehensions about what is to be included in computer education constitutes another source of tension between schools and parents.

An observation in the United Kingdom, which has been confirmed in other parts of the world, suggests that more affluent school communities are purchasing computers in greater numbers than school communities in poorer areas (Dillon, 1985). One Australian independent school, for example, was reported recently as having ten 512K Macintosh computers, sixty-three Apple IIe's and IIc's, an assortment of other brands and a Vax 750. The school's Director of Computing stated, 'We see the computers as a vital part of our educational services and believe that our students must be prepared for the technological world they're entering'. This tendency for affluent schools (that is, those with affluent parent bodies) to acquire computers more readily, compounded by the fact that students from such schools are also more likely to have computers at home, points to yet another imbalance for the education system to seek to redress.

These are just some of the sources of tension between school and home arising from the dissemination of this all-purpose machine, the microcomputer. But the signs are not all gloomy.

The shape of things to come

Let me recount an experiment that took place during 1985 and is continuing into 1986 at one high school in Adelaide, South Australia. As part of the National Computer Education Program, one class of students in Year 10 was given a set of lap-held computers. The purpose was quite simple: to find out what effect this tool would have on students' work patterns. At the beginning of the trial, the computing co-ordinator overseeing the experiment commented:

> The concept of students gaining some degree of ownership of a personal computer which they are able to take home and to use in all aspects of their work is an innovation which may herald the future of students' learning in many parts of the curriculum. (quoted in Cooke, 1986, p. 34)

It is this aspect of the experiment that is of most interest here, since it involves a study of how computers are being utilised, at school and at home.

The class teacher leading the project takes the class for English and humanities but the students use their computers for all subjects and carry them home in their bags each evening. The computers are NEC PC8201A models, similar to the kind used by reporters at one of Adelaide's daily newspapers, and come with an in-built word processor. Some students have rechargeable battery packs at home and can thus use their computers anywhere: in the playground, on the bus, wherever the need arises; other students exchange batteries with a stockpile of rechargeable batteries at school.

What is the reaction of parents to this experiment? For a start, all wanted their children to be involved. The class teacher recorded what happened when students took their microcomputers home:

> It was interesting to hear the reactions of students when they first took their units home. One of the biggest problems was finding time to do their homework because everyone wanted to play with the computer. What started out as curiosity has been an added bonus in that parents and families have shown an interest in what their children are doing on the units and have often become more directly involved in their child's development as a writer. (Cooke, 1986, p. 36)

When the experiment continued into its second year, the lap-held micros were passed on to a new Class 10. This parting was not easy for, as the teacher noted, the computers 'have become such an important part of their learning experience . . . that they all feel they will really miss them'. Perhaps the last word should rest with one of the more reluctant writers in the group: 'I never knew,' he said, 'that English could be so much fun!'

A technological revolution can be said to occur when a particular technology comes within the reach of virtually everyone. This is happening with computers for, as a Japanese engineer noted as early as 1983, microprocessor chips are rather like perishable foods: they must be sold quickly before the price falls. Hence, the commonly held view that the new information technologies have brought about a revolution in the workplace and in our daily lives, dramatically changing patterns of interaction in the different communities in which we all participate.

As far as schools are concerned, it seems that most of the change is yet to come. Perhaps the Adelaide experiment points the way, for the harbinger of this change is likely to be the truly portable, battery-powered micro, with the capabilities of the new generation of computers. This development, together with associated developments in compact disk technology where single 12 cm disks can hold 600mb or the equivalent of 200 000 pages of typed text, is set to have a major impact on education.

Currently, there does not seem to be any way for schools to acquire computers in sufficient numbers for the needs of students. Nor is it realistic to envisage the government increasing funding above the present inadequate levels. However, with the advent of the truly portable microcomputer, which students can carry between school and home, a solution to the impasse may be envisaged. If student purchases of personal computers were tax-exempt, and with further reductions in price which would be considerable for a mass market, one can imagine parents being prepared to purchase computers, as now generally happens with handheld calculators. The micro will thus become a personal and indispensable tool for school, home and work.

References

AHERRAN, A. (1986) 'Survey: the extent and nature of primary school children's access to computers in homes', *ACE News*, February.
COOKE, J. (1986) 'A glimpse of the future: computers and English', *Pivot*, vol. 13, (1), pp. 34–6.
DILLON, D. (1985) 'The dangers of computers in literacy education: Who's in charge here?', in Chandler, D. and Marcus, S. (eds) *Computers and Literacy* (Milton Keynes: Open University Press).
FERRIS, R. J. (1985) 'The incredible indispensable computer', *United*, vol. 3, May.
POGROW, S. (1983) *Education in the Computer Age: Issues of Policy, Practice and Reform* (Beverly Hills: Sage Publications).
WELLINGTON, J. J. (1985) *Children, Computers and the Curriculum* (London: Harper & Row).

# Part III

Achieving Literacy in a Multilingual Society

Chapter 21

Challenge and Opportunity for Literacy in the English-Medium, Multilingual School

Joyce M. Morris

Following precedent, the International Reading Association allocated one Precongress Institute to the United Kingdom Reading Association as host national affiliate for the Eleventh World Congress on Reading. Following precedent too, as honorary arrangements chair, I accepted responsibility for choosing an appropriate topic for the Institute, for organising it, and for editing its proceedings.

Choice of topic

The broad theme 'Achieving Literacy in a Multilingual Society' was a starting point for discussions with colleagues about what the published topic of the Institute should be. This was because it complemented the 'Parents and Teachers Together' theme of the UKRA strand programme in that parent–teacher co-operation is particularly important for literacy in multilingual societies such as the United Kingdom. Moreover, it provided opportunities to make a distinctly British contribution to the current international debate about the educational implications of linguistic diversity.

The 'multilingual' theme also allowed due recognition to be paid to the fact that, because all the Congress presentations would be in English, many delegates would have to be at least bilingual. Furthermore, it was particularly appropriate, considering the Congress's venue, as over 160 languages are now spoken in the schools of the Inner London Education Authority (ILEA).

Whatever their mother tongue or community languages, all children in the United Kingdom must learn to be literate in English and, in most schools, English is the medium of instruction. Nevertheless, all teachers need to appreciate fully the implications of linguistic diversity, and to regard it with respect as a 'challenge' and 'opportunity' for literacy rather than as a 'problem'. Accordingly, it was decided that the published topic of the UKRA Precongress Institute should be worded, 'Challenge and Opportunity for Literacy in the English-Medium, Multilingual School'.

It was also suggested that, if sponsorship could be found, the Institute should be supported by a similarly-entitled display of work by teachers and pupils in multilingual classrooms around Britain. Fortunately, this suggestion could be followed up owing to grants awarded by the Commission for Racial Equality and the Hilden Charitable Trust, and the first national exhibition of unpublished, multilingual materials was mounted at the University of London Institute of Education. Moreover, the grants were generous enough to cover the cost of an annotated catalogue, and to allow the exhibition to be open throughout the four days of the Congress.

As will be seen, John Broadbent has contributed the last chapter in this collection on the 'ideas' behind the national display which he helped to organise. He gives reasons for a view, apparently shared by the other contributors, that these ideas fly in the face of social reality. Educational provision for linguistic diversity has serious weaknesses, and tends to be 'tokenistic'. Consequently, he concludes, the skills of potentially bilingual children are not fully developed, with a loss to them and to the British nation as a whole.

In the first chapter, arguments for the different responses to bilingualism are given by John Singh, who also acted as co-chair for the Institute. As Her Majesty's Inspector with special responsibility for the education of ethnic minorities, he is particularly concerned about the implications of these responses for the staffing, organisation and methodology of schools which serve developing bilingual pupils.

This 'general' exposition of the situation is followed by David Houlton's contribution which focuses on the need for a coherent policy to cater for linguistic diversity in *primary* schools. While recognising mother-tongue literacy needs, and the role of parents and the community in meeting them, he emphasises the central importance of the teachers' attitudes and expertise. He also illustrates what he means with reference to scenes recently witnessed in a multi-ethnic primary school.

The next chapter, by Mohammed Nazeer-Ud-Din draws mainly on his personal experience as a multilingual speaker and teacher of Urdu in *secondary* schools. He sympathetically explains why ethnic minority pupils often opt out of language studies, and pleads for far greater attention to be given to helping them make 'creative' use of their mother tongue and cultural heritage.

The following chapters are concerned with teacher-training for a multilingual society. Silvaine Wiles outlines the models of in-service education which are used at the ILEA Centre for Urban Educational Studies, where she is director of the Language Division. According to her, if schools are to offer genuine equality of opportunity, they must provide for children to develop their community languages as well as English. Using a table format she summarises the disadvantages of the changing nature of this provision over time, and highlights the issues that still need to be resolved. She also identifies urgent teacher-training tasks in relation to the multilingual school, and brings life to some of her main points with a simple classroom example.

In his chapter, the bilingual Arturo Tosi stresses the need to give bilingualism a positive value, and describes the national scheme for training teachers of community languages pioneered by the Royal Society of Arts. Most importantly, he draws attention to a principle which is not often adequately recognised, namely, that the techniques used in teaching reading and writing must be 'language-specific'. In other words, they cannot be transferred from one language to another.

Beryl Thomas is bilingual too, and she explains the complexities of the current linguistic situation in Wales against its historical background. In doing so, she provides some very interesting information including the fact that, in her country, most of the pupils in bilingual schools come from non-Welsh-speaking homes. Significantly, some schools are introducing 'language awareness' lessons during the first two years of secondary education in an attempt to foster greater understanding of other languages and cultures.

Additional considerations

In the United Kingdom, teacher-training for literacy in a multilingual society should obviously include consideration of the varieties of English spoken by the population. Contributions on this aspect were prepared for the Precongress Institute but, because of space limitations, they have had to be omitted from this collection. For the same reason, it was not possible to include the papers given at the UKRA Symposium on 'Language, Literacy and the Bilingual Child'.

It is hoped that at least some of these omitted contributions will eventually be published, not only for their intrinsic value but also because they would help to draw further attention to the importance attached to this topic at the Eleventh World Congress on Reading. For only when widespread recognition is given to the importance of catering for linguistic diversity is there any real prospect that educational provision will be such as to give children in our multilingual society the best possible opportunities to achieve their full potential for literacy.

Chapter 22

Responding to Language Diversity

John Singh

Bilingualism among individuals and groups is a common phenomenon in many countries. However, as discussed in this brief chapter, national responses to it vary according to the circumstances which brought it about and the social, cultural and political imperatives that have applied at various times in the past, or apply now.

Reasons for bilingualism in national populations

The most common reason for bilingualism in national populations is the integration of differing cultural groups located in specific regions or areas into one nation state. In some cases bilingualism has developed as the result of a perceived need for a national lingua franca in an attempt to ease social and political cohesion and more pragmatically to ease the business of state. It is quite common in such circumstances to recognise and accept that the languages associated with the cultures of certain regions or areas will be the normal means of expression within those contexts and are officially recognised as such. There are many examples of this which include the USSR, India, China, Yugoslavia and, nearer home, in parts of Wales. Another, related, approach has been to recognise more than one official national language and reflect that fact in the social and political administration of the country. This applies, for example, to countries such as Belgium and Canada.

But there are other factors which have contributed to bilingualism among national populations. Not least of these has been colonialism which has left a legacy of a range of languages in different parts of the world not indigenous to those areas. Sometimes such languages have become the lingua franca of the state, as in some African and Caribbean countries, or they may have become one of a range of languages commonly spoken, as is the case in countries of the Indian sub-continent, where English is still widely used. However, perhaps the immediate concern is to consider how, through education, to respond to the bilingual or developing bilingual skills of pupils and students whose families raise their children in a mother tongue which is not the national language of the country where they have settled.

Consequences of United Kingdom immigration

In the United Kingdom and many other countries within and outside Europe this issue has become emphasised as a result of immigration. It is an issue that raises strong passions. Some individuals or groups feel that if the factors in their cultural backgrounds are not recognised or respected by the society of which they are full members it will diminish their self respect and development. On the other hand, some sectors of majority communities see any responses to aspects of minority cultures as potentially divisive, ultimately leading to a fragmentation of the society along ethnic grounds. Education has to detach itself from the passions, while recognising the strength of the feelings expressed, and address itself to the educational advantages to the individual and society of responding to pupils' first languages, within a framework of what is practical in schools and colleges.

In the United Kingdom, immigration has resulted in a large number of languages in addition to English being spoken by families settled in different parts of the country. The range of languages in any location depends on settlement patterns, so it is possible to find LEAs such as that of Inner London (ILEA, 1986) where over 160 languages are spoken by a cross-section of over 20 per cent of the pupil population. In other LEAs the numbers of languages may be substantial but much smaller. In individual schools there may also be a large number of languages, but the normal pattern is that in such schools one or two languages will be substantially represented, with others being spoken by small numbers or individual pupils.

Arguments for different reponses to bilingualism

It is inevitably a concern of the education service that the first priority in responding to children for whom English is not their first language is to teach them English, based on the fact that being thoroughly fluent and literate in the national language will enable educational success and social mobility. This argument often presumes that a response to a first language will slow down the development of competence in English. Moreover, although both action and descriptive research has shown this not to be so, there is still a residual doubt which to some extent may have inhibited developments in schools. Another concern is that the responsibility for maintaining the language and culture of ethnic minority groups should rest principally with the communities themselves and, indeed, that it would be most effectively carried out within a context where the language and culture are a normal part of the interaction among individuals within the communities concerned.

Given these arguments, one returns to what will be educationally valuable to the individual and society and what is practical in schools given our present state of knowledge. Here it is a fact that, although born locally, many young children enter nursery and infant reception classes speaking a mother tongue with little or no English. It is, therefore, logical to assume, and the Bradford 'Mother Tongue and English Teaching' Project has confirmed it (Bradford College, 1980), that if the school is able to respond to the pupils' first language and enable its use in early learning, there will be educational benefits for the child. These include a greater involvement of parents in the educational process, a more rapid rate of cognitive and conceptual development, and no detrimental effect on the speed and effectiveness in the learning of English. It has also been demonstrated in the primary language survey conducted by the Assessment of Performance Unit (HMSO, 1981), that pupils who are literate in their first language are more successful than those who are not in learning to read English effectively. This suggests implications for the staffing, organisation and methodology of those schools that serve developing bilingual pupils.

In secondary schools there are many pupils who are already bilingual. Some of them may be orally competent in their first language, while others may be both orally competent and literate. It extends their learning opportunities if they can study those languages to as high a level as they are able. It also extends the range of languages available to society at large in its international relations, including cultural and commercial contacts. Additionally, it increases the opportunity of employment in those areas where a variety of ethnic community groups have settled. At the secondary level it is logical to include the languages of ethnic minority communities within the normal framework of modern languages provision and make them accessible to all pupils, whether or not they are mother-tongue speakers. As in primary schools there are implications for the staffing, organisation and methodology of those schools if a demand for such provision is to be properly accommodated in the teaching and learning offered.

There are, of course, other aspects of a response to pupils' developing bilingualism about which there is uncertainty as to how the formal education system should respond. One of these is the extent to which schools and local authorities should respond to demands for the maintenance of languages beyond the two types of responses indicated above. It is a fact that response to children's first languages in primary or secondary schools will to some degree contribute to their maintenance, but beyond that there are complications. One such complication is that referred to earlier regarding the efficacy of the school taking on a responsibility which could be better carried out within cultural community groups. Another is the extent to which the normal provision of a school would be distorted for the individual child if pupils were detached from other elements of the curriculum to be taught their first language. The answer, given the present state of knowledge and practice, would seem to lie in schools,

LEAs and community groups co-operating with one another in making community language provision within a community context, and ensuring that the methods and resources used do offer a learning experience compatible with good educational practice.

A further important issue is that of reflecting the cultural backgrounds of pupils in schools in order that pupils will feel that their backgrounds and experiences are part of the school's concern and that, in all schools, all pupils are being educated to appreciate the ethnic diversity of society. This has implications for the resources available in schools, and the themes and topics chosen for study. It will include, among other aspects of ethnic and cultural diversity, knowledge about the languages of the different groups that now constitute society.

A basis for future developments

The following quotations drawn from *We are All Immigrants to this Place* (Toronto Board of Education, 1976), may offer a reasonable basis for informing the developments necessary in multicultural societies responding to ethnic and cultural diversity, which naturally includes language:

> Multiculturalism may be viewed as the development of a consciousness of one's ancestral roots or ethnicity for creative purposes...
>
> The emphasis on creativity at the core of multiculturalism is an emphasis on cultural development as well as cultural preservation. In the past, the emphasis has been mainly on the preservation and the result has been much alienation of the young, who cannot readily identify with norms, institutions and customs imported from other parts of the world.
>
> Language is important... The better one understands the ancestral language, the deeper will be the understanding of the group's culture and the stronger will be the creative base for the talent that exists.

Multicultural education is an education in which the individual child of whatever origin finds not mere acceptance or tolerance but respect and understanding. It is an education in which cultural diversity is seen and used as a valuable resource to enrich the lives of all. It is an education in which differences and similarities are used for positive ends. It is an education in which every child has the chance to benefit from the cultural heritage of others as well as his or her own.

References

BRADFORD COLLEGE (1980) *Mother Tongue and English Teaching* (The MOTET research project sponsored by the Department of Education and Science).
HMSO (1981) *Language Performance in Schools* (APU Primary Survey Report No. 1).
ILEA (1986) *Inner London Education Authority Language Census.*
TORONTO BOARD OF EDUCATION (1976) *We are All Immigrants to this Place.*

Chapter 23

Focus on the Multilingual Primary School

David Houlton

Although, in the context of British society, multilingualism is not a new phenomenon, it is only recently that primary teachers have begun to acknowledge its implications for the curriculum. Significant developments are underway as a result, but these may stand to be criticised as being merely tokens unless they are incorporated into a more coherent policy for supporting linguistic diversity. This chapter identifies three major areas of focus for fuller consideration as part of such a policy, namely 'the teacher's role', 'mother tongue literacy needs' and 'parents and the community'.

The current situation

The following scenes, witnessed on a recent visit to a multi-ethnic primary school, serve as a backdrop to our discussion. Four- and 5-year-old bilingual children were conversing comfortably in their mother tongues as they went about their activities in the home area, in sand and water play and with constructional toys. Older infants could be seen in a listening corner making use of story tapes in their own languages. Others were taking part in 'live' mother-tongue story sessions. Commercially-produced reading materials in a range of languages were freely available. Class-made storybooks were in evidence and drew strongly on the cultural and linguistic experiences that the children and their families had to offer. Signs and labels declared the fact that linguistic diversity was the norm in the school. And in numerous other ways, some incidental and some planned, children were being encouraged to share their linguistic resources with their teachers and their peers. The headteacher, when asked about the thinking behind the school's approach, spoke of her belief in child-centredness and the importance of giving status to what the children had to offer. A nursery teacher described how she had seen young children's learning and general development benefit through being able to enter a school environment which bore cultural and linguistic resemblance to that of the home. A teacher of 10-year-olds explained how recognition of children's languages and dialects fitted into her overall strategy for combating racism. In short, the school was beginning to acknowledge its multilingualism.

Multilingualism – a new concept?

It should be understood, however, that the concept of a 'multilingual' primary school is a relatively recent one. This is not to imply that multilingualism itself is a new development. Quite the contrary: linguistic variation has long been a feature of many children's daily lives in Britain, whether it takes the form of an indigenous language – Welsh, Gaelic, Manx or Cornish (Price, 1984), a regional variety of English such as 'Scouse' or 'Geordie' (Trudgill, 1982), a language such as Greek, Yiddish, German or Cantonese which arrived in the last century (Edwards, 1983), or one of the South Asian languages of post-war immigration (Linguistic Minorities Project, 1985). What is new, rather, is that primary teachers have begun to recognise their pupils' bilingualism and bidialectalism: in other words, the multilingualism of their classrooms as having a positive role to play in the educational process.

Traditionally, children have been expected to leave the languages of their homes 'at the school gates' (Rosen and Burgess, 1980), for schools have worked from an assumption that possession of a mother tongue other than English will be an impediment to learning and, if encouraged, a source of tension in the classroom (Edwards, 1983). Class and regional dialects of English have received similar treatment, being regarded as debased and deficient forms of the standard language to be eradicated at the earliest possible opportunity (Hollingworth, 1977). To suggest that these assumptions and the attitudes underpinning them have completely disappeared would be a distortion, but in some multi-ethnic primary schools more linguistically-enlightened policies are emerging. The school described earlier offers an illustration of the curricular developments that are coming about as a result.

Encouraging as these trends are, it is my contention that in their present form they are essentially a series of piecemeal beginnings which, in order to have any lasting impact, need to be incorporated into a more coherent policy for langauge development. Indeed, failure to do this may merely serve to reinforce existing criticisms of multicultural practice in the primary school as being superficial and tokenistic (Richardson, 1982; Rushdie, 1982). What, then, is to be done? I would identify three major areas of focus.

The teacher's role

First, and pivotal to the quality of learning in the multilingual classroom, is the teacher. Much has been written elsewhere about the effect of teachers' expectations on children's attainment (Green, 1985) and it is unnecessary to reiterate this. But interwoven with it is the question of teaching style and, particularly, the enabling or inhibiting influence this can exert within the multilingual classroom. It is in the nature of such classrooms that children frequently possess skills and knowledge which far surpass those of the teacher (Houlton, 1986). In these circumstances the teacher can no longer see herself in the traditional sense as the embodiment of all knowledge. She needs, instead, to assume a more interactive role, functioning at times as a partner in children's learning (Rowland, 1984), and on other occasions as a facilitator, encouraging children to learn from each other, whilst always being willing herself to learn from them (Hester, 1982). In the literary domain the implications of this changed role for the teacher are quite far-reaching. In terms of monitoring, for example, if a child is engaged with reading material in a language unfamiliar to the teacher, that teacher is immediately faced with the need to review her practice and assumptions. No longer can she expect to maintain direct control over all that occurs in the classroom. And where systematic monitoring is called for it may be necessary to approach it on a more collaborative basis, involving the children themselves, as well as colleagues and others with bilingual skills. A similar review is necessary when we take account of the bidialectical child's facility for appropriating and reformulating text when reading aloud in English (Goodman and Buck, 1973). We know that in such cases deviations from text are frequently dialect-based and indicative of the child actively engaging with the passage. Treating these 'miscues' as errors for correction is not just inappropriate but may devalue the home dialect and render the child a self-conscious and reluctant reader (Berdan, 1981).

Mother tongue literacy needs

Secondly, if we accept the premise, underlying much of current primary school practice, that there should be parity of status between English and the other languages of the classroom, the question of literacy development in the mother tongue, or the appropriate community language, becomes paramount. At present, following the nursery/infant phase where, for some children, the foundations of mother tongue literacy are being laid, there is a substantial gap in provision until the secondary years where opportunities for formal study of the language might be offered. Disruption on this scale, amounting to four or five years, is likely to be quite deleterious to a child's literacy development. But it becomes additionally disturbing when we recognise that these middle years of schooling happen to coincide with a crucial stage in the growth of children's ethnic identities and cultural perceptions (Milner, 1983), the net effect of which might be to reduce greatly their desire to maintain their language, and widen any gulf which might already be emerging between them and the cultural worlds of their families and communities (Taylor, 1981; Wilson, 1978).

Parents and the community

Thirdly, it is well established that parents have a vital role to play in their children's literacy development, and the benefits resulting from this are well documented (Hamilton and Griffiths, 1984). On the multilingual situation there is an added dimension, for many parents also have literacy skills in languages other than English. Already some primary schools involve their bilingual parents as classroom assistants, storytellers and translators (Houlton, 1985), but relatively unexplored is the role that parents have to play within a co-ordinated mother tongue literacy programme. Equally unexplored is the contribution that the wider communities can make through their supplementary schools. A fuller picture of the scale of this self-help undertaking is gradually becoming available (Linguistic Minorities Project, 1985), and a number of writers have argued the case for the mainstream sector forging links with the language-teaching expertise that resides within it (Houlton and Willey, 1983; Tansley, 1986). Unfortunately, we have yet to see any major moves towards effecting such links with a view to developing a co-ordinated response to children's literacy needs. No doubt a substantial amount of trust-building would need to precede any moves in this direction, but it is my contention that co-ordination between these two sectors of children's education would go a long way towards filling the gap in existing mother-tongue teaching provision, and ensuring that multilingual schools have more than the tacit support of their communities.

References

BERDAN, R. (1981) 'Black English and Dialect – Fair Instruction', in Mercer, N. (ed.), *Language in School and Community* (London: Edward Arnold).
EDWARDS, V. (1983) *Language in Multicultural Classrooms* (London: Batsford).
GOODMAN, K. and BUCK, C. (1973) 'Dialect Barriers to Reading Comprehension Revisited', *The Reading Teacher*, vol. 27.
GREEN, P. (1985) 'Multi-Ethnic Teaching and Pupils' Self-Concept', in Swann, M., *Education for All* (London: HMSO).
HAMILTON, D. and GRIFFITHS, A. (1984) *Parent, Teacher, Child* (London: Methuen).

HESTER, H. (1982) *Language in the Multicultural Primary Classroom Project: Broadsheet 2* (London: Schools Council Publications).
HOLLINGWORTH, B. (1977) 'Dialect in School – an Historical Note', *Durham and Newcastle Research Review*, vol. 8 (39), pp. 15–20.
HOULTON, D. (1985) *All Our Languages* (London: Edward Arnold).
HOULTON, D. (1986) *Cultural Diversity in the Primary School* (London: Batsford).
HOULTON, D. and WILLEY, R. (1983) *Supporting Children's Bilingualism* (York: Longman Resources Unit for the Schools Council).
LINGUISTIC MINORITIES PROJECT (1985) *The Other Languages of England* (London: Routledge & Kegan Paul).
MILNER, D. (1983) *Children and Race – ten years on* (London: Ward Lock Educational).
PRICE, G. (1984) *The Languages of Britain* (London: Edward Arnold).
RICHARDSON, R. (1982) *Culture, Race and Peace: Tasks and Tensions in the Classroom* (Occasional Paper no. 2, Centre for Peace Studies, St Martin's College, Lancaster).
ROSEN, H. and BURGESS, A. (1980) *Languages and Dialects of London School Children* (London: Ward Lock Educational).
ROWLAND, S. (1984) 'What is Really Meant by the Teacher as Co-Learner?', *Dialogue in Education*, vol. 1, no. 1.
RUSHDIE, S. (1982) 'The New Empire Within Britain', *The Listener*, November 9.
TANSLEY, P. (1986) *Community Languages in Primary Education* (Windsor: NFER–Nelson).
TAYLOR, M. (1981) *Caught Between* (Windsor: NFER).
TRUDGILL, P. (1982) *On Dialect: Social and Geographical Perspectives* (Oxford: Basil Blackwell).
WILSON, A. (1978) *Finding A Voice* (London: Virago).

This can prove fatal with regard to the teaching of Urdu, which at present carries little social esteem. Often pupils show resistance towards learning the language of their ancestors. They wish to distance themselves from their culture in the hope that, by doing so, they will become more acceptable to the community which surrounds them. They may, perhaps, feel that a person only speaks Urdu because he or she is unable to master English.

Normally, a language only becomes relevant in its cultural context. The opportunities available to the minority groups for participating in any activities at a cultural level, are severely limited. There are few occasions (other than speaking in the language at home) where they can experience the living Urdu. This unfamiliarity coupled with an acute sense of inferiority stemming from being associated with a low-status culture, makes them react negatively towards the community languages and cultures. Instances where youngsters cannot speak to their parents in the language spoken by them are not too uncommon.

Moreover, much of the uniqueness of a language is lost upon a person who is not literate in more than one language. Among those pupils for whom English has become the first language, there is a compulsive desire to compare Urdu with English. Rightly or wrongly, the dominant language at school comes to be regarded as a 'standard' or 'norm' against which any other language to be learnt is judged. The phonic and syntactic differences found are viewed as peculiarities and the demanding task of acquiring the new linguistic skills is made even more difficult.

The present accepted practice of starting to teach Urdu in the fourth year (at the age of 14) adds to the social and psychological discomforts experienced by the pupils. As they are not exposed to the written language earlier, their vocabulary is fairly limited. This lack of competence, at their age, makes them feel inadequate. Learning such 'elementary' things as alphabets, simple words and sentences, is seen as an insult to their intelligence and abilities. In this emotionally-charged situation, the mastering of the new sound patterns and different intonations becomes an unsettling challenge to the students' adopted identity.

The urge to translate into English whatever is read can prove a hindrance to understanding the meaning so that, if the words and concepts are not translatable, their value becomes redundant. Modes of expression have their roots in the culture from where they have been derived. Therefore, to appreciate the nuances and the fullest meanings, one needs to acquaint oneself intimately with the sensibilities of the cultural groups concerned: their conventions and their particular way of relating the experiences in words have to be studied.

Making creative use of a language

Once the uniqueness of a language is acknowledged and the basic skills are acquired, pupils will feel the need to extend their mastery of the language by using it for the purpose of self-expression. Admittedly, Urdu for oral and written communication serves an important purpose in informal and formal situations, but there is a need to encourage pupils to make creative use of the language. For it is then that the value of the language is heightened. It ceases to be something externally imposed and becomes an integral part of one's being.

To be able to use a language creatively in different contexts, the pupils need to familiarise themselves with models of good writing. The literature of the past and present can offer a link with the culture and also be a source of immense enjoyment and inspiration. The desirability of such contact cannot be over-emphasised: by developing this tradition, the survival of Urdu will be ensured beyond the school years of a person's life. Furthermore, imaginative involvement with one's own language can have a profoundly liberating effect.

To achieve some of the objectives set out above, we need to create an atmosphere in our secondary schools where all pupils are able to use their language and participate in their respective cultures unselfconsciously. Those who can speak more than one language are not some kind of 'less than civilised' beings; they are pupils who happen to have an

Chapter 24

Focus on the Multilingual Secondary School

Mohammed Nazeer-Ud-Din

The fact that we live in a multicultural, multilingual society is slowly being recognised in Britain. In some inner-city secondary schools, languages which have long been used here are at last beginning to be taught. This is a significant development which needs to be followed-up by creating circumstances for pupils to use their languages unselfconsciously. With special reference to the teaching of Urdu, this short chapter draws attention to what is fundamentally involved in making the most of cultural and linguistic diversity, particularly at the secondary stage of schooling.

Cultural and linguistic diversity

Cultural diversity is by no means exclusive to the United Kingdom. Sometimes it is not fully appreciated that the collective experiences of populations living in a large number of countries throughout Europe, Asia, America, Canada and Australia is not so very unlike our own, in that a wide range of cultures is represented within them. For such societies to earn the description of 'pluralist' would require a full acknowledgement of the existence of differences between the groups of people and a positive endeavour to use such differences as a source of inspiration. When this kind of understanding is reached, various cultures can flourish side by side and provide individuals and communities with a rich and more varied way of life. In such a society nobody would feel ashamed of themselves; they could all live out their lives, without feeling they owed any apology to others for their existence.

The recognition of linguistic diversity can play an essential role in achieving some of these objectives. Language is the expression of culture in words; it starts in infancy and lasts throughout a person's life. It provides individuality whilst linking a person to the rest of the world and the most valued treasures of inherited culture are contained in it. Apart from being a means of communication, language also assists human beings with concept-forming processes and thought patterns and, above all, language gives the speaker an identity and a sense of belonging to a particular community.

Attitudes towards the teaching of languages

The demand for the teaching of mother-tongue and community languages does not in any way constitute a rejection of the dominant language or culture: it is an attempt to rescue the ethnic languages and cultures from being completely obliterated in this country. 'Reviving' them is essential, if only to give back to their users some of their lost self-respect and sense of personal identity. There is no longer any need to justify, for example, the teaching of Urdu to our young people. The first steps have been taken, and we can make the most of this opportunity if we are prepared to recognise the nature of the challenges it presents.

A general point must first be made about the attitude of schools towards the teaching of languages. With our emphasis on 'the market-value of the subject', we tend to force languages towards the periphery of the curriculum framework. They became second-rate subjects. The function of a language is seen as being 'instrumental', with very little intrinsic value or worth. The attitude is that 'O' Level GCEs are needed in this or that language, merely to apply for certain jobs. The importance of language as a source of enjoyment and self-fulfilment is, to say the least, underestimated.

The challenge of teaching Urdu

There is a tendency for able, interested pupils to opt out of language studies in order to improve their job prospects.

agenda but in the most tokenistic of ways, tacked on rather than central to the issue of education in a multicultural society. And the teaching force wasn't about to become more representative either: the group contained only one teacher with bilingual qualifications and that for an area that desperately needs more bilingual teachers.

Clearly, in-service education for practising teachers will remain an urgent task for the foreseeable future. This is confirmed by the number of teachers coming forward for courses at the Centre for Urban Educational Studies (CUES), an Inner London Education Authority (ILEA) specialist teachers' centre concerned broadly with the issue of equal opportunities but more specifically, through its Language and Community division, with exploring language issues in multilingual schools and relationships between the home, the school and the community.

Models of INSET

In-service education for teachers is ultimately about improving the quality of children's learning by providing opportunities for teachers to enhance their professional skills. How best to do this is an issue of constant debate. It has been traditional to provide courses of varying length in a range of institutions (universities, colleges, teachers' centres). More recently school-focused INSET has been seen as a model likely to be more dynamic and productive. Instead of courses drawn up and led by individuals outside schools, staff of a particular school identify their needs and priorities and set about addressing them in the school context itself (Hargreaves, 1984; Thomas, 1985). Another model of in-service education is the drafting of additional staff to schools to work alongside teachers in some form of advisory/support/team-teaching capacity for varying periods of time: the nature of the 'contract' and the expected outcomes are often negotiated in advance. Curriculum development work in the form of action-research projects built round the active participation of class teachers is also an exciting model of in-service education. We use all these models at CUES: centre-based courses, school-based courses, school-focused curriculum development work and advisory teachers working alongside class teachers in schools: all have their advantages and disadvantages.

From separate provision to mainstream support

Today, one of the major tasks of the Language Division of CUES is to explore with teachers ways of approaching and organising their work that enable all children, even bilingual learners at an early stage in their development of English, to take a full and active part in the mainstream class. This will inevitably involve enabling children to use their first languages as well as English. Such linguistic resources must be nurtured, not allowed to wither. In the 1960s and 1970s the focus was different: then the concern was to train specialist teachers of English as a second language (ESL). These teachers would work in language centres or as peripatetic teachers, and bilingual children would be withdrawn for varying periods of time from their mainstream classes to be given special help with English. It took us a long time to recognise that this was ineffective and unacceptable. Today we are intent on getting the support back into the mainstream and our courses are focused not at specialists but at class and subject teachers.

Table 25.1 attempts to sketch out (albeit crudely) the way thinking in the field has evolved over time along with the changing nature of provision, the obvious and generally agreed disadvantages and the current unresolved issues.

In London, all types of provision can be found (with the exception of reception centres) and this is doubtless the pattern in other parts of the country. There is general agreement about the direction in which we should be moving, but a good deal of disagreement about how to get there. Looking at the disadvantages listed in Table 25.1 related to different forms of withdrawal, it is hardly surprising that ESL support as it is currently delivered has recently come to be viewed as racist. In retrospect, well-intentioned structures which were set up to help bilingual children can be seen as subtle forms of institutional racism. Separate, central funding has encouraged separate, tack-on provision and it has extra cultural heritage to draw upon. All languages are important and equally relevant to the needs of the people who use them. Respect for others or their symbols of self-identity is not a concession to be granted or withdrawn at will. The dominant influence of one language or form of language over others deprives a society of some of the valuable contributions the minority groups can make towards the growth and enrichment of that society.

Chapter 25

Bilingual Children and In-Service Education

Silvaine Wiles

There is a continuing need to expand in-service education in the field of equal opportunities. In particular, this paper argues that the mainstream class is the only legitimate learning environment for bilingual children whatever their level of English. Only when it is fully understood that learning through the curriculum is not only as important as the children's development of English, but influential in it, will schools begin to offer genuine equality of opportunity. And real equality will also entail provision for children to develop their community language as well as English. Teachers need in-service support, time and resources if they are to implement these changes effectively.

INSET: a continuing need

'How many of you attended courses where equal opportunities issues were included on the programme?' A sea of hands. Before surprise had given way to expressions of delight, a teacher in the front row muttered, 'One session only'. Further questioning revealed that this was indeed the customary format. Of a group of over one hundred London 'first appointments' only a handful had had the equivalent of half a dozen sessions on issues such as racism, sexism, bilingualism, biculturalism and language variation – and for some of these it had been optional. This was a group of teachers about to embark on a career in an area of London that has over 40 per cent bilingual children in primary schools; indeed many of the schools have almost 100 per cent bilingual pupils. So nothing had changed – equal opportunities might be on the

A simple classroom example might help to bring to life some of the points made above. A nursery class teacher chooses the theme of 'construction' to work on over a period of several weeks. As part of a continuing programme of anti-sexist work she decides that she will actively encourage the participation of the girls in the class, many of whom are bilingual. The children engage in a range of construction activities culminating in the construction of a house (big enough to walk into) which they help the teacher to design, build, decorate (wallpaper inside, paint outside), and which they will go on to furnish with junk furniture built by themselves.

Observed at the decorating stage, a group of girls (English and Gujarati-speaking) successfully manage to paper the interior of the house entirely on their own using real wallpaper and paste, a trestle table and all the appropriate tools. They work collaboratively. A good deal of discussion is essential to complete the task . . . 'Is that enough paste?', 'Where shall we hang this?', 'Can you help me carry it?' They use English and Gujarati as appropriate and learn to handle brushes, rollers, scissors for trimming the edges, and so on. Pictures of the tools are posted around the working area and labelled in Gujarati and English.

On several occasions, boys try to take over the activity and the house (they want it for a police station) but are firmly held at bay by the girls, supported when necessary by the teacher. When the girls eventually tire, a good hour later, a couple of boys who had waited patiently are allowed to have a go. During the session the teacher is needed only to encourage, to give advice and to respond to questions. But, of course, the teacher's skill had gone into creating an exciting learning environment which exemplifies many of the criteria listed above.

The task ahead

It is therefore possible to identify three urgent teacher-training tasks in relation to the multilingual school:

1. Making it clear that training in ESL is desirable for all teachers who work with bilingual children, class and subject teachers alike, not just for language specialists – expanding current provision to meet this need.
2. Providing INSET for specialist ESL teachers to help them as their role changes from separate ESL support to collaborative, team-teaching situations.
3. Providing INSET for the managers – unless the senior teachers in a school understand the need for change in relation to support for bilingual children, individual teachers and departments will have little impact on the quality of provision.

Currently a good deal of INSET provision in this field attracts only the convinced and committed. Until all schools see these issues as central to their concerns we cannot hope to change teacher attitudes and expectations. Deficit models of bilingual children will only recede when they are brought in from the fringes and enabled to speak with their own voices.

References

HARGREAVES, D. H. (1984) *Improving Secondary Schools* (Report of the Committee on the Curriculum and Organisation of Secondary Schools, ILEA).
SWANN, LORD (1985) *Education for All* (Report of the Committee of Inquiry into the Education of Children from Ethnic Minority Groups).
THOMAS, N. (1985) *Improving Primary Schools* (Report of the Committee on Primary Education, ILEA).

TABLE 25.1 *Support for bilingual children's development of English (From separate language provision to learning through the curriculum in the mainstream class.)*

Provision	Disadvantages
RECEPTION CENTRES	Unacceptable segregation, racially and socially divisive, focus on language rather than learning, decontextualised.
RECEPTION CLASSES	Non-curriculum-based teaching, adult the only English-speaking model, restricted contact with English speaking peers.
LANGUAGE CENTRES	Isolation and marginalisation of ESL pupils and teachers, withdrawal associated with remedial support, de-skills.
WITHDRAWAL CLASSES	Mainstream teachers, encourages notion that only specialists can work successfully with bilingual children.
RESOURCE CENTRES	Solution still outside the mainstream class/school.

Issues still to be resolved

IN-CLASS SUPPORT	Nature of support, a negotiated contract between class or subject teacher and ESL specialist status of ESL teacher.
ESL TEACHER AS CO-ORDINATOR/ADVISER (*resources, monitoring progress*)	Status of co-ordinator, time for co-ordination, mainstream teachers' role in monitoring progress.
TEAM-TEACHING (*class teacher, bilingual teacher, ESL teacher*)	Adequate planning time to allow for genuine collaboration.
CLASS AND SUBJECT-BASED TEACHERS TRAINING TO WORK IN MULTILINGUAL CLASSROOMS	Provision of adequate training and resources, genuine commitment of all teachers, school managers and administrators to this as the only legitimate goal.

encouraged the view that ethnic-minority children present problems which need special remediation. It has encouraged the setting-up of support structures that are proving difficult to dismantle, and it has allowed mainstream teachers to think that the solution lies outside their classrooms.

Solutions will not be easy, but they must be found. As the Swann Report (1985) made clear, we are talking about such fundamental issues as justice and equality. We are talking about education for all in a plural society. Teachers need time to articulate their anxieties, time to consult with colleagues, time to review their teaching approaches and resources in order to cater adequately for mixed ability, multilingual classes. In the short term they need time to establish ways of working with ESL teachers that demean neither group and enable them to learn from each other. In the long term they need time to take on board full responsibility for organising a learning environment that will genuinely meet the needs of all the children.

Language and learning through the curriculum

What sort of learning environment are we talking about? It will certainly involve some of the following:

- thinking carefully about the phasing of the learning tasks
- providing opportunities for listening and talking
- organising for peer group interaction and collaboration
- understanding more fully the relationship between language and learning
- providing maximum support for understanding
- understanding more fully the nature of bilingualism and biculturalism
- using bilingual children's linguistic and cultural experiences as resources for learning
- creating an ethos of respect and tolerance in the class/school
- taking a clear stand on racism, sexism and classism
- understanding that learning through the curriculum is not only as important as the children's development of English, but is influential in that development.

remain 'moderates' as to its eventual outcome, while being 'radicals' in their underlying philosophy and objectives.

The RSA scheme's philosophy

An important premise behind the scheme is that what should determine the method of language teaching is the experience of the language acquired by the learners as much as the structural features of it. Thus, when the learners are bilinguals not monolinguals the pedagogy to develop bilingualism must be different from that appropriate for mother-tongue or foreign-language teaching. Accordingly, the scheme sees itself as independent of other language schemes, including the modern languages scheme, which is designed for teachers of truly *foreign*, not community, languages.

The second principle of this approach is that the training programme must include a strong language-specific component. Here the claim is that, although many teachers may already be familiar with classroom organisation and techniques of language teaching, the process involved in learning the reading and writing of a particular language (for example, French) cannot be transferred to another (for example, Arabic). Teachers then will learn how a specific language group first encounters English and how this may influence the bilingual learners' initial competence.

The third main element in the philosophy behind the new scheme is an interest in the relationship between community-language learning and the wider educational context. Its promoters hope to demonstrate that bilingual education, far from being Utopian, is a realistic and constructive innovation in our schools, both for pupil and teacher. First, there is evidence that young speakers of community languages are increasingly looking for an opportunity in their school curriculum to develop their bilingual and biliterate competence. Their choice is certainly more likely to lead to real intellectual benefit than is any smattering of a foreign language. The introduction of such innovation also makes sense professionally: community teachers who have done so much to help the survival of their languages in this country are now seeking functional co-ordination and appropriate teaching responsibility within the mainstream system. This is not only impressive evidence of their sense of commitment, it is also a great chance for the system to acquire the vast body of knowledge and experience of teaching language so as to develop genuine bilingualism, something which has never previously existed in the English language-teaching tradition.

Giving bilingualism a positive value

This latter could lay the foundation for an important development in the role of education in England. In the new world of technological development and international exchange bilingualism will be a future passport. Skill in the cognitive use of a second language cannot, in fact, be acquired via instruction in communicative competence in a foreign language. Most educational systems have recognised this and many countries have taken appropriate measures to introduce bilingual education, especially necessary where the economy needs to be promoted within a politically but not linguistically homogeneous context, as in Canada, Scandinavia, the Indian sub-continent and the EEC.

So far, in general, Britain has not seen fit to make a contribution to the efforts of the rest of the world, and the EEC in particular, by giving bilingualism a positive value and function in society. Once this blind spot is removed from our educational system, ethnic minorities will have demonstrated that, while the Welsh learned to defend their bilingual heritage through political activism, they were able to achieve the same results through education. The RSA investment in the Community Language Scheme could then come to be seen as a historic step towards a richer society, both culturally and materially, for all the inhabitants of the British Isles, whatever their ethnic origins.

Chapter 26

Training Bilingual Teachers to Support and Develop Pupils' Bilingualism

Arturo Tosi

An introduction to the Royal Society of Arts Scheme for the Training of Teachers of Community Languages (TTCL).

More than a decade has now passed since the first discussions on the need to educate all children to live in our multicultural society and on the importance for schools to respect the diverse cultural background of all people living in Britain. A central issue in that debate was the role of other mother tongues, and the opportunity to teach them to children whose first language was not English. In the 1970s many projects concerned with mother-tongue teaching were also set up by international political organisations such as the EEC and UNESCO, and several policy recommendations were made by professional bodies such as the National Council for Mother Tongue Teaching and the National Association for Multicultural Education.

Today we hear less and less about mother-tongue teaching in our multicultural schools and teacher-training colleges, but we increasingly encounter discussions about the *bilingualism* of minority communities and about the education in the *community language* of bilingual children. Not surprisingly, many teachers have begun to wonder what bearing this has on our previous concern for minority children's other *mother tongue* and whether it is going to be another short-lived 'fad' of academic debate. I would suggest that not only are the two issues closely related, but that the current one actually points to a growing political and professional maturity on the part of those involved in this area compared with the earlier approach.

A pioneer training scheme

That it has established itself politically is a tribute to the experience and efforts of a large number of 'minority' and 'majority' teachers in multicultural schools: people who strenuously defended children's rights to diversity in education and have rebelled against the national tradition by maintaining that the experience of growing up with two languages rather than one is an asset rather than a handicap. As for the pedagogic development of this new approach, the Royal Society of Arts Scheme for the Training of Teachers of Community Languages (TTCL) is probably the first attempt on the part of professionals in Britain to address the challenging but fascinating question of what is the most effective way of teaching something which is neither a mother-tongue nor a foreign language.

The RSA Community Language Scheme was launched in 1983 and after the first pilot year was introduced by several colleges in England and Scotland. Today it involves as many as fourteen languages (Arabic, Bengali, Cantonese, Farsi, Greek, Gujarati, Hindi, Italian, Mandarin, Punjabi, Spanish, Tamil, Turkish and Urdu). Teachers are being trained to teach these languages to children who speak them already in their home and ethnic community alongside English. This is the important new dimension of the scheme and its ten advisers help to implement it in new programmes at the different centres. The approach, in fact, is based neither on presumed mother-tongue competence, which children obviously cannot achieve in this country, nor on linguistic expectations associated with foreign language learning, which are quite irrelevant to the experience of young bilingual speakers. In this sense the RSA scheme is pioneering an important experiment in the field of language education, as with any such innovation those who have set it in motion

(i) finding enough time for oral and written work in both languages;
(ii) the early introduction of reading schemes brings with it added difficulties in the choice between Welsh and English as the medium of reading. Welsh orthography has a more 'regular' sound–symbol correspondence than does the English writing system. Consequently, switching from one to the other can cause problems;
(iii) the use of English within the community, especially the mass media, indicates that English is not really a second language, even when technically it is so. Many teachers are emphatic in stating that the teaching and learning of English are easier now in predominantly Welsh-speaking areas than they were ten years ago because of the increasingly supportive language environment. The implications for the Welsh language are less fortunate.

The Schools Council Research and Development Project on the 'Teaching and Learning of English in Wales 8–13', directed by D. W. H. Sharp at the University College of Swansea, made a detailed study of the problems involved in teaching English in Wales. It included an analysis of the errors most commonly made, a study of the methods of teaching English including the language textbooks in use, and a survey of pupils' interests as reflected in their popular reading. The results show that, in terms of textbooks used and pupils' reading, no distinction can be made between English first-language and English second-language pupils in Wales. This is especially true at secondary school level and when preparing for external examinations.

English as a first language

English is the first language of the vast majority of pupils in the schools of Wales and to them learning a second language (be it Welsh, French or German) is often a matter of choice. The methods adopted to teach English in Wales do not differ from the methods used in England. The same range of readers are to be found in schools, so are the same textbooks and set books. Teachers in training are made aware of the range of approaches and language registers. 'Unfortunately oral work, in most schools, is given less prominence than reading and writing' (Welsh Office, 1984). In many ways, however, there is an increasing awareness that the development of oral skill is important at both primary and secondary level. It is vital for pupils to have frequent opportunities to speak in a variety of situations calling for a range of vocabulary and idiom in order to extend their experience and powers of expression. Teachers must be sensitive to children's language and careful not to make them feel that their accent or use of language is 'inferior' or wrong.

Bilingual schools

In 1939, the first official Welsh-medium primary school was opened in Aberystwyth. It was an independent school sponsored by the Urdd (the Welsh League of Youth). In 1947, the first Welsh School maintained by a local authority was opened in Llanelli. By 1984 there were sixty-three Welsh primary schools, most of them in anglicised areas. Running parallel with this development at primary level was a demand for bilingual secondary education and, by 1984, fourteen bilingual comprehensive schools had been established, with more schools being planned (Welsh Office, 1985).

Most of the pupils in the bilingual schools come from non-Welsh-speaking homes. (In one comprehensive school it is estimated that 98 per cent of the pupils come from non-Welsh-speaking-homes.) These pupils' first language is, therefore, English. The primary approach is an 'immersion' approach, although English is taught using first-language methods to a large extent. At both primary and secondary level both languages are used as teaching media so that the children develop into effective and efficient bilinguals. In some cases the children's linguistic dominance will change, and Welsh will become the preferred language for both academic and social expression. All teachers at the bilingual schools must also be fully bilingual.

Chapter 27

Teacher-Training for Bilingualism in Wales

Beryl Thomas

In Wales, Welsh is taught as a first or second language in the majority of primary and secondary schools. Naturally, teacher-training has to take account of that fact, the estimated 11 per cent of pupils speaking Welsh as a first language, and the growing numbers of bilingual schools. This chapter briefly indicates the complexities of the current linguistic situation against its historical background.

Historical background to English-medium education in Wales

The Acts of Union between England and Wales in 1536 and 1542 declared that English should be the only official language in Wales. Consequently the newly-established Tudor grammar schools totally ignored the Welsh language and the long-standing cultural tradition associated with it. Day-school education in Wales followed the English pattern – the Commonwealth schools of the seventeenth century, the schools of the Society for the Propagation of Christian Knowledge (SPCK) in the eighteenth century, the schools of the British and National Societies and the board schools (after the 1870 Education Act) in the nineteenth century – all were almost exclusively English-medium institutions, whereas the teaching of Welsh relied on the charity schools and the Sunday schools.

The grammar schools that were established in Wales from 1889 onwards with the Welsh Intermediate Education Act (by 1903 there were 96 intermediate schools in Wales) contained no provision for teaching Welsh. Consequently, thousands of Welsh children experienced the same language loss as did Idris Davies, a twentieth-century poet from Rhymney in Gwent, who said:

> I lost my native language
> For the one the Saxon spake
> By going to school by order
> For education's sake.

During this century the status of Welsh has improved, but the number of first language Welsh speakers has declined from over 80 per cent in 1901 to below 20 per cent in 1981.

English as a second language

Latest estimates suggest that around 11 per cent of the pupils in the schools of Wales have English as their second language. However, the number of native Welsh speakers is not evenly distributed throughout the eight Local Education Authorities. For example, a report published by the Aberystwyth Faculty of Education (1986) states that, although Welsh is under siege in Wales, it is still the first language of 53 per cent of Gwynedd's children, 25 per cent of Dyfed's children and 6 per cent of the children of Powys. Gwent, on the other hand, makes no provision for Welsh-medium teaching.

Teachers in training have to be made aware of the existence of these children and need to consider what special provision, methods and materials are called for in their teaching of English in schools. In particular, how and when the approach should differ from that used for the majority of pupils whose first language is English. The Welsh first-language pupil has to become as fully bilingual as possible. The aim in schools must be native-speaker proficiency in English – full bilingualism in fact. In some cases the child's proficiency in his second language will surpass his first-language competency, and English may become his preferred or first language. Achieving this aim of full bilingualism can present the teacher with a number of problems:

encouraging literacy in a wide variety of languages, from preschool provision through to adult education. The display included materials which related to more than thirty languages – South Asian languages such as Bengali, Gujarati, Hindi, Malayalam, Punjabi, Sinhalese, Tamil and Urdu; African–English Creoles; European languages including French, Greek, Italian, Polish, Portuguese, Spanish, Turkish and Welsh; Chinese languages including Cantonese, Hakka and Putong'hua. There were also materials for literacy in Farsi, in Japanese and in Ukrainian. Behind each example of pupils' work in any one of these languages currently used in Britain lies a very important idea, a proud affirmation of language loyalty.

The great strength of our practice in all of these languages lies in the presence in Britain of teachers, students and whole communities who proudly speak them as a mother tongue. Because these languages are in use in Britain today they can no longer be studied as a sterile academic exercise; they are a living resource, and the multilingual display mounted at the Eleventh World Congress on Reading gloriously demonstrated this reality.

Within each language and within each associated culture there are intrinsic assumptions about language acquisition and about literacy which are specific to the particular language, or to the particular variety of language which pupils are bringing into British classrooms. Each single language, once a certain level of proficiency is reached, can open the door to a treasure-house of excitement and shared experience. None of us alone in a whole lifetime could ever do justice to the richness of diversity in thinking and expression revealed by the display: what this paper attempts instead is to extrapolate the unifying factors in terms of opportunities and challenges facing all teachers who show a concern for literacy in whatever language.

Guiding principles beind the work displayed

Three guiding principles appear to lie behind most if not all of the work displayed, as far as the teachers are concerned:

1. The intention to develop the latent potentialities of each and every child, and to encourage in every citizen a confident sense of personal identity, self-esteem and worth;
2. The intention to facilitate a smooth continuity between the language(s) and culture(s) of the home to the language and culture of the school;
3. The intention to open up to all members of the society full opportunities to enjoy equal access to information and the power that socially relevant information can bestow.

Social reality

It has then to be said that all these intentions fly in the face of reality as far as our monolingual English-medium education system is concerned. The latent potentiality of each and every child is far from fully developed, especially when the child happens to have access to the use of more than one language as a result of family circumstances. Eminent sociolinguists, including Michael Stubbs (1976), have drawn attention to the tendency of the British school system to produce a passive resistance to knowledge and self-expression. Despite the discovery that a sound basis of literacy in the home language is a prerequisite for the acquisition of further linguistic and cultural resources, the majority of pupils who do succeed in our schools seem to do so at the tragic expense of a denial of their cultural roots. This is as true of children from British working-class backgrounds as it is of children from, for example, Italian or Pakistani backgrounds.

Social reality in Britain today does not celebrate or even accept difference. Current statistics tell us that, in the UK, fewer students from working-class backgrounds are reaching university than since before the Second World War. University admission requirements tell us that a pass in, for example, Urdu at the Ordinary General Certificate of Education Level is not an adequate qualification for those subjects which require the knowledge of a language in addition to English. For many university departments a modern language means only French, German, Italian, Spanish or Russian. For most other languages there are no

Welsh as a first and second language

In Wales, there is no national language policy. Each Local Education Authority is responsible for formulating and developing its own. In September 1983, a total of 1398 primary schools in Wales were teaching Welsh as a first or second language, and at only 426 schools was no Welsh taught. At secondary level a similar picture emerges in that 205 secondary schools out of a total of 236 taught Welsh to their pupils.

Students training to be teachers are made aware of the methods and approaches most commonly adopted in schools. Here the 'graded objectives' courses are the most popular ways of presenting second-language materials at present and are closely linked to the GCSE examination. This is equally true about the teaching of French, German or Spanish in the schools of Wales. Much emphasis is also placed on the development of language awareness as applied to the first-language or second-language situation. As a result, some schools are introducing language awareness lessons during the first two years of secondary education, integrating as many languages as possible, and attempting to foster greater understanding of other languages and cultures.

References

ABERYSTWYTH FACULTY OF EDUCATION (1986) *Secondary Education in Rural Wales* (Report of the Aberystwyth Policy Group, University College of Wales).
WELSH OFFICE (1984) *Curriculum and Organisation of Primary Schools in Wales* (HMI Report, HMSO).
WELSH OFFICE (1985) *Statistics of Education in Wales* (HMSO).

Chapter 28

Ideas Behind the Congress Display of Work by Teachers and Pupils in Multilingual Classrooms

John Broadbent

This chapter analyses the intentions lying behind the production of materials designed to encourage literacy in more than thirty of the languages brought into British classrooms by the pupils themselves. Many such materials were displayed at the Eleventh World Congress on Reading in 1986. Each piece of work by a teacher or pupil in a language other than English confronts a largely monolingual education system in Britain with a proud affirmation of difference. A general recognition of that dimension of difference has been shown to be a cultural and educational resource of value to all.

Teachers and pupils in British schools have a very real contribution to make towards a more genuinely international understanding of some of the issues involved in learning to read and to write in more than one language. The current multilingual population in our inner-city schools does present challenges to a monolingual education system but, more importantly, it also presents opportunities which a great many of our colleagues are still failing to recognise.

Languages represented in the first national display

The display referred to in this chapter was mounted with the assistance of a large number of colleagues working in different areas of Britain, some of whose names are listed in the Appendix. Their work constituted the first national display in Britain of teacher- and pupil-made classroom resources for offered by the Teaching of English as a Foreign Language. It is certainly interesting to note the various material resources which have enabled multilingual materials to be produced to date. Some of them have arisen from specially funded and necessarily short-lived projects, others from agencies funded under Section 11, such as Curriculum Development Units, and yet others from teacher-training institutions.

Teacher/pupil-produced reading materials

Most of the existing work has been put together by practising teachers with little or no support beyond the willingness and gifts of their students. Shahla White (1986) of the Language Division at the ILEA Centre for Urban Educational Studies expresses the situation this way:

> The rather scant supply of reading materials in community languages has prompted many teachers to produce their own. This initiative has resulted in more appropriate and personalised reading material as these teachers are sensitive to the individual needs of their pupils. Often the children will have contributed to the production of these materials and feel more involved and attached to them. They identify with the text, are more familiar with it and thereby are able to 'predict' more easily while reading. This inevitably leads to a better appreciation of the texts and strengthens the children's confidence and pride in their community language and culture. Such teacher/pupil produced reading material also presents a greater variety of resources which will be culturally relevant and authentic to the language and needs of the children involved. These materials tend to match closely the interests and the reading ability of the individuals for whom they are produced.

The ideas which can be shown to lie behind the production of the best multilingual materials in Britain today offer the possibility of triumphing over all the obstacles mentioned in this chapter. That triumph will not be possible without the kind of co-ordination and dissemination that a worldwide professional organisation of even greater dimensions and scope than the International Reading Association can ensure. I end therefore with a plea for much closer collaboration in the future on the part of the wide range of voluntary professional language associations in the world today: let us face the challenges and use the opportunities together.

Appendix

The Multilingual Display was mounted with the help of numerous colleagues, including the following:

Ashraf Awa, Bradford Community Languages Programme.
Jill Bourne, National Foundation for Educational Research.
John Broadbent, EC Pilot Project, Community Languages in the Secondary Curriculum.
Judy Craven, Central Manchester Caribbean English Project.
Matiullah Dard, Birmingham Community Languages Unit and Joseph Chamberlain Sixth Form College.
Shukla Dhingra, Nottingham Language Centre.
Mona Gabb, Woking ESL Support Service.
Barbara Grayson, Newham In-Service Education Centre.
Jean Greaves, Walsall Learning Support Service.
Hilary Hester, ILEA Centre for Language in Primary Education.
Qamar Husain, Cleveland Centre for Multicultural Education.
Muhammad Shah Khan, Birmingham Community Languages Unit and Smallheath School.
Maurice Launders, London Borough of Hounslow.
Jan McAleavy, Brent Language Service.
Joyce Morris, Chairperson, Eleventh World Congress on Reading.
Bhupinder Kaur Nakai, Birmingham Community Languages Unit and Handsworth Wood Girls School.
Mohammend Nazeer-Ud-Din, EC Pilot Project, Community Languages in the Secondary Curriculum and Nottinghamshire County Council.
Sue Perry, Peterborough Centre for Multicultural Education.
Mike Powell, Coventry Community Language Aides Unit.
Rupleka Ray, Cleveland Centre for Multicultural Education.
Maria Roussou, Schools Council Mother Tongue Project.
Perminder Sandhu, Bradford Bililingualism in Education Project.
Chris Shearsby, Coventry Minority Group Support Service.
Teresa Skibinski, Ufficio Scolastico Italiano and Bishop Vaughan RC Comprehensive School, Swansea.
Jean Solity, Mary Ward Centre, London WC1.
Rachel Thackray, University of Lancaster, Department of Linguistics.

Advanced Level examinations. These are just a few of the factors which militate against equality of opportunity in our multilingual society.

Thus it seems that each of the principles which underlies the first national multilingual display is, in fact, in conflict with social reality. The teachers and children who have contributed to the display – quiet, gentle and creative as they are – are at war with the surrounding society. In Sweden, or in France, or in any other country with a nationally-centralised education system, such teachers and children would be engaged in fairly obvious and open warfare with the institutions of the state. In Britain, where devolution encourages experimentation, the conditions much more closely resemble the conditions of guerrilla warfare.

Weaknesses of educational provision

Each teaching strategy for a language other than English, each piece of work in a language other than English, represents a valuable precedent, a piece of territory conquered. But a closer analysis of these strategies, and of the resultant work, reveals the weaknesses of our overall campaign. Within each local education authority there are at least five kinds of providing agency, and the efforts of these five agencies are rarely concerted. What are the agencies? Two have been mentioned already – the home and the school. Other chapters of this volume explore in great detail the opportunities which arise from greater parental involvement in the educational process. In most schools, especially secondary schools, this parental involvement is rejected. Rejected also is a proper collaboration with the voluntary sector, with the community schools, which can be considered as a third type of providing agency. The fourth and fifth kinds of provision in Britain are add-ons within the local authority provision, made possible under Section 11 of the 1966 Local Government Act which central government funds available for the teaching of English to speakers of other languages and, increasingly, since a 1977 Directive of the European Community, for the teaching of community languages. Even between these last two kinds of provision there is little by way of a concerted effort: monolingual strategies predominate.

To date, very little work has been done to relate the acquisition of literacy in the home language to the acquisition of literacy in the medium of instruction, or indeed to the delivery of the school curriculum as a whole. The providers of language education and the providers of teacher education have so far failed to bring together the different kinds of practice. With one or two notable exceptions, linguistic development is still largely seen as the development of skills within discreet linguistic and cultural boundaries rather than the offer, to each potentially bilingual child, of opportunities to decide confidently and consciously, on the balance of linguistic and cultural identities, which he or she wishes to adopt or reflect.

Even among those teachers who support 'multicultural' education, there still lurks a refusal to recognise that the varieties of language which each child brings into the school is valid in its own right, and important to the child's self-image. There is little in terms of teaching materials, other than those recently developed to expand the repertoires of speakers of African–English Creoles, which can challenge the prevailing notion that literacy needs necessarily to be channelled towards standardised versions of the various languages in use in the UK. Is it then necessarily the case that literacy becomes more difficult to achieve if one speaks a variety of language which differs from accepted educated norms? Or do the opportunities for literary or other forms of self-expression extend as the range of a person's linguistic repertoire becomes extended? In a devolved system of education in which each local education authority, even each school, is autonomous and supposedly responsive to local circumstances, we should by now have come much closer to adequate solutions to these issues.

This chapter could have concentrated in greater depth on the challenges which result from a lack of co-ordination across the geographical boundaries of more than a hundred local education authorities in Britain, or from the lack of willingness on the part of educational publishers to risk funding less lucrative publishing language projects than those

List of Contributors

Eleanor Anderson
Senior Lecturer in Education
Hertfordshire College of
Higher Education

Professor Jonathan Anderson
Professor of Education
Flinders University
South Australia

Rosemary Bacon
Head of Science
The Lancashire Reading
and Language Service
Lancaster

John Bald
Tutor-in-Charge
Reading and Language Centre
Colchester Institute

Dr Roger Beard
Lecturer in Education
School of Education
University of Leeds

Wendy Bloom
Senior Lecturer in Education
St Mary's College, Twickenham

John Broadbent
Research Officer and Co-ordinator
EC Pilot Project
Community Languages in the
Secondary Curriculum
Institute of Education
University of London

Professor Elizabeth Goodacre
Head of School of Education
Middlesex Polytechnic

Nigel Hall
Lecturer in Education
School of Education
Manchester Polytechnic

David Houlton
Lecturer in Primary Education
School of Education
University of Nottingham

Margaret Litchfield
Team Leader
Leicestershire Literacy
Support Service
Leicester

Elizabeth May
Teacher
School of Education
Manchester Polytechnic

Dr Moira G. McKenzie
(Formerly Adviser/Warden
Centre for Language
in Primary Education)
ILEA, London

Professor John E. Merritt
Emeritus Fellow, Leverhulme
Trust
Charlotte Mason College
of Education
Ambleside

Janet Moores
Teacher
School of Education
Manchester of Polytechnic

Dr Joyce M. Morris
Reading Consultant and Author
London

Mohammed Nazeer-Ud-Din
Teacher of Urdu,
EC Pilot Project
Community Languages in the
Secondary Curriculum
Nottingham Language Centre

List of Contributors

Alan Porter
Teacher
The Lancashire Reading and
Language Service
Lancaster

Frank Potter
Senior Lecturer in Education
Edge Hill College of
Higher Education
Ormskirk

Flo Robinson
Consultant
Community Education
Development Centre
Coventry

Janette Shearer
Teacher
School of Education
Manchester Polytechnic

John Singh
HM Inspector
Department of Education and
Science

Brigid Smith
Director of Studies
Communications Faculty
Stewards School, Harlow

Peter Smith
Adviser and Author
Education Department, Hounslow

Helen C. Tite
Senior Lecturer in Education
Faculty of Education
and Social Science
Nene College, Northampton

Beryl Thomas
Senior Lecturer
Department of Education
University College, Swansea

Dina Thorpe
Schools Librarian
Hertfordshire Library Service

Arturo Tosi
Chairman, Community
Languages Scheme
Royal Society of Art

Lyn Weldon
Author and Remedial Teacher
Barton, Cambridge

Silvaine Wiles
Director, Language Division
ILEA Centre for
Urban Educational Studies

Susan Williams
Teacher
School of Education
Manchester Polytechnic

David Wray
Lecturer in Education
Department of Education
University College, Cardiff

Catherine Wallace, Ealing College of Higher Education.
Shahla White, ILEA Centre for Urban Educational Studies.
Qudsia Yousuf, ILEA and University of London School Examinations Board.

References

STUBBS, M. (1976) *Language, Schools and Classrooms* (London: Methuen).
WHITE, S. (1986) 'Reading in Two Languages' in *Issues* (London: National Anti-Racist Movement in Education), Spring.